DIFFERENTIAL EQ WITH *MAPLE*™

Kevin R. Coombes
Brian R. Hunt
Ronald L. Lipsman
John E. Osborn
Garrett J. Stuck

University of Maryland at College Park

John Wiley & Sons, Inc.
New York • Chichester • Brisbane • Toronto • Singapore

ISBN 0-471-10875-8

Printed in the United States of America

10 9 8 7 6 5 4 3

Printed and bound by Malloy Lithographing, Inc.

Preface

As the subject matter of differential equations continues to grow, as new technologies become commonplace, as old areas of application are expanded, and as new ones appear on the horizon, the content and viewpoint of courses and their textbooks must also evolve.

Boyce & DiPrima, **Elementary Differential Equations**, Fifth Edition.

Traditional introductory courses in ordinary differential equations (ODE) have concentrated on teaching a repertoire of techniques for finding formula solutions of various classes of differential equations. Typically, the result was rote application of formula techniques without a serious qualitative understanding of such fundamental aspects of the subject as stability, asymptotics, dependence on parameters, and numerical methods. These fundamental ideas are difficult to teach because they have a great deal of geometrical content and, especially in the case of numerical methods, involve a great deal of computation. Modern mathematical software systems, which are particularly effective for geometrical and numerical analysis, can help to overcome these difficulties. This book changes the emphasis in the traditional ODE course by using a mathematical software system to introduce numerical methods, geometric interpretation, symbolic computation, and qualitative analysis into the course in a basic way.

The mathematical software system we use is *Maple*. (This book is also available in a *Mathematica* version.) We assume that the user has no prior experience with *Maple*. We include concise instructions for using *Maple* on three popular computer platforms: *Windows*, *Macintosh*, and the *X Window System*. This book is not a comprehensive introduction or reference manual to either *Maple* or any of the computer platforms. Instead, it focuses on the specific features of *Maple* that are useful for analyzing differential equations. It also describes the features of the *Maple* "Worksheet" interface that are necessary for creating a finished document.

We designed this book to supplement the fifth edition of the textbook **Elementary Differential Equations**, by Boyce & DiPrima, the text we use in our own course. It could, however, easily be used in conjunction with most other ODE texts. It addresses most of the standard topics in ODE, but with a strikingly different emphasis.

We had two basic goals in mind when we introduced this supplement into our course. First, we wanted to deepen students' understanding of differential equations by giving them a new tool, a mathematical software system, for analyzing differential equations. Second, we wanted to bring students to a level of expertise in the mathematical software system that would allow them to use it in other mathematics, engineering, or science courses. These basic goals have guided our project from start to finish. We believe that we have achieved these goals in our own classes. We hope this supplement will be useful to students and instructors on other campuses in achieving the same goals.

Acknowledgements

We thank Peter Olver of the University of Minnesota, and our colleague Jonathan Rosenberg, both of whom contributed material to this book. We are grateful to all of our colleagues who have used earlier versions of this material in their classes at the University of Maryland at College Park. We are particularly indebted to the many students who have used these materials, and have communicated to us their comments and suggestions. We are grateful to our departmental administrators for giving us the freedom to experiment in what has been a very stable course. Finally, we thank Barbara Holland, mathematics editor at Wiley, for her enthusiastic and thoughtful support of our project.

Kevin Coombes
Brian Hunt
Ron Lipsman
John Osborn
Garrett Stuck

College Park, Maryland
April 10, 1995

Contents

1 Introduction   1
    Guiding Philosophy   1
    Student User's Guide   3
    Instructor's Guide   5
2 Getting Started with *Maple*   11
    Maple in *Windows*   11
    Maple on a *Macintosh*   14
    Maple in the *X Window System*   17
3 Doing Mathematics with *Maple*   21
    Problem Set A: Practice with *Maple*   31
4 Using *Maple* Worksheets   35
5 Solutions of Differential Equations   43
6 A Qualitative Approach to Differential Equations   51
    Problem Set B: First Order Equations   59
7 Numerical Methods   67
8 Features of *Maple*   85
    Troubleshooting   106
    Problem Set C: Numerical Solutions of Differential Equations   109
9 Qualitative Theory of Second Order Linear Equations   117
    Problem Set D: Second Order Equations   127
10 Series Solutions   137
11 Laplace Transforms   143
    Problem Set E: Series Solutions and Laplace Transforms   151
12 Higher Order Equations and Systems of First Order Equations   159
13 Qualitative Theory for Systems of Differential Equations   173
    Problem Set F: Systems of Equations   181

    Glossary   195
    Sample Worksheet Solutions   203
    Index   225

Chapter 1

Introduction

We begin by describing the philosophy behind our approach to the study of ordinary differential equations. This philosophy has its roots in the way we understand, use, and apply differential equations; it has influenced our teaching and guided the development of this book. This chapter also contains two user's guides, one for students and one for instructors.

Guiding Philosophy

In scientific inquiry, when we are interested in understanding, describing, or predicting some complex phenomenon, we use the technique of *mathematical modeling*. In this approach, we describe the state of a physical, biological, econometric, or other system by one or more functions of one or several variables. For example, the position $s = s(t)$ of a particle is a function of the time t; the temperature $T = T(x, y, z, t)$ in a body is a function of the position (x, y, z) and the time t; the gravitational or electromagnetic force on an object is a function of its position; the money supply is a function of time; the populations $x = x(t)$ and $y = y(t)$ of two competing species are functions of time. Next, we attempt to formulate, in mathematical terms, a fundamental law governing the phenomenon. Typically, this formulation results in one or more differential equations; *i.e.*, equations involving derivatives of the functions describing the state of the system with respect to the variables they depend on. Frequently, the functions depend on only one variable, and the differential equation is called *ordinary*. To be specific, if $x = x(t)$ denotes the function describing the state of our system, an *ordinary differential equation* in $x(t)$ might involve $x'(t)$, $x''(t)$, higher derivatives, or other known functions of t. By contrast, in a *partial differential equation*, the functions depend on several variables.

In addition to the fundamental law, we usually describe the initial state of the system. We express this state mathematically by specifying *initial values* $x(0)$, $x'(0)$, *etc.* In this way, we arrive at an *initial value problem*—an ordinary differential equation together with initial conditions. If we can solve the initial value problem, then the solution is a function $x(t)$ that predicts the future state of the system. Using the solution, we can describe qualitative or quantitative properties of the system.

At this stage, we compare the values predicted by $x(t)$ against experimental data that we accumulate by observing the phenomenon. If the experimental data and the function values match, we congratulate ourselves on a job well done and go on to the next challenge. If they do not match, we go back, refine the model, and start again. Even if we are satisfied with the model, we may later arrive at a time when new technology, new requirements, or newly discovered features of the phenomenon render our old data obsolete. Again, we respond by reexamining the model.

The subject of differential equations consists in large part of building and solving mathematical models. Many results and methods have been developed for this purpose. These results and methods fall within one or more of the following themes:

(1) Existence and uniqueness of solutions

(2) Dependence of solutions on initial values

(3) Derivation of formulas for solutions

(4) Numerical calculation of solutions

(5) Graphical analysis of solutions

(6) Qualitative analysis of differential equations and their solutions.

The basic results on existence and uniqueness (theme 1), and dependence on initial values (theme 2), form the foundation of the subject of differential equations. The derivation of formula solutions (theme 3) is a rich and important part of the subject; a variety of methods have been developed for finding formula solutions to special classes of equations. Although many equations can be solved exactly, many others cannot. However, any equation, solvable or not, can be analyzed using numerical methods (theme 4), graphical methods (theme 5), and qualitative methods (theme 6). The ability to obtain qualitative and quantitative information without the aid of an explicit formula solution is crucial. That information may suffice to analyze and describe the original phenomenon (which led to the model, which gave rise to the differential equation).

Traditionally, introductory courses in differential equations focused on methods for deriving exact solutions to special types of equations, and included some simple numerical and qualitative methods. The human limitations involved in compiling numerical or graphical data were formidable obstacles to implementing more advanced qualitative or quantitative methods. Computer platforms have reduced these obstacles. Sophisticated software and mainframe computers have enhanced the use of quantitative and qualitative methods in the theory and applications of differential equations. With the arrival of comprehensive mathematical software systems on personal computers, this modern approach has become accessible to undergraduates.

In this book, we use the mathematical software system *Maple* to implement this new approach. We introduce symbolic, numerical, graphical, and qualitative techniques, and show how to use *Maple* to analyze differential equations and their solutions with these techniques. As you encounter each new technique, you should ask: Under which of the six themes listed above does it fit? Answering that question will help you to organize the course material.

In order to take advantage of this modern approach, you must learn to use a computer platform effectively. We give detailed instructions for using *Maple* on three specific types of computers. In this way, we minimize the time required to learn to use the computer platform.

Finally, the software system we have chosen provides an additional valuable opportunity: it enables the production of "Worksheets" that combine textual commentary with the numerical, symbolic, and graphical output of the mathematical software system. Engineers and scientists have to develop not only skills in analyzing problems and interpreting solutions, but also the ability to present coherent conclusions in a logical and convincing style. You should use the Worksheet capabilities of the software to submit solutions to the computer assignments in such a style. This is excellent preparation for the professional requirements that lie ahead.

Student User's Guide

The chapters of this book can be divided into three classes: descriptions of the computer platform, supplementary material on ordinary differential equations (ODE), and computer problem sets. Here is a brief description of the contents.

The computer platform chapters require no prior knowledge of computers. Chapter 2 explains how to start *Maple* on three kinds of computers: *Windows*, *Macintosh*, and the *X Window System*. Chapter 3 introduces some basic *Maple* commands. You should work through Chapters 2 and 3 while sitting at your computer. Then you should work the problems in Problem Set A. These steps will bring you to a minimal level of competence in the use of *Maple*. You should complete these tasks within one week after the semester begins. After that, read Chapter 4, which contains detailed instructions for manipulating the *Maple* Worksheet interface on your computer. Finally, Chapter 8 is an introduction to the more sophisticated *Maple* commands that will be useful in later problem sets. It is best to read this chapter after working some problems in Problem Set B, but before starting on Problem Set C.

Keep in mind that the computer platform chapters are intended to teach you enough about *Maple* to study ordinary differential equations. If you want to explore the mathematical software system in more depth, then you should consult a book devoted to that topic. The standard reference is: B. Char, *et al.*, **First Leaves: A Tutorial Introduction to Maple V**, Springer-Verlag, 1992. Guides to the *Maple* interface on various computers are also available from Waterloo Maple Software.

The eight ODE chapters are intended to supplement the material in your text. The emphasis in this book differs from that found in a traditional ODE text. The main difference is less emphasis on the search for exact formula solutions, and greater emphasis on qualitative, graphical, and numerical analysis of the equations and their solutions. Furthermore, the commands for analyzing differential equations with *Maple* appear in these chapters.

Although you are expected to devote considerable time to the material in this book, you should remember that it is a *supplement* to your main text. Your instructor should supply a syllabus that explains how to coordinate the chapters in this supplement with the sections of your text. As an example, here is a list of the ODE chapters in this supplement, and the corresponding chapters in the textbook Boyce & DiPrima, **Elementary Differential Equations**, 5th edition.

Title of ODE Chapter	Corresponds to Boyce & DiPrima
Solutions of Differential Equations	Chapter 2
A Qualitative Approach to Differential Equations	Chapter 2
Numerical Methods	Chapter 8
Qualitative Theory of Second Order Linear Equations	Chapter 3
Series Solutions	Chapter 5
Laplace Transforms	Chapter 6
Higher Order Equations and Systems of First Order Equations	Chapters 4 & 7
Qualitative Theory for Systems of Differential Equations	Chapter 9

You should keep up with the syllabus, read carefully all the assigned sections in your text, and do many of the problems at the end of those sections.

The third collection of documents in this book consists of six sets of computer problems. The problem sets form an integral part of the course. Solving these problems will expose you to the qualitative, graphical, and numerical features of the course. Each set contains about fifteen problems; your instructor will decide which problems to assign, and when and how you are to submit them.

You can most profitably attack the problem sets if you plan to do them in two distinct sessions. Begin by reading the problems and thinking about the issues involved. Jot down some notes about how *Maple* can help you solve the problems. Although it is tempting to sit at the computer and start typing immediately, you will find that approach to be inefficient and potentially frustrating. Some preparation with pencil and paper will be useful. Then go to the computer and start solving the problems. If you get stuck, save your work and go on to the next problem. You should expect to spend at least one hour per problem. If there are things you'd like to discuss with your instructor, print out the relevant parts of the Worksheet to take with you. Then log out, go home, and try to digest what you've done— decide what's right, what's wrong, what could be done better, what surprises you encountered, *etc.* Talk to your instructor or your peers about anything you don't understand. This first session should be attempted a week before the assignment is due. After you have reviewed your output and obtained answers to your questions, you are ready for your second session. At this point, you should fill the gaps, correct your mistakes, and polish your Worksheet. This will take another hour or so per problem. Although you may find yourself spending extra time on the first few problems, if you read the *Maple* chapters carefully, and follow the suggestions above, you should steadily increase your level of competence in using *Maple*.

The end of this book contains two useful sections: a Glossary and a collection of Sample Worksheet Solutions. The Glossary contains a brief summary of some *Maple* commands, options, and built-in functions. The Sample Worksheet Solutions show how we solved several problems from this book. These samples will serve as guides when you prepare your own Worksheet solutions. Emulate them. Strive to prepare coherent, organized solutions. Combine *Maple*'s input, output, and graphics with your own textual commentary and analysis of the problem. Edit the final version of your solution to remove syntax errors and false starts. You will soon take pride in submitting complete, polished solutions to the problems.

Instructor's Guide

The philosophy that guided the writing of this book is explained at the beginning of this chapter. Here is a capsule summary of that philosophy. We seek:

- To guide students into a more interpretive mode of thinking.
- To use a mathematical software system to enhance students' ability to compute symbolic and numerical solutions, and to perform qualitative and graphical analysis of differential equations.
- To develop course material that reflects the current state of ODE and emphasizes the mathematical modeling of physical problems.
- To minimize the time required to learn to use the computer platform.

Our material consists of computer platform documents, ODE supplements, and computer problem sets. Here are our recommendations for integrating this material into the course.

Platform Documents. These are discussed in the preceding section. Proper use of these documents will quickly propel students to a reasonable level of proficiency. Students should read Chapters 2 and 3, and work Problem Set A within the first week of the semester. They should read Chapter 4 immediately after that, but they can delay reading Chapter 8 until after they start Problem Set B.

ODE Chapters. These eight chapters supplement the material in a traditional text. We use *Maple* to study differential equations using symbolic, numerical, graphical, and qualitative methods. We emphasize the following topics: stability, comparison methods, numerical methods, direction fields, and phase portraits. These topics are not emphasized to the same degree in a traditional text. We suggest that you incorporate this new emphasis into your class discussions. You should devote some class time to each chapter. Specific guidelines are difficult to prescribe, and the required time varies with each chapter, but on average we spend 30–40 minutes per chapter in class discussion. Of course, students will pay greater attention to the chapters if the material appears on quizzes and exams.

The structure of this book requires that numerical methods be discussed early in the course, immediately after the discussion of first order equations. The discussion of numerical methods should be directed toward the use of *Maple*'s numerical ODE solvers.

Computer Problem Sets. There are six computer problem sets. The topics addressed in the problem sets are:

(A) Practice with *Maple*
(B) First Order Equations
(C) Numerical Solutions of Differential Equations
(D) Second Order Equations
(E) Series Solutions and Laplace Transforms
(F) Systems of Equations

Problem Set A is a practice set designed to acquaint students with the basic symbolic and graphical capabilities of *Maple*, and to reacclimate them to calculus. It should be assigned on the first day of class, to be completed within one week. It is best to assign each remaining problem set at least two weeks before the due date. The course material corresponding to the problem set should be covered during those two weeks. It is good practice to set aside a small amount of class time to discuss questions that arise in students' first attempts to work the problems. That should typically be 3–5 days before the due date. (In the student guide, we suggested a two-stage plan of attack for completing the problem sets. Your class discussion should ideally occur after the first stage.)

We recommend that you assign all of Problem Set A and 3–6 problems from the other problem sets. Students should be required not only to analyze the problems critically, but also to present their analysis in coherent English and mathematics, displayed appropriately on their printouts. To accomplish this, students must master the editing features in the Worksheet interface of *Maple*. These features are discussed in the computer platform chapters. This skill is very important: Engineers and scientists do not just solve problems; they must also present their ideas in cogent and convincing fashion. We expect students to do the same in this course.

It is important to keep in mind that computer files can be copied effortlessly. You should choose a policy regarding student collaboration, and make this policy clear. For example, you might allow students to discuss the assignments, but require them to create the solution Worksheets themselves. Or you might allow students to work jointly and to submit collective solutions. We have found that allowing students to collaborate (in teams of no more than three) can be very beneficial. You should also vary the problems you assign from semester to semester.

Hardware Considerations. Before using these materials, you should make sure that your institution has enough machines with enough computing power to run *Maple*. To solve the problems in this book in a reasonable amount of time, you need a computer with 8–12 megabytes of random access memory (RAM). On some platforms, *Maple* requires a numeric coprocessor (sometimes called a floating point unit, or FPU); it is recommended for all platforms. Note that the student version of *Maple* does not use the numeric coprocessor.

Software Considerations. New versions of software appear frequently. When a complex system like *Maple* changes, many commands work better than they did before, some work differently, and a few may no longer work at all. As this book goes to press, the current version of *Maple* is Version V.3; this is the version we describe. If you use a different version of the software, then the interface you see may differ slightly from the one we describe. Most problems in the book can also be solved using *Maple* Version V.2. You should not expect to be able to solve the problems using a version of *Maple* older than Version V.2.

Generalities. You do not have to be a *Maple* expert to use this course supplement. On the other hand, both you and your students will benefit if you spend some time working with *Maple*. We recommend that, in addition to working through Problem Set A, you work through the problems you assign in each set, preferably on the same computers that the students will use.

Our practice is to spend almost no class time discussing *Maple* per se. We try not to lose sight of the fact that we are teaching a course in *mathematics*, not *Maple*. We expect students to gain expertise in *Maple* from this book, from experimentation, from online help, from talking to each other, from questions addressed to the instructor after class and in office hours, and by consulting outside literature such as the manual **First Leaves: A Tutorial Introduction to Maple V**, by B. Char, *et al.*

Students often try to establish the following mode in their mathematics courses: "Give me a formula, I will give you a number!" However, we want students to understand the motives and methods behind a formula and its use. In the graphical environment offered by *Maple*, students sometimes try to establish a new mode: "Give me a program, I will give you a picture!" We ask not only that students produce a picture, but also that they interpret it, analyze the phenomenon it represents, and describe clearly and coherently the conclusions they derive from it.

Sample Syllabus. In this section, we assume that the text for the course is the fifth edition of **Elementary Differential Equations** by Boyce & DiPrima. Suitable modifications of these instructions must be made if you use a different text. This supplement contains enough material to address the topics in the first nine chapters of Boyce & DiPrima. This material is more than ample for one semester or two quarters of study. If the course is given in a 15-week semester, then it is likely that some portions of the first nine chapters of Boyce & DiPrima will have to be omitted.

For example, at the University of Maryland in College Park, we omit Chapters 5 and 6. Because of the heavy emphasis on *Maple*'s numerical ODE solver, it is imperative that numerical methods be treated early in the course.

The following syllabus is for a typical Fall Semester. It assumes a MWF schedule with 38 lectures (14 weeks less one day for Thanksgiving and three days for exams).

Boyce & DiPrima Sections	Material from this book Chapters	Problem Sets	Number of Lectures
2.1–2.8	1–6	A, B	10
8.1–8.4	7, 8	C	3
3.1–3.9	9	D	10
4.1–4.2	12		1
7.1–7.7	12	F	7
9.1–9.5	13	F	7

The following schedule indicates where exams and problem set due dates could be placed. Each problem set should be assigned at least two weeks in advance of the due date.

Item	Lecture Number
Problem Set A	5
Exam 1	11
Problem Set B	13
Problem Set C	20
Exam 2	25
Problem Set D	27
Exam 3	38
Problem Set F	40

Here is a sample grading scheme that gives ample weight to the *Maple* assignments: 3 Exams (@ 15% each) = 45%; 4 Computer Problem Sets (@ 5% each) = 20%; Quizzes or Standard Homework = 5%; and the Final Exam = 30%.

The culmination of the course is Chapter 13 and Problem Set F, which correspond to Chapter 9 in the text by Boyce & DiPrima. This material unites the numerical, geometric, and qualitative approaches to the study of differential equations, and applies them to systems of equations that model real problems. Many of our students do achieve a synthesis of this material; we believe that they leave the course with a deeper understanding of and a better appreciation for the subject of differential equations.

Instructors have a great deal of flexibility in deciding how to integrate the material from this supplement into a course. By choosing among the ODE chapters (Chapters 5–7 and 9–13), the instructor can decide which aspect of the course to emphasize. In order to emphasize numerical methods, you could stress Chapter 7 and Problem Set C. In order to emphasize symbolic computation, you could stress Chapters 5, 10, and 11 and Problem Set E. In order to emphasize geometric methods, you could stress Chapters 6, 9 and 13 and Problem Sets B and D. Chapter 12 incorporates both symbolic and geometric methods.

By adjusting the number of problems assigned from each problem set, the instructor can adjust the level of intensity. For example, some of our colleagues spread the problems out in a more uniform way during a semester, instead of assigning several substantial problem sets. Although we prefer to assign a few substantial problem sets, the material accommodates either mode.

Chapter 2

Getting Started
with *Maple*

In this chapter, we describe the basic skills needed to use *Maple* on several different computer platforms. In particular, we describe how to open, save, and print files. These are all features of the *interface* between *Maple* and the particular computer operating system that you are using. These instructions are distinct from the actual commands you will use to do mathematics with *Maple*. The next chapter introduces the mathematical aspects of *Maple*.

This chapter has three parts, one for each of the following user interfaces: *Windows*, *Macintosh*, and the *X Window System*. You should find out what kind of computer and operating system you will be using, and then sit down at the computer with this guide and read the appropriate section. We note that *Windows* is most commonly found on PCs, and the *X Window System* on *UNIX* workstations. If you are using *Windows* or the *Macintosh* operating system on a networked computer, some of the features we describe below may be different for your particular installation.

All of the systems we describe are window-based interfaces, which are manipulated using the keyboard and the mouse. Moving the mouse moves a small arrow (called a *pointer*) on the screen. To *click* on an object, place the pointer over the object and click the mouse button (if your mouse has more than one button, use the left button). To *double-click*, position the pointer and press the button twice in rapid succession. To *drag* an object, position the pointer over it, press and hold the mouse button, slide the object to where you want it, and then release the mouse button. A window can be dragged by its titlebar.

Maple in *Windows*

When you sit down at the computer, it may be turned off or it may be running a screensaver program. If it's off, turn it on and wait until it finishes booting. If a screensaver is running, move the computer's mouse to refresh the display. If all goes well, the screen should now contain various windows and/or icons.

In *Windows*, the "Program Manager" is the name of the program that is used to manage other programs, or *applications*. If you do not see a window on the screen with the title "Program Manager", you should try clicking on various things until

11

you find it. (If you are using a networked PC, it's possible that the Program Manager has been replaced on your system by a custom-designed application.) Each of the icons in the Program Manager window represents an application, or a window containing several applications. Double-clicking on an application icon will start the application it represents. Double-clicking on a window icon will open the window and allow you to view the applications inside it.

Along the top of the Program Manager window you should see a series of buttons labeled **File**, **Edit**, **Options**, **Windows**, and **Help**. If you click on one of these buttons, a menu will appear with a list of various commands and options. You can invoke one of these by clicking on the appropriate button.

If a window is partially obscured, you can bring it to the front by clicking on any part of it. Double-clicking in the small box in the upper left-hand corner of a window will make the window disappear.

Online Help for *Windows*. If you have never used *Windows* before, it's probably a good idea to go through the tutorial called "Windows Tutorial", which is started by selecting the appropriate button in the Program Manager **Help** menu. The tutorial covers the basics of managing windows and applications.

Starting *Maple*. The *Maple* program uses a lot of memory, so you should close other applications before starting *Maple*. An application can be closed by choosing the **Quit** or **Exit** button in the **File** menu belonging to the application.

Once you have closed the other applications, you are ready to start *Maple*. The icon for the *Maple* application is a maple leaf with the name "Maple" printed on it. The location of this application will depend on your particular machine, so you may have to hunt around to locate it. Try looking in windows that have the word "Application" or "Math" in their titles. When you've found the icon, double-click on it. After a brief delay, a new window labeled "Maple V Release 3-(Untitled)" will appear on the screen. This window is a *Maple* "Worksheet". You can now start typing in the Worksheet.

Saving Your Worksheet on a Diskette. To save your Worksheet onto a diskette, you'll need to buy some diskettes for the computer you are using (usually 3.5 inch, 1.44 megabyte High Density (HD) diskettes). These are inexpensive and available in many book stores and computer stores.

Insert a diskette in the slot in the front of the computer. If the disk is unformatted, or formatted for a different kind of computer, you will have to format it before you can use it. To do this, go back to the Program Manager window, and find the window labeled "Main". (If this window is iconified, you'll have to open it by double-clicking on it.) Now open the application called "File Manager". Then click the button **Format Disk**... in the **Disk** menu of the File Manager window. A dialog panel will appear. In this panel, you should select the proper disk drive if your machine has more than one. You can give a name to the diskette by typing in the **Label** box. Once you have selected the proper drive and typed in a name, click on the "OK" button. A new panel will appear warning that formatting will erase everything on the diskette. If you click "Yes", the diskette will be formatted. This will take a few minutes.

Once you have a properly formatted diskette inserted in the drive, make sure that your *Maple* window is active by clicking in it. A darkened titlebar indicates that the window is active. Now select **Save As**... from the **File** menu. A dialog panel will appear on the screen. Near the bottom of the panel is a box labeled "Drives:". The drive that has your diskette should be either "A:" or "B:", depending on whether you have one or two drives, and depending on which one you're using. Select the proper drive by clicking on its name. (If you don't see the name of the drive, use the arrow button to move around in the list of drives.) Once you have the proper drive selected, click in the box labeled "File Name:" (near the upper left-hand corner) and then type the name you'd like to use for the Worksheet. The name should have no more than eight characters and the extension ".ms"; for example, "Problem1.ms". Then click "OK". If you get an error message, it is likely that you've inserted the disk incorrectly or in the wrong drive, or the disk is not formatted correctly. If all goes well, a copy of the file will be saved on the diskette, and the name of the *Maple* window will change to the name you typed. To verify that the file has been copied, you can use the File Manager application.

Once a Worksheet has a title, you can save further changes by simply selecting **Save** from the **File** menu. *Maple* automatically keeps track of the filename. If you want to save the Worksheet under a different name, you'll have to use the **Save As**... button again. You should save your work frequently.

If the computer you are using is networked, and you have an account on the network, you may be able to save your Worksheet on a central file server. Consult your system administrator for instructions.

Opening a Previously Saved Worksheet. In *Maple*, you can have only one Worksheet open at a time. Opening a new or previously saved Worksheet will close the current one, so be sure to save the current Worksheet before you open a new one. To open a saved Worksheet, click on the **File** button, and then click on the **Open** button. A new dialog panel will appear. This panel is essentially identical to the one that appeared as a consequence of selecting the **Save As**... button. You can navigate in this panel by clicking on drives and/or directories until the file you want appears in the box labeled "File Name:". After selecting the file you want, click on the "OK" button. *Maple* files have the filename extension ".ms". To open a new Worksheet, click the **New** button in the **Worksheet** submenu.

Graphics. In *Maple*, the output of a plotting command comes up in a separate window. To paste the plot into your Worksheet, you should make the graphics window active by clicking in it, and then select **Copy** from the **Edit** menu. Then click at the desired insertion point in the active Worksheet, and select **Paste** from the **Edit** menu. A copy of the plot will appear in the Worksheet. Once you have the plot pasted into the Worksheet you should close the graphics window by double-clicking the small box in the upper left-hand corner of the graphics window.

Printing Your Worksheet.   To print a Worksheet, first make sure the Worksheet you want to print is the active window. Then select **Print**... from the **File** menu. A new panel will appear offering various options. One option is to print a selected range of pages. You can do this by typing the appropriate page numbers in the "From" and "To" boxes. When you're ready to print, click on the "OK" button.

Interrupting Calculations.   In the "Tool Bar" near the top of the Worksheet is a button with a stop sign on it. If *Maple* is hung up in a calculation, you can usually stop it by clicking on this button.

Ending the *Maple* Session.   It is important to quit *Maple* when you are done working. First make sure that you have saved your work. Then select the **Quit** button from the **File** menu. If you haven't saved all your work, *Maple* will give you one last chance to save it. When you have exited *Maple*, its menu and any open Worksheets will disappear. Be sure to quit any other programs you have been using before you leave the machine.

Don't forget to eject your diskette before you leave. On most machines, you eject the diskette by pushing the button just below the slot for the diskette.

Maple on a *Macintosh*

When you sit down at a *Macintosh* it may be turned off, or it may be running a screensaver program. If it's off, turn it on and wait until it is finished booting. If a screensaver is running, move the computer's mouse to refresh the display. If all goes well, along the top of the screen you should see the following (from left to right): an Apple icon; a series of menu buttons; the time; a "Balloon Help" icon; and in the upper right-hand corner, an "Application" icon. Click and hold on the Application icon. A menu will appear that will show, among other things, a list of applications running on the *Macintosh*. There will be a check mark on the button corresponding to the current application. Drag the mouse down to the "Finder" button, and then release. Your screen may change, depending on which application was active, and you should see one or more windows or panels on the screen. You are now in the Finder.

The Finder is the *Macintosh* program for finding, copying, moving, and organizing files. Each of the icons in the Finder represents either a file or a folder; a folder is a group of files bundled together. Clicking on a file or folder icon will *select* the icon, and the icon will be darkened. Double-clicking on a folder icon will cause the Finder to bring up a new window displaying a set of icons representing the files in that folder. Double-clicking on a file icon will open the file. The *Macintosh* tries to open a file using an appropriate *application*, or program. For example, *Maple* files will be opened using the *Maple* program. Double-clicking on such a file will open it in *Maple*. You can usually tell the type of a file by looking at its icon. For example, the icon for *Maple* files is a maple leaf.

If a window is partially obscured you can bring it to the front by clicking on any part of it. Clicking in the small box in the upper left-hand corner of a window will make the window disappear.

Moving files from one folder to another is done as follows: find the folder into which you want to move (or copy) a file. This folder can be either in iconic form, or in the form of an open window showing its contents. Then find the file you want to move and drag it to the target folder. An icon representing the file will appear in the target folder. (The file will be moved or copied, depending on who owns the file and folder.) To delete a file, drag its icon into the trash can at the bottom right-hand corner of the screen. Then select **Empty Trash**... from the **Special** menu at the top of the screen. A warning panel will appear on the screen asking you to confirm that you want to delete the files in the trash can.

Online Help for the *Macintosh*.   If you have never used a *Macintosh* computer before, it is probably a good idea to go through the *Macintosh* tutorial called "Macintosh Basics". You can start this tutorial by double-clicking on its icon. The tutorial will cover the basics of managing files and opening applications and will help you become comfortable using the *Macintosh*. You can also get a rudimentary kind of help by turning on the **Show Balloons** option in the **Balloon Help** menu.

Starting *Maple*.   The *Maple* program uses a lot of memory, so before you start *Maple* you should quit any other applications that are running on the *Macintosh*. To do this, use the menu attached to the Application icon in the upper right-hand corner of the screen.

The icon for the *Maple* application is a maple leaf with the name "Maple" or "MapleFPU" printed below. It should be in a folder called "Maple", or something similar. The location of this folder will depend on your particular machine, so you may have to hunt around in the Finder to locate it. Try looking in folders that have the word "Application" or "Math" in their titles. When you've found the icon, double-click on it to open it. (Select the "MapleFPU" icon if it's available; "FPU" stands for "floating point unit", and is designed to take advantage of a special floating point processor present in some computers.) After a brief delay, a new window labeled 'Worksheet "Untitled-1" ' will appear on the screen, and the menu buttons along the top of the screen will change. You can now start typing in the Worksheet.

Saving Your Worksheet on a Diskette.   To save your Worksheet onto a diskette, you'll need to buy some diskettes for the computer you are using (usually 3.5 inch, 1.44 megabyte High Density (HD) diskettes). These are inexpensive and available in many book stores and computer stores. Insert a diskette in the slot in the front of the *Macintosh*. If the disk is unformatted, or formatted for a different kind of computer, a panel will appear asking you whether you want to format it. If you click **Initialize**, a panel will appear asking whether you really want to erase the diskette. If you click **Erase**, the *Macintosh* will prompt you for a name for the diskette. Type in a name, then hit RETURN. It will take a few minutes to initialize the diskette.

Once you have a properly formatted diskette inserted in the drive, an icon representing the diskette will appear along the right-hand edge of the screen. Make sure that your *Maple* window is active by clicking the mouse in it. A darkened titlebar indicates that the window is active. Now select **Save As**... from the **File** menu. A new panel will appear on the screen. Select the button **Desktop** on the right-hand side. In the center of the panel you should see the name of your diskette. Click on the name, and then click **Open**. The panel will change, and there will be a box labeled "Save this document as:". Type the name you'd like to use for the Worksheet ("Assignment 1", for example), and then click **Save**. A copy of the file will be saved on the diskette, and the name of the main window will change from "Untitled-1" to the name you typed. To check that the file has been copied, double-click on the diskette icon. A new window will appear containing a list of files on the diskette. To continue working with *Maple*, click on your Worksheet.

Once a Worksheet has a title, you can save further changes by simply selecting **Save** from the **File** menu. *Maple* automatically keeps track of where you want to save it. If the diskette on which you originally saved the file is not in the drive, the *Macintosh* will pop up a panel with an error message, or prompt you to insert the diskette. In the latter case, you can get rid of the panel by typing "COMMAND-." (see below). If you want to save the Worksheet under a different name, you'll have to use the **Save As**... button again. If you want to save a copy of the Worksheet with the same name, but on a different diskette, you can use the button **Save a Copy In**.... You should save your work frequently.

If the computer you are using is networked, and you have an account on the network, you may be able to save your Worksheet on a central file server. Consult your system administrator for instructions.

Opening a Previously Saved Worksheet.   There is only one way to open a previously saved Worksheet as the *active* Worksheet on the *Macintosh*. First, you must quit *Maple* if it is already running. Then find the icon on your diskette that represents the Worksheet you'd like to open. Double-click on the icon representing the Worksheet. *Maple* will start up with the selected Worksheet as the active worksheet. (For instructions on opening a Worksheet as a "Scratchpad", see Chapter 4.)

To open a new *Maple* Worksheet, quit *Maple* and then restart it by clicking on the "Maple" or "MapleFPU" icon.

Graphics.   In *Maple*, the output of a plotting command comes up in a separate window. To paste the plot into your Worksheet, you should make the graphics window active by clicking in it, and then select **Copy** from the **Edit** menu. Then click at the desired insertion point in the active Worksheet, and select **Paste** from the **Edit** menu. A copy of the plot will appear in the Worksheet. Once you have the plot pasted into the Worksheet you should close the graphics window by clicking the small box in the upper left-hand corner of the graphics window.

Printing Your Worksheet. To print a Worksheet, first make sure the Worksheet you want to print is the active window. Then select **Print**... from the **File** menu. A new panel will appear offering various options. One option is to print a selected range of pages. You can do this by typing the appropriate page numbers in the "From" and "To" boxes. When you're ready to print, click on the **Print** button.

The COMMAND Key. On either side of the space bar is a key with both an apple and a cloverleaf-like symbol on it. We refer to these keys as the COMMAND keys. We will describe some uses for the COMMAND key in the next few chapters. For now, you should remember one important use. If the *Macintosh* is hung up, or is doing something you don't want it to be doing, you can often free it up by typing "COMMAND-." (*i.e.*, hold down the COMMAND key and type a period). In particular, this usually works if you want to interrupt a *Maple* calculation. It also works when the *Macintosh* puts up a panel prompting you to insert a nonexistent or missing diskette.

Ending the *Maple* Session. It is important to quit *Maple* when you are done working. First make sure that you have saved your work. Then select the **Quit** button from the **File** menu. If you haven't saved all your work, *Maple* will give you one last chance to save it. When you have exited *Maple*, its menu and any open Worksheets will disappear. Be sure to quit any other programs you have been using before you leave the machine. (You can check to see which programs are running by using the Application menu in the upper right-hand corner of the screen. You do not have to quit the Finder.)

Don't forget to eject your diskette before you leave. You can eject the diskette by selecting **Eject Disk** from the **Special** menu in the Finder, or by dragging the diskette icon into the trash can.

Maple in the *X Window System*

We assume that you are using a computer running some version of the *UNIX* operating system and that you are using the *X Window System*. We also assume that you have an account on the computer and know how to log on. The *X Window System* is highly customizable, and you will have to learn the idiosyncrasies of your particular installation. In many installations, windows or panels will appear with a titlebar at the top, with buttons in the right- and left-hand corners. You can bring a partially obscured window to the front by clicking its titlebar. To do much more than this with your windows, you will have to consult site-specific documentation and/or your system manager.

One of the windows on your screen should be a terminal window (probably titled "xterm" or "login"). You can type *UNIX* commands in this window. Here is a list of the basic *UNIX* commands for locating, moving, copying, and deleting files.

<u>*UNIX* Command</u>	<u>Effect</u>
ls	lists your files
cp file.a file.b	puts a copy of file.a into file.b
mv file.a file.b	renames file.a to file.b
rm file.a	deletes file.a

In fact, you should be able to do most of the necessary file manipulation of your *Maple* files from within the *Maple* program (to be explained below), but on occasion you may need to maneuver your *Maple* files exactly as you would any other files in the *UNIX* environment.

Online Help for the *X Window System*.   The usual way to obtain help in a *UNIX* environment is to consult the manual pages using the "man" command. For example, by typing the command "man ls" you can learn about the features of the "ls" command, including options that can be used with it. If you are a *UNIX* novice, you may find it instructive to try the "man" command on some of the basic system commands listed above.

Starting *Maple*.   *Maple* is often started from an xterm window by typing a special command at the *UNIX* prompt. The command may be "maple" or "xmaple". Alternatively, *Maple* might be started on your system by clicking on a special menu button. You may need to ask your system administrator for the precise command or start-up procedure. Whatever the procedure, a new window will appear containing a *Maple* "Worksheet". Near the top of the window will be a row of menu buttons. You can now start typing in the Worksheet.

Saving Your Worksheet.   To save a Worksheet, click on the **File** button in the menu row. A new menu will appear below the button. Click on the **Save As**... button. A panel will appear in the middle of the screen. This panel has four regions: a Filter region, which displays the current directory; a Directories region, which lists the subdirectories in the current directory; a Files region, which lists the files in the current directory; and a Selection region. There are also four buttons at the bottom of the panel. By double-clicking on a directory name in the Directories region, you cause the selected directory to become the current directory; the Directories and Files regions will change to show the subdirectories and files in the new current directory. The current directory always contains two subdirectories labeled "." and "..". The directory "." is the current directory. The directory ".." is the directory immediately above the current directory (the parent directory). Thus to move back up the directory tree you double-click on the ".." directory in the Directory region. If there are more subdirectories in the current directory than will fit in the

Directories region, you can use the mouse to manipulate the slider to the right of the Directories region to scroll up and down through the list of subdirectories. You can also navigate the directory tree by typing a pathname into the Filter region, and then clicking the **Filter** button.

Once you have reached the directory in which you wish to save the Worksheet (by double-clicking on successive subdirectories or typing a pathname into the Filter region) you should place the pointer at the end of the pathname in the selection box and click. Then type in the name you wish to give to your Worksheet. The name should end with the suffix ".ms". Then click on the **Save** box in the menu row. The panel will disappear, the Worksheet will be saved, and its title will change to the name you typed. If after working some more you want to save your Worksheet again using the same name, all you have to do is click on the **Save** button instead of the **Save As**... button. If you want to save it under a new name, you must repeat the steps above. You should save your work frequently.

Opening a Previously Saved Worksheet. To open a saved Worksheet, click on the **File** button, and then click on the **Open** button. A panel that is essentially identical to the one that resulted from selecting the **Save As**... button will appear. You can navigate the directory tree by double-clicking on directories (or by typing a pathname into the Filter region and clicking the Filter button) until the file you want appears in the File region of the panel. Then double-click on the name of the appropriate file (or click on the name and select **Load**). *Maple* saves files with the filename extension ".ms".

To open a new Worksheet, click the **New** button in the **File** menu. Make sure that you save the current Worksheet before you open a new or previously saved one, because opening another Worksheet will cause the current one to be closed, and unsaved changes to be lost. *Maple* gives a warning when you open a new Worksheet, but it does *not* give a warning when you open a previously saved Worksheet, so you should be especially careful in this situation.

Graphics. In *Maple*, the output of a plotting command comes up in a separate window. To paste the plot into your Worksheet, you should make the graphics window active by clicking in it, and then select **Copy** from the **Edit** menu in the graphics window. Then click at the desired insertion point in the Worksheet, and select **Paste** from the **Edit** menu in the Worksheet window. A copy of the plot will appear in the Worksheet. Once you have the plot pasted into the Worksheet you should close the graphics window, by choosing **Exit** from the **File** menu.

Printing Your Worksheet. To print a Worksheet, select **Print** from the **File** menu. A panel will appear in the center of the screen. Near the top of the panel are two small buttons labeled "Output to File:" and "Printer Command:". If you click on the button labeled "Printer Command:", your Worksheet will be directed to the printer. If you click on the button labeled "Output to File:", the Worksheet will be written to a PostScript file with suffix ".ps". The default filename will be shown in the box to the right of the label. If you want to send the output to a PostScript file with a different filename, you can click in this box and type in a new filename. Finally, when you have everything as you want it, click on the "OK" button at the bottom of the panel.

Interrupting Calculations.   Near the top of the Worksheet is an **Interrupt** button. If *Maple* is hung up in a calculation, you can usually stop it by clicking on this button.

Ending the *Maple* Session.   When you are done working, it is important to quit *Maple*. First make sure that you have saved your work. Then select the **Exit** button from the **File** menu. If you haven't saved all your work, *Maple* will give you one last chance to save it. Be sure to quit any other programs you have been using before you log out and leave the machine.

Chapter 3

Doing Mathematics
with *Maple*

These instructions are designed to get you started with the *Maple* software. The software is fairly easy to use, and with the help of these instructions you should quickly master the basic skills necessary to work with it. Before you read this chapter you should already have read the appropriate section of the preceding chapter, *Getting Started with Maple*. After you have read that section, you will know how to get *Maple* up and running. Then you should read this chapter, trying out the commands in a *Maple* Worksheet as you go along. For further practice with these *Maple* commands, work the problems in Problem Set A.

Input and Output. You interact with *Maple* using Worksheets. On your computer screen a Worksheet appears as a window with various kinds of text and graphics in it. But *Maple* also treats a Worksheet as a *document*, and in particular *Maple* knows how to break the Worksheet into pages to produce a finished, printed version of the Worksheet. A Worksheet is divided into *regions*, which can be of five different types: input, output, graphics, separator and text. We'll discuss this region structure in detail later, but in this section we discuss only two types of regions: input regions and output regions. An input region is a place where you type expressions for *Maple* to evaluate. An output region is a place where *Maple* gives its response.

To enter a command in *Maple*, you type the command in an input region, put a semicolon at the end of the command, and then push the RETURN key (on the *Macintosh*, you must push the ENTER key in the number pad at the lower right corner of the keyboard). If you type RETURN without first typing a semicolon, *Maple* will sit there, waiting for more input. If this happens, just type a semicolon and hit RETURN again. If you want a simple linefeed in an input region, you type SHIFT-RETURN (on the *Macintosh*, just RETURN). This is useful when typing a long formula, or when you want to group several commands or expressions together in a single input region. You can enter several commands in a single input region as long as you end each command with a semicolon.

As an example, try typing **1 + 1;** (with the semicolon). It should appear on the screen near the top. You have given *Maple* an expression to evaluate. To find out the answer, press RETURN (or ENTER, on the *Macintosh*). *Maple* will display the answer. Your Worksheet should now look something like this:

>   **1 + 1;**

2

The symbol ">" is the input prompt in *Maple*, and it appears at the beginning of every input region. (It is possible to customize the visible features of the *Maple* Worksheet, so you may see a different symbol for the input prompt.) The output of the command (in this case "2") is in an output region. Material in the output regions is specially formatted in mathematical notation.

Arithmetic.   As we have just seen, *Maple* can do arithmetic like a calculator. You can add with "+", subtract with "−", multiply with "*", divide with "/", and exponentiate with "^". For example:

>   **2*5 + 3^2 − 4/2;**

17

>   **(5 + 3)*(5 − 3);**

16

Maple requires you to use the "*" symbol explicitly to express multiplication. Typing "2 5" instead of "2*5", or "2x" instead of "2*x", will cause a *syntax error*—*Maple*'s way of letting you know that it didn't like the way you typed the expression.

Maple differs from a calculator in that it often does exact arithmetic rather than using decimal approximations. For example, if you type in **4/7**, *Maple* will simply respond $\frac{4}{7}$. To force *Maple* to give you a decimal approximation, you must use the built-in *Maple* command **evalf** (which means "evaluate as a floating-point number").

>   **evalf(4/7);**

0.5714285714

To get 20 digits rather than 10 in the answer, you would type **evalf(4/7,20)**. Another way to force *Maple* to use decimal approximations rather than exact numbers is to use a decimal point. For example, in *Maple*, **2.0** is different from **2** (enter the fractions **1/2** and **1/2.0** in *Maple* and see what happens). It is important to remember this distinction because approximate, or floating point, arithmetic is usually faster than exact arithmetic. Floating point output is also quite different in appearance. To see an example of this, evaluate the following two commands in your Worksheet.

>   **solve(x^3 − x − 2 = 0, x);**
>   **solve(x^3 − x − 2.0 = 0, x);**

Notice that while *Maple* is doing a computation, the pointer changes from an arrow to a watch.

Errors in Input.   If you make an error in an input line and *Maple* can't understand you, it will print an error message. For example:

```
> 5 + 3x - 2;
syntax error:
5 + 3x -2;
     ^
```

The error here is that there is a missing multiplication operator "*". Note that *Maple* places a marker at the place where it first notices the error; however, the actual error may have occurred earlier. Missing multiplication operators, brackets and parentheses are the most common errors on input lines.

   If you have made a mistake on an input line, you can edit the input line by using the mouse to position the pointer at the desired insertion point, clicking the button on the mouse, then typing (or deleting with the delete key), and finally pressing RETURN to reenter the line. When you reenter the line, *Maple* will write over the old output in the output region directly below.

Online Help.   There are several ways to get online help in *Maple*. To get help on a particular topic, enter **?<topic>**. For example, the command **?evalf** will open a window that contains help on the **evalf** command. You can also access specific parts of the online help by typing **??** or **???** before a command name. Two question marks produce the syntax of the command, while three question marks produce examples.

   You can also browse through the online help by pressing the **Help** menu button, and selecting the *Maple* Help browser. You might also try the *Maple* tutorial. To do this, enter the command **tutorial();** (remember the parentheses and the semicolon), and then follow the directions.

Algebra.   You can add, subtract, multiply, and divide variables as well as numbers. Consider the following series of commands:

```
> (x + y)*(x + y)^2;
```

$$(x + y)^3$$

```
> expand((x + y)^3);
```

$$x^3 + 3x^2y + 3xy^2 + y^3$$

```
> factor(x^3 + 3*x^2*y + 3*x*y^2 + y^3);
```

$$(x + y)^3$$

   Maple often makes minor simplifications to the formulas you type in, but does not make any big changes unless you tell it to. The **expand** command forced *Maple* to multiply the formula out, and the **factor** command told *Maple* to put it back in factored form.

Maple also has a **simplify** command that tries to express a formula as simply as possible; sometimes this involves factoring, and sometimes multiplying things out. For example:

> **simplify((x^2 – y^2)/(x – y));**

$$x + y$$

> **simplify(exp(a + ln(b*exp(c))));**

$$be^{a+c}$$

Equations and Assignments. In *Maple*, you use the combination ":=" (colon equals) to assign values to a variable. For instance,

> **x := 5;**

$$x := 5$$

will give the variable **x** the value 5 from now on. Whenever *Maple* sees an **x** it will substitute the value 5.

> **x^2 + 3*x*y + y;**

$$25 + 16y$$

To clear a variable, type **x := 'x'** . This reassigns to **x** its name, **x**.

> **x := 'x';**

$$x := x$$

> **x^2 + 3*x*y + y;**

$$x^2 + y + 3xy$$

Assignments can be quite general.

> **z := x^2 + 3*x*y + y;**

$$z := x^2 + 3xy + y$$

> **z + 7* y;**

$$x^2 + 3xy + 8y$$

> **y := 5;**

$$y := 5$$

> **z;**

$$x^2 + 15x + 5$$

The input **x := x + 5** (which would be legitimate in FORTRAN) will produce the warning "recursive definition of name". If you get such a warning you should immediately unassign the variable by typing **x := 'x'**, because evaluating an expression with a recursive definition will almost certainly cause *Maple* to crash.

Important: A common source of puzzling errors in a *Maple* session is to forget that you have defined variables (*Maple* never forgets). You can check the current definition of a variable by typing the variable name (followed by a semicolon) by itself on an input line. For example, to find the current value of the variable **z**, type **z**. If *Maple* returns z, it means that **z** has not been assigned a value. If it returns anything else, **z** has been assigned a value.

An equation in *Maple* is indicated by an equals sign (without a colon). For example, to solve the equation $x + \sin y = 3$ for y, we type

> **solve(x + sin(y) = 3, y);**

$$-\arcsin(x - 3)$$

Built-in Commands and Functions. The commands **evalf, expand, factor**, and **solve** are examples of *Maple*'s built-in commands. *Maple* also has many built-in functions, including familiar mathematical functions like **sqrt, cos**, or **log**. *Maple* also has a few built-in constants, such as **Pi** (the number π), **E** (the base e of the natural logarithm), **I** (the complex number $i = \sqrt{-1}$), and **infinity** (∞).

Some examples:

> **log(E^2);**

$$2$$

Notice that **log** and **ln** are both names for the natural logarithm function, called "ln" in many texts.

> **sin(Pi/3);**

$$\frac{1}{2}\sqrt{3}$$

(To get a numerical answer one would use the **evalf** command.)

> **solve(x^3 − x = 0, x);**

$$0, 1, -1$$

> **fsolve(exp(−x) = x, x);**

$$0.5671432904$$

We have not described the command **fsolve**, but you can find out about it by entering **?fsolve** in your *Maple* Worksheet. We will explore many other *Maple* commands and functions in this book (including commands that can differentiate, integrate, or solve differential equations).

User-defined Functions and Expressions.   It is also possible to define new functions in *Maple*. In the following example a polynomial function is defined and then evaluated at one point:

> f := x –> x^3 + 7*x – 5;

$$f := x \to x^3 + 7x - 5$$

> f(2);

17

The arrow is typed as a minus sign "–" followed by a greater than sign ">". The arrow represents a *transformation rule*: the function f takes a variable or value x and *transforms* it to $x^3 + 7x - 5$.

In *Maple*, it is important to distinguish a *function* from a simple *expression*. For example, x^3 + 7*x – 5 is an expression. We can assign a name to an expression, as follows:

> g := x^3 + 7*x – 5;

$$g := x^3 + 7x - 5$$

Although this *expression* looks very much like the *function* we defined above, it is in fact quite different. The function is a transformation rule, while the expression is merely a quantity involving x. In particular, typing **g(2)** will not give the value of the expression at $x = 2$ (try it to see what happens!). To evaluate an expression at a particular point, we must use the substitution command **subs**.

> subs(x = 2, g);

17

This command means "substitute the value of 2 for x in the expression g".

Aborting Calculations.   If *Maple* gets hung up in a calculation, or seems to be taking too long, you can usually abort it by selecting the **Interrupt** or **Stop** button. It may take a while for *Maple* to abort the calculation. It's a good idea when using any computer program to save your work often, for an unexpected crash or power outage can wipe out all your unsaved work.

Graphics.   The basic plotting command in *Maple* is **plot**. It can be used to plot both functions and expressions.

> plot(x^3 – x, x = –1..1);

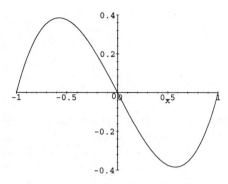

Notice that in this command we have plotted an expression, as opposed to a function. The syntax for plotting a function is similar:

> **plot(f(x), x = −1..1);**

An alternative syntax for plotting functions is **plot(f, −1..1)**. In these commands, **−1..1** indicates that the function or expression is to be plotted on the interval $-1 < x < 1$.

Plots can be misleading at times because the scale of the plot may not be what you expect and the origin may not be where you expect it to be. You should pay careful attention to the labeling of the axes. To get a plot with a specified vertical range, give the **plot** command a second range, as follows:

> **plot(x^3 − x, x = −1..1, y = −2..2);**

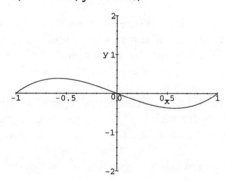

Referring to Previous Output.   *Maple* automatically remembers the output of the last three statements you entered. A double quote (") refers to the output of the previous command. Two double quotes ("") refer to the second-to-last output, and three double quotes (""") to the third-to-last output. For example:

> **2 + 2;**

4

> `"^2;`

$$16$$

> `""*5;`

$$20$$

A safer and more effective way to refer to past output is to assign the output to a variable. For example, we could type:

> `a := 2 + 2;`

$$4$$

> `a^2;`

$$16$$

> `a*5;`

$$20$$

This is more effective because it allows you to refer to the output by name anywhere in the Worksheet. It is safer because the output in the preceding region is not necessarily the most recent output generated by *Maple*. In fact, there is no way to tell by looking at the Worksheet which output is the most recent.

Visible State vs. Internal State.   When *Maple* saves a Worksheet, it saves the *visible state* of the Worksheet, *i.e.*, it saves exactly what you see on the screen and nothing else. If you open your Worksheet in a new *Maple* session, the Worksheet will contain the input and output statements, but the actual results will not be available to *Maple*'s internal computation engine. In order to use the results of your previous work in your current calculation, you must redo the old calculations. You can do this by stepping through the Worksheet, evaluating each input region. (There is also a menu button to evaluate the entire worksheet.)

Packages.   The *Maple* system actually consists of three parts. The part that reads input, displays output and manipulates Worksheets is called the *interface*. *Iris* is *Maple*'s internal name for the interface. The other two parts of *Maple*—the *kernel* and the *library*—execute the commands you type. The kernel contains the core parts of *Maple* that are always available. The library contains additional commands that are only loaded into memory as needed. Most commands are loaded automatically without any intervention on your part. You don't need to concern yourself with these; for all practical purposes, you can pretend that they are part of the kernel.

To use certain *Maple* commands, however, you must tell *Maple* explicitly to load them. If you try to use a command that is not automatically loaded without explicitly loading it, *Maple* will not know the command and will simply echo the input line in the output area. For example,

> **contourplot(x^2 + y^2, x = −5..5, y = −5..5);**

$$\text{contourplot}(x^2 + y^2, x = -5..5, y = -5..5)$$

The command **contourplot** is a library command and must be loaded explicitly.

Most of the library routines that are not loaded automatically are bundled in *packages*. The two packages you will need for most of the problem sets are called **plots** and **DEtools**. The former contains a collection of specialized plotting routines including **contourplot, implicitplot, display,** and **odeplot**. The latter contains additional routines such as **dfieldplot** and **DEplot** for studying differential equations. You can load all the commands in a package with a single command. For example, the command

> **with(plots):**

loads all the routines from the **plots** package. (If you end the command with a semicolon instead of a colon, then *Maple* prints a list of the commands contained in the package.) You can conserve memory by loading a single command from a package instead of the entire package. For example, to load the single command **contourplot** from the **plots** package, type **with(plots, contourplot)**.

There are a few commands that are not automatically loaded and are not part of a package. These can be loaded using the command **readlib**. You should rarely need to use this command. The online documentation warns you when you need to use **readlib** to load a command from the library.

Suppressing Output.   Certain commands produce output that might be considered superfluous. For example, when you assign a value to a variable *Maple* echoes the value. When you load a package using the **with** command, *Maple* prints a list of all the commands in the package. The output of a *Maple* command can always be suppressed by ending the command with a *colon* rather than a *semicolon*. Note that ending a statement with a colon has no effect on what *Maple* does internally; it only affects what you see in the Worksheet.

The Restart Command.   A simple and effective way to clear all the assigned values in a *Maple* session is to use the **restart** command. This command shuts down *Maple*'s computational engine, clears everything from memory, and then restarts the computational engine. Nothing will change on the screen. After you have typed **restart**, you can continue working. But keep in mind that all the variable assignments have been cleared, so you will have to evaluate the appropriate input regions to restore any assignments you want to use. We recommend that you use the **restart** command frequently. In particular, you should put the **restart** command at the top of every worksheet so that *Maple* starts with a clean slate each time you evaluate the Worksheet from the beginning.

Problem Set A

Practice with *Maple*

In this problem set, you will use *Maple* to do some basic calculations, and then to plot, differentiate and integrate various functions. This problem set is the minimum you should do in order to reach a level of proficiency that will enable you to use *Maple* throughout the course. In this problem set you should concentrate on the mathematics, but if you wish to try out some of the editing features of the Worksheet interface, you can read about them in the next chapter.

1. Evaluate:

   (a) $3 + 9$

   (b) 2^{123}

   (c) π^2 and e to 35 digits

   (d) the fractions $\frac{22}{7}$, $\frac{311}{99}$, and $\frac{355}{113}$, and determine which is the best approximation to π.

2. Evaluate to ten digits:

   (a) $\dfrac{\sin(0.1)}{0.1}$

   (b) $\dfrac{\sin(0.01)}{0.01}$

   (c) $\dfrac{\sin(0.0001)}{0.0001}$.

3. Factor the polynomial $x^3 - y^3$.

4. *Maple's* **plot** command plots the graph of one or more functions. Type **?plot** for a brief explanation of its syntax (or see Chapter 3). Use *Maple* to graph the following:

   (a) $y = 3x + 2$ for $-5 \leq x \leq 5$

   (b) $y = x^2 + x - 1$ for $-5 \leq x \leq 5$

(c) $y = \sin x$ for $0 \le x \le 4\pi$

(d) $y = \tan x$ for $-\pi/2 \le x \le \pi/2$

(e) $y = e^{-x^2}$ for $-2 \le x \le 2$.

5. Plot the functions x^4 and 2^x on the same graph, and determine how many times their graphs intersect. (*Hint:* You will probably have to make several plots, using intervals of various sizes, in order to find all the intersection points. You may have to limit the y-range in your plots.) Now find the values of the points of intersection by using the **fsolve** command.

6. The **contourplot** command takes a function of two variables (say $f(x,y)$) and plots several *level curves* of the function (that is, curves of the form $f(x,y) = c$, where c is a constant). For example, **contourplot(x^2 + y^2, x = −5..5, y = −5..5)** plots the level curves of the function $f(x,y) = x^2 + y^2$, in the square $-5 \le x \le 5$, $-5 \le y \le 5$. (Remember to enter **with(plots)** before using the **contourplot** command.)

   (a) Use **contourplot** to plot level curves of the function $f(x,y) = 3y + y^3 - x^3$, in the region where x and y are between -1 and 1 (to get an idea of what the curves look like near the origin) and in a larger region (to get the big picture).

   (b) A particular level set of a function can be plotted with the **implicitplot** command (also in the **plots** package). Plot the curve $3y + y^3 - x^3 = 5$.

   (c) Plot the level set of the function $f(x,y) = y \ln x + x \ln y$ that contains the point $(1,1)$.

7. The derivative of a function can be found by typing **diff(f(x), x)**. Find the derivatives of the following functions. In each case, if it appears that the answer *Maple* gives can be simplified, investigate the possibility by using **simplify**.

   (a) $f(x) = 7x^3 + 3x^2 - 2x + 1$

   (b) $f(x) = \dfrac{x+1}{x^2+1}$

   (c) $f(x) = \cos(x^2 + 1)$

   (d) $f(x) = \arcsin(2x + 3)$

   (e) $f(x) = \sqrt{1 + x^4}$

   (f) $f(x) = x^r$

   (g) $f(x) = \arctan(x)$.

8. Consider the polynomial $x^6 - 21x^5 + 175x^4 - 735x^3 + 1624x^2 - 1764x + 720$.

   (a) Factor it.

   (b) Find the roots using the *Maple* command **solve**.

(c) Plot the polynomial for $0.5 \le x \le 6.5$.

(d) Plot the polynomial and its derivative on the same interval. Explain your plot using calculus.

9. Use the *Maple* command **limit** to evaluate the following limits:

(a) $\displaystyle\lim_{x \to 0} \frac{\sin x}{x}$

(b) $\displaystyle\lim_{x \to \pi} \frac{1 + \cos x}{x - \pi}$

(c) $\displaystyle\lim_{x \to \infty} x\, e^{-x}$

(d) $\displaystyle\lim_{x \to 0^-} \frac{1}{x}$

(e) $\displaystyle\lim_{x \to 0} \sin\left(\frac{1}{x}\right)$.

10. The integration command in *Maple* is **int**. Type **?int** to see the general syntax for both indefinite and definite integration. As an example, **int(sin(x), x)** gives the output $-\cos x$. Notice that the constant of integration is left out; *Maple* gives you one possible antiderivative of the function you specified. As an example of the definite integral, the command **int(sin(x), x = 0..Pi)** gives the answer 2.

See if *Maple* can do the following integrals. For the indefinite integrals, use *Maple* again to check the results by differentiating:

(a) $\int_0^{\pi/2} \sin x \, dx$

(b) $\int x \cos(x^2) \, dx$

(c) $\int \sin(3x) \sqrt{1 - \cos(3x)} \, dx$

(d) $\int \ln x \, dx$

(e) $\int x^2 \sqrt{x + 4} \, dx$

(f) $\int \sqrt{x^4 + 1} \, dx$

(g) $\int e^{\cos x} \, dx$

(h) $\int_{-\infty}^{\infty} e^{-x^2} \, dx$.

11. *Maple* can also integrate functions numerically, to get an approximate answer. This is useful in cases where *Maple* cannot perform the symbolic integration. The command that does this is **evalf(Int())**, which has the same syntax as **int**, but note the capital **I**. Find numerical values for the following integrals:

(a) $\int_0^\pi e^{\cos x} dx$

(b) $\int_0^1 \sqrt{x^4 + 1} \, dx$

(c) $\int_{-\infty}^\infty e^{-x^2} dx$.

For part (c), figure out how much the numerical answer differs from the exact answer found in the previous problem.

Chapter 4

Using *Maple* Worksheets

In this chapter we describe some aspects of the Worksheet feature of *Maple*. In particular, we describe some of the formatting tools that will help you to create an attractive and polished finished document. Since we refer frequently to menu buttons, we establish the following convention: When referring to a button in a submenu of another menu, we type first the name of the button in the top menu, then a colon, then the name of the button in the submenu. For example, **Format:Math Style:Small** means the **Small** button of the **Math Style** submenu of the **Format** menu. To get to this button, press and hold the mouse button on the **Format** button at the top of the screen, drag down to the **Math Style** button, and then drag right and select the **Small** button.

We describe the Worksheet interface for *Windows*, the *Macintosh*, and the *X Window System*. Most of the differences between platforms occur because menu options are rearranged.

Keyboard Equivalents.   You may have noticed that some of the menu buttons have not only a name but also some extra symbols on the right. For example, the **Copy** button from the **Edit** menu is marked with a "Ctrl+C" on the right. (On the *Macintosh* a special symbol referring to the COMMAND key precedes the "C".) This represents a *keyboard equivalent*. If you hold down the CONTROL key (on the *Macintosh*, the COMMAND key) and type the "C" key, it has the same effect as clicking on the **Copy** button. Experienced users often find these keyboard equivalents to be efficient alternatives to using the mouse. You can read the keyboard equivalents off the menu buttons. On some systems, certain menu buttons refer to the *function keys* along the top of the keyboard, or to the ALT key. For example, in Windows, "F5" will toggle a region between input and text. In the *X Window System*, you may have to experiment to find the key that functions as the ALT key. It is not necessarily the key labeled "Alt".

Regions.   A *region* is a line or group of lines in a *Maple* Worksheet containing information of a particular type. There are five types of regions in a *Maple* Worksheet: input, output, text, graphics, and separator. An input region begins with an input prompt (usually ">"), and is used for passing commands to *Maple*'s computational engine. An output region does not have a separate prompt, but can usually be recognized by its elaborate formatting. A text region also does not begin with a prompt, and is used for inserting commentary into your Worksheet. A graphics region is an area containing pasted graphics (see the section *Graphics* in Chapter 2). A separator region is simply a horizontal black line.

Somewhere in the Worksheet there should be a small vertical bar, called the *insertion point*. The letters and symbols that you type will appear at the insertion point. (To be precise, typed characters will only show up in input and text regions, though the insertion point may appear in any type of region.) Note that the insertion point is independent of the position of the pointer (the arrow controlled by the mouse). The insertion point can be moved to the position of the pointer by clicking the mouse button. You can also use the arrow keys on the keyboard to move the insertion point around.

There are special commands for inserting regions and changing their type. To insert a new input region, set the insertion point in an existing region and then select **Format:Insert New Region:Below** (on the *Macintosh*, **Format:Insert Prompt**, and in the *X Window System*, **Edit:Insert Prompt**). An input prompt will appear below the current region. (In *Windows*, this will only work on Input and text regions.) To insert a new text region on the *Macintosh* select **Format:Enter Text**, and in the *X Window System* select **Edit:Insert Text**. (You may find it useful to make note of the keyboard equivalents for the above commands, which are different for each platform.) To insert a text region in *Windows*, you must first create an input region and then change the new region to a text region by typing the "F5" function key, or by selecting **Format:Text Region**. On the *Macintosh* and in the *X Window System*, you can change the type of a region by using the **Input:Text** button just above the Worksheet.

Editing Text and Input.   The basic editing features are under the **Edit** menu, namely, the **Cut**, **Copy**, and **Paste** commands (note the keyboard equivalents listed on the menu buttons). You select text to cut or copy by holding down the mouse button and dragging the mouse across the relevant text. To paste material that you have cut or copied, move the pointer to the desired insertion point, click the mouse button (to set the insertion point), and choose **Paste** from the **Edit** menu or press CONTROL-V (on the *Macintosh*, COMMAND-V).

Manipulating Worksheets.   Only a portion of the Worksheet is displayed in the window on the screen. To scroll through the Worksheet use the "page up" and "page down" buttons on the keyboard, or drag the slider up and down in the scroll bar on the right side of the window. (See the section *Memory Management* for some tips on how to speed up scrolling.)

You can have only one Worksheet active at a given time. To switch to a different Worksheet, select **File:Open**. (The *Macintosh* works differently; see the section *Scratchpads* in the special section on the *Macintosh* at the end of this chapter.)

Page Breaks.   When you print your Worksheet, *Maple* automatically breaks the Worksheet into pages. In some cases you may want to force *Maple* to start a new page in a different place than it chooses. In *Windows*, you can do this with the command **Format:Insert Page Break**. In the *X Window System*, insert two consecutive region separators using **Edit:Insert Separator Line**. In either case, the page break will show up as a thick black line. If you are using a *Macintosh*, see the special section at the end of this chapter.

Graphics.   In Chapter 2, we described how to cut and paste a plot from a graphics window into the Worksheet. In this section we describe a few more things you can do with graphics.

In one of the corners of a graphics window there should be a small box that can be used to resize the plot (in *Windows*, you can resize by dragging any edge). Press and hold the mouse button in this area and then drag the corner to resize the window. When you cut and paste the plot into the Worksheet, the pasted plot will be the same size as the one in the graphics window.

The **Axes** menu of a graphics window allows you to choose among three styles of axes: **Normal, Boxed,** and **Frame.** You may want to use **Boxed** axes for contour plots and direction field plots. (For help finding the **Axes** menu on the *Macintosh*, see the special section at the end of this chapter.)

One last thing you can do with a graphics window (but not with a pasted graphic) is to find coordinates of points in the plot. Position the pointer over the point you're interested in, and click the mouse. The coordinates of the point will appear in the window.

Be sure to close graphics windows when you're finished with them. Each window uses a substantial amount of memory, and having too many of them open could cause *Maple* to crash.

Online Help.   In Chapter 3, we described some aspects of *Maple*'s extensive online help facility. We now describe an additional help feature available in *Windows* and on the *Macintosh*. If there is a command in your Worksheet that you'd like to find out about, you can select it by dragging the mouse across it, and then choose the command **Help:Help On**... (the name of the command you selected appears in quotes in this menu button), or use the *Windows* keyboard equivalent CONTROL-F1. (On the *Macintosh*, the equivalent menu command is **Windows:Help for Selection**....) This will bring up a help window for the selected command. This is a useful feature when using the Help Browser, since the documentation contains many cross-references that can be followed using the above procedure.

Setting Defaults.   There are several ways to customize your *Maple* Worksheets, and once you become comfortable using *Maple* you may want to experiment with them. For now we suggest that at the beginning of each *Maple* session you select **Format:Math Style:Small** (on the *Macintosh*, **Format:Output:Small**, and in the *X Window System*, **Options:Output Fontsize:Small**). This will make the output slightly smaller, and will allow you to see a larger piece of the Worksheet in the window. Before you print the Worksheet you should also turn off **View:Separator Lines** (in the *X Window System*, **View:Display Region Boundaries**) if it has been turned on in your session. (On the *Macintosh*, you can delete these lines with **Format:Remove Separator Lines**.) Although the horizontal lines can be useful while you're working on the document, the printed Worksheet looks better without them.

If you are using a public computer and you find that your Worksheet looks substantially different than you think it should, it may be because a previous user has changed some of the defaults. You may have to change the defaults back. If the computer you are using reboots from a central fileserver, you may be able to restore the defaults by rebooting the machine.

Memory Management.   *Maple* uses a lot of computer memory, for computations as well as for the interface (or *front end*). These memory demands can put a severe strain on computers that do not have either a large amount of RAM or a hard disk and virtual memory. Here are some things you can do to economize on memory. In Chapter 8, we give some more tips on managing memory.

1. Use the **restart** command. This command restarts the *Maple* kernel and clears all definitions.
2. Every open window uses up memory, so windows should be closed when no longer needed. This applies to help windows, graphics windows, and (on the *Macintosh*) Scratchpads.
3. Graphics require a great deal of memory. If you are having problems with a shortage of memory, you may want to postpone pasting the graphics into the Worksheet until you are done with everything else. For example, you might fiddle with a plotting command until you have it just the way you want it. Then delete all the graphics windows, but leave the plot command in the Worksheet. Continue working on the Worksheet. Then just before you print, go back and evaluate the plotting commands and cut and paste the plots into the Worksheet. This strategy has the additional benefit that the Worksheet scrolls faster without graphics.
4. *Maple* prints output in standard math notation, with integral signs, fancy symbols, *etc.* This kind of printing uses a lot of memory and causes the Worksheet to scroll slowly. To speed things up and economize on memory, select **Format:Math Style:Character** (in the *X Window System*, **Options:Output Mode:Pretty Print**, on the *Macintosh*, **Format:Output:Character**). This causes output to be displayed in "pretty-printed" form using standard characters. After you are finished working on the Worksheet, and before you print, switch to **Format:Math Style:Small** (in the *X Window System*, **Options:Output Mode:Hi-res Print**, on the *Macintosh*, **Format:Output:Small**), and then evaluate the Worksheet to put the output back into standard math notation.

5. Do each problem in a separate Worksheet. When you are finished with one problem, save and close the Worksheet, and then open up a new Worksheet for the next problem. You can print out each Worksheet separately, then bundle them together when you turn in your assignment. This strategy also limits the amount of work you will lose if the worksheet becomes corrupted.

6. If all else fails, save your Worksheet, quit *Maple*, and then restart it.

Monitoring Memory Use.   If you have problems with insufficient memory, you can monitor memory usage by keeping an eye on the statistics at the bottom of the Worksheet. (On the *Macintosh*, select **Windows : Status**. A panel will appear with memory statistics for both the interface and computations. You can move this panel to the edge of the screen and leave it open so that you can keep an eye on the memory statistics.)

Save Your Work Often.   *Maple* is a complex program, and as with any complex program, you will almost certainly experience unexpected problems and crashes while using it. The best protection against such problems is to save your work often. If *Maple* does crash, you'll only lose the work you've done since the last save.

Special Features of Worksheets in *Windows*

Just below the menu bar of a Worksheet in *Windows* there is a bar with various buttons on it. These buttons perform some of the menu functions described above. To learn what a particular button does, place the pointer over the button and hold down the mouse button. A description of the function will appear at the bottom of the window. If you do not want to perform the function, move the pointer away from the button before releasing the mouse. One button that does not have a menu equivalent is the "Stop Sign" button, which is used to interrupt calculations. You can turn off the tool bar with the toggle switch in **View : Tool Bar**.

Special Features of Worksheets on the *Macintosh*

There are some additional features of the interface which are available only on the *Macintosh*.

The Ruler.   Just below the title bar of a Worksheet on the *Macintosh* there is a ruler with various buttons below it. The first four of these buttons determine how the material in a region is positioned: flush left, centered, flush right, or flush left and right. Next to these are buttons labeled **Input**, **Output**, and **Text**. When the insertion point is in a region, one of the position buttons will be darkened and one of the region type buttons will be darkened. These buttons indicate what kind of region the insertion point is in and what the default positioning is for items in that region. For example, a text region is, by default, positioned flush left. If you wanted to have centered text, say in a title, you would type the text in a text region and then click on the appropriate positioning button. You can also change the type of an empty input region by selecting the region and then clicking on the text button in the ruler.

Scratchpads. On the *Macintosh*, you can open more than one Worksheet at a time by choosing **File:Open**. A panel will pop up that will allow you to select a Worksheet to open. The new Worksheet will be opened as a "Scratchpad". A Scratchpad Worksheet is quite different from the Active Worksheet. If you enter input from the Scratchpad, it will be automatically pasted into the Active Worksheet and the output will also appear in the Active Worksheet (but not in the Scratchpad).

The principal use for Scratchpads is to transfer material from previously saved Worksheets into the Active Worksheet. For example, to transfer all the input regions from Worksheet B into Worksheet A, you proceed as follows: Open Worksheet A as the Active Worksheet by clicking on its icon. Select **File:Open**, and in the panel find Worksheet B. Once Worksheet B is open as a Scratchpad, position the pointer at the top of Worksheet B and then step through Worksheet B by repeatedly hitting the ENTER key. The input and output will appear in Worksheet A. When you are finished with Worksheet B, close its window and then continue working on Worksheet A.

There can be only one Active Worksheet in a *Maple* session. To open a different Worksheet as the Active Worksheet you must quit the *Maple* session and then open the new Worksheet by clicking on its icon.

Mathematical Typing. When inserting commentary in Worksheets, it is often useful to be able to type certain mathematical symbols (∞ or π, for example). Some mathematical symbols are easily accessible from the keyboard of a *Macintosh*. For example, here is a table of some keystroke combinations that generate mathematical symbols.

Keystrokes	Symbol
OPTION-5	∞
OPTION-.	$\geq$
OPTION-,	$\leq$
OPTION-=	$\neq$
OPTION-+	$\pm$
OPTION-p	π
OPTION-b	$\int$

Note that the OPTION key should be held down while the other key is pressed. (The OPTION key is next to the COMMAND key.)

It is also possible to create subscripts and superscripts. For example, to create the expression "x_1", first type "$x1$", then select the 1 (drag the mouse across it to highlight it), then select **Format:Style:Subscript**. Superscripts are created in a similar way. (Be sure to click on a new insertion point before you resume typing or you will delete the text you have highlighted.) A similar procedure can be used to create italic and bold type: after highlighting the appropriate text, select **Format:Style:Bold** to create bold text. To create Greek letters, type a letter, select it, then select **Format:Font:Symbol**. If you do this with the letter "D", for example, you obtain the Greek letter Δ.

Another way of using different fonts in your Worksheet is to emphasize titles and section headings. Suppose, for example, that you want to enlarge the font used for the title of your Worksheet. Select the title by dragging across it so it's highlighted. Then select **Format:Size:18**. You could select a different font and style as well. Finally, you could center the title by clicking the centering button in the Ruler. Section headings could be set in a boldface, larger font (14, bold, for example) to make them easier to find. You should experiment with these formatting features and try to develop a style you like.

Showing and Using Page Breaks. On the *Macintosh*, you can avoid bad page breaks by inspecting and modifying the page breaks before printing. First select **Settings:Show Page Breaks**. The page breaks should appear as dotted horizontal lines in the Worksheet. Inspect the Worksheet to see whether there are any bad or clumsy page breaks. For example, it is generally undesirable to have a page break between an input region and the output region it generates. The best way to alter the page breaks is to type additional carriage returns (using the RETURN key) to create extra white space. Another way is to use the command **Format:Insert Page Break**. Selecting this command will cause a new page break to be inserted at the current insertion point. This page break will appear as a faint dotted line. To delete the page break, click on the line to highlight it and then press the delete key.

Graphics Window Options. Near the top of a graphics window is a button labeled **Options**.... Clicking on this button will bring up a new window labeled "Plotting Options". The **Axes** option was described in the *Graphics* section earlier in this chapter. The **Title** option allows you to type in a title for the plot. This title will appear both at the top of the graphics window, and also just above the plot. It is seldom necessary to put a title on a plot because the input statement in the Worksheet usually conveys adequate information about the plot.

Recovering from Errors. We have already described how to interrupt a *Maple* evaluation using "COMMAND-.". There is one other thing you can try when things go wrong on a *Macintosh*. The command **File:Revert** will replace the Active Worksheet with the most recently saved version, although it does not change *Maple*'s internal state.

Chapter 5

Solutions of Differential Equations

In this chapter, we show how to solve differential equations with *Maple*. For many differential equations, the *Maple* command **dsolve** produces the general solution to the differential equation, or the specific solution to an associated initial value problem. We also discuss the existence, uniqueness, and stability of solutions of differential equations. These are fundamental issues in the theory and application of differential equations. An understanding of them helps in interpreting and using results produced by *Maple*.

Finding Symbolic Solutions

Consider the differential equation

$$\frac{dy}{dx} = f(x, y). \tag{1}$$

A solution to this equation is a function $y(x)$ of the independent variable x that satisfies $y'(x) = f(x, y(x))$. It is sometimes possible to find a formula for the solutions to (1); we call such a formula a *symbolic solution*. In *Maple*, the command that finds symbolic solutions is **dsolve**. To find a symbolic solution of the differential equation (1), type

   dsolve(diff(y(x), x) = f(x, y(x)), y(x));

Notice that you must type **y(x)** instead of **y** to let *Maple* know that y is the dependent variable and x is the independent variable. *Maple* produces the answer in terms of an arbitrary constant _C1. (For higher order equations, there will be several arbitrary constants.) For example, consider the differential equation

$$\frac{dy}{dx} = x + y.$$

You can solve this equation in *Maple* by typing

   dsolve(diff(y(x), x) = x + y(x), y(x));

The output from this command is

$$y(x) = -x - 1 + e^x \, \_C1$$

You can then obtain specific solutions by choosing specific values for _C1. For example, the solution satisfying a given initial condition can be obtained by choosing _C1 appropriately. This value of _C1 can be found by imposing the initial condition on the general solution and solving for _C1. Alternatively, you can specify the initial condition as well as the differential equation when you use **dsolve**. To solve the initial value problem

$$\frac{dy}{dx} = f(x, y), \qquad y(x_0) = y_0,$$

you would type

dsolve({diff(y(x), x) = f(x, y(x)), y(x0) = y0}, y(x));

For example, the command

sol1 := dsolve({diff(y(x), x) = x + y(x), y(0) = 2}, y(x));

produces the output

$$sol1 := y(x) = -x - 1 + 3e^x$$

The solution of the differential equation is the expression following the equals sign. In this example, we have given the name **sol1** to the output.

Next, suppose you want to plot the solution, or find its value at a particular value of x. You can't just tell *Maple* to plot **y(x)** or evaluate **y(x)** at $x = 5$, say, because **dsolve** presents the solution in the form of an *equation*, not a function. The most straightforward way to plot or evaluate the solution is to define a function equal to the expression following the equals sign,

y1 := x -> -x - 1 + 3*exp(x);

and then plot or evaluate **y1(x)**. You can also use the *Maple* commands **rhs** and **unapply** to extract the function automatically from **sol1**. The command

y1 := unapply(rhs(sol1), x);

will extract the right-hand side (using **rhs**) of the solution equation and convert it (using **unapply**) into a function of the variable x.

We often want to study a family of solutions obtained by varying the initial condition. Here is a natural way to do this in *Maple*. Begin by solving the differential equation with a generic initial value. For example,

sol2 := dsolve({diff(y(x), x) = x + y(x), y(0) = c}, y(x));

produces a solution formula in terms of the initial value c. The result of this command is

$$sol2 := y(x) = -x - 1 + e^x(1 + c)$$

Next, view the right-hand side as a function of both x and c. To define such a function in *Maple*, type

y2 := unapply(rhs(sol2), x, c);

Now suppose we want to plot a family of solution curves with initial values $y(0) = -2, -1, \ldots, 4$ on the interval $0 \leq x \leq 3$. We can type

   plot({y2(x, c) \$ c = −2..4}, x = 0..3);

The result of this command is shown in Figure 1. (The *Maple* syntax used here is the *sequence operator*, represented by a dollar sign. You can get more information about this operator by typing **?dollar** in a *Maple* session, or by consulting Chapter 8.)

Figure 1

The **dsolve** command is robust; it can solve many differential equations. In fact, it can solve most of the differential equations that can be solved with the standard solution methods one learns in an introductory course. However, there are many other equations, some of which can be solved by more advanced solution methods, that *Maple* cannot solve.

REMARK. Although we have focused on first order equations in this section, **dsolve** also solves higher order equations and systems of equations. See the *Differentiation* section in Chapter 8, Chapter 12 and the Sample Worksheet Solutions for examples.

Existence and Uniqueness

The fundamental existence and uniqueness theorems for differential equations guarantee that every initial condition $y(x_0) = y_0$ leads to a unique solution near x_0, provided that the right-hand side of the differential equation (1) is a "nice" function (to be specific, provided that f and $\partial f / \partial y$ are continuous functions). Graphically, these theorems say that there is a solution curve through every point, and that the solution curves cannot cross. Thus, initial value problems have exactly one solution, but, since there are an infinite number of initial conditions, differential equations have an infinite number of solutions. This principle is implicit in the results obtained above with **dsolve**; when we do not specify an initial condition, the solution depends on an arbitrary constant; when we specify an initial condition, the solution is completely determined.

It is important to remember that the existence and uniqueness theorems only guarantee the existence of a solution *near* the initial point x_0. Consider the initial value problem

$$\frac{dy}{dx} = y^2, \qquad y(0) = 1.$$

From the *Maple* command

sol3 := dsolve({diff(y(x), x) = y(x)^2, y(0) = 1}, y(x));

we get the output

$$sol3 := y(x) = -\frac{1}{x - 1}$$

To understand where the solution exists, we can graph the expression given by **dsolve** in Figure 2.

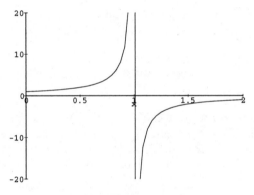

Figure 2

We see that the graph has two branches. Since the left branch passes through the initial data point $(0, 1)$, it is the desired solution. Furthermore, we see that the solution exists from $-\infty$ to 1, but does not extend beyond 1. In fact, it becomes unbounded as x approaches 1 from the left. Note that *Maple* includes the asymptote.

Stability of Differential Equations

In addition to existence and uniqueness, the sensitivity of the solution of an initial value problem to the initial value is a fundamental issue in the theory and application of differential equations. We introduce this issue through the following examples.

EXAMPLE 1. Consider the initial value problem

$$\frac{dy}{dx} + 2y = e^{-x}, \qquad y(0) = y_0.$$

We ask: How does the solution $y(x)$ depend on the initial value y_0? More specifically: Does the solution depend continuously on y_0? Do small variations in y_0 lead to small, or large, variations in the solution? Since the solution is

$$y(x) = e^{-x} + (y_0 - 1)e^{-2x},$$

we immediately see that, for any fixed x, the solution $y(x)$ depends continuously on y_0. We can say more. If we let $\tilde{y}(x)$ be the solution of the same equation, but with the initial condition $\tilde{y}(0) = \tilde{y}_0$, then $\tilde{y}(x) = e^{-x} + (\tilde{y}_0 - 1)e^{-2x}$. So, we have

$$|y(x) - \tilde{y}(x)| = |y_0 - \tilde{y}_0|e^{-2x}.$$

Thus for $x \geq 0$ we see that $|y(x) - \tilde{y}(x)|$ is never larger than $|y_0 - \tilde{y}_0|$. In fact, $|y(x) - \tilde{y}(x)|$ decreases as x increases. For $x \leq 0$ the situation is different. When x is a large negative number, the initial difference $|y_0 - \tilde{y}_0|$ is magnified by the large factor e^{-2x}. Even though $y(x)$ depends continuously on y_0, small changes in y_0 lead to large changes in $y(x)$. For example, if $|y_0 - \tilde{y}_0| = 10^{-3}$, then $|y(-7) - \tilde{y}(-7)| = 10^{-3}e^{14} \approx 1203$. These observations are confirmed by Figure 3, a plot of the solutions corresponding to initial values $y(0) = 0.97, 1, 1.03$ for $-3 \leq x \leq 3$.

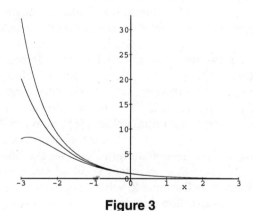

Figure 3

EXAMPLE 2. The solution of the initial value problem

$$\frac{dy}{dx} - 2y = -3e^{-x}, \qquad y(0) = y_0$$

is $y(x) = e^{-x} + (y_0 - 1)e^{2x}$. Again, $y(x)$ depends continuously on y_0 for fixed x. Letting $\tilde{y}(x)$ be the solution with initial value $\tilde{y}_0$, we see that

$$|y(x) - \tilde{y}(x)| = |y_0 - \tilde{y}_0|e^{2x}.$$

Now we see that $y(x)$ is very sensitive to changes in the initial value for x large and positive, but insensitive for x negative. These observations are confirmed by Figure 4, a plot of the solutions corresponding to initial values $y(0) = 0.97, 1, 1.03$ for $-2 \leq x \leq 2$.

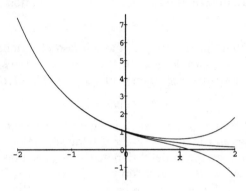

Figure 4

Often, we are primarily interested in positive values of x, such as when x corresponds to time in a physical problem. If an initial value problem is to predict the future of a physical system effectively, the solution for positive x should be fairly insensitive to the initial value, *i.e.*, small changes in the initial value should lead to small changes in the solution for positive time. To see the importance of this principle, note that for a physical system the initial value y_0 is typically not known exactly, but is found by measurement. When measuring y_0, we usually get only an approximate value $\tilde{y}_0$. Then, if $\tilde{y}(x)$ is the solution corresponding to $\tilde{y}_0$ and the solution is very sensitive to the initial value, $\tilde{y}(x)$ will have little relation to the actual state y (x) of the system as x increases.

A differential equation (like the equation in Example 1) whose solution is fairly insensitive to the initial value as x increases is called *stable*, while a differential equation (like the equation in Example 2) whose solution is very sensitive to the initial value as x increases is called *unstable*. As we have seen, if an equation is unstable and is used over a long time interval, a small error in the initial value can result in a large error later on. Caution should be exercised when using an unstable equation to model a physical problem.

REMARK. We have considered stability as x increases, *i.e.*, stability to the right. We can also consider stability to the left. There are equations that are stable both to the left and to the right, and equations that are unstable both to the left and right.

The following theorem, which we state without proof, is often useful in assessing stability.

THEOREM. *Suppose $f(x, y)$ has continuous first order partial derivatives in the vertical strip*

$$R = \{(x, y) \; : \; x_0 \le x \le x_1, -\infty < y < \infty\},$$

and suppose there are numbers K and L such that

$$K \le \frac{\partial f}{\partial y}(x, y) \le L, \quad \text{for all } (x, y) \in R.$$

If $y(x)$ and $\tilde{y}(x)$ are solutions of $dy/dx = f(x, y)$ on the interval $x_0 \le x \le x_1$ with initial values $y(x_0) = y_0$ and $\tilde{y}(x_0) = \tilde{y}_0$, respectively, then

$$|y_0 - \tilde{y}_0|e^{K(x-x_0)} \le |y(x) - \tilde{y}(x)| \le |y_0 - \tilde{y}_0|e^{L(x-x_0)},$$

for all $x_0 \le x \le x_1$.

If $L \le 0$, then the right-hand inequality in the theorem shows that

$$|y(x) - \tilde{y}(x)| \le |y_0 - \tilde{y}_0|, \quad \text{for all } x_0 \le x \le x_1.$$

Thus the solutions differ by no more than the difference in the initial values, and the differential equation is stable. Moreover, if $L > 0$, but not too large, and $x_1 - x_0$ is not too large, then

$$|y(x) - \tilde{y}(x)| \le M|y_0 - \tilde{y}_0|, \quad \text{for all } x_0 \le x \le x_1,$$

where $M = e^{L(x_1-x_0)}$ is a moderate sized constant. Thus the equation is only mildly sensitive to changes in the initial value, and the equation is only mildly unstable. On the other hand, if $K > 0$, then the left-hand inequality in the theorem shows that the solution is sensitive to changes in the initial value, especially over long intervals. We can briefly summarize these results by saying that if $\partial f/\partial y \le 0$, then the differential equation is stable; but if $\partial f/\partial y > 0$, then the equation is unstable.

REMARK. The right-hand inequality in the theorem is an example of a *continuous dependence* result; it shows that the solution depends continuously on the initial value.

Let us examine our examples in light of these observations. Rewriting the equation in Example 1 as $dy/dx = -2y + e^{-x}$, we see that $f(x, y) = -2y + e^{-x}$ and $\partial f/\partial y = -2$. We can apply the theorem with $x_0 = 0, x_1 = \infty$, and $L = K = -2$ to find that

$$|y(x) - \tilde{y}(x)| = |y_0 - \tilde{y}_0|e^{-2x}, \quad \text{for all } x \ge 0,$$

as we found above from the solution formula. Thus the equation is stable. We could also conclude that the equation is stable just by noting that $\partial f/\partial y < 0$. Likewise, for the equation of Example 2, $f(x, y) = 2y - 3e^{-x}$ and $\partial f/\partial y = 2 > 0$, so the equation is unstable.

Of course, we can understand the stability of the differential equations in these two examples by examining the solution formulas. But $\partial f/\partial y$ can be calculated and its sign and size found, even if a solution formula cannot be found. For example, we can immediately tell that the differential equation $dy/dx + x^2 y^3 = \cos x$ is stable because

$$f(x, y) = -x^2 y^3 + \cos x$$

and $\partial f / \partial y = -3x^2 y^2 \leq 0$. Yet neither **dsolve** nor any other standard technique enables us to find a formula solution to this differential equation.

Throughout the course we will see many examples that illustrate the dependence (either sensitive or insensitive) of the solution to an initial value problem on the initial value.

Caveats.   It is important to realize that *Maple*, like any software system, may occasionally produce misleading results. Consider, for example, the initial value problem

$$\frac{dy}{dx} = -\frac{x}{y}, \qquad y(0) = -1.$$

In Versions V.2 and V.3 of *Maple*, the command

> **sol4 := dsolve({diff(y(x), x) = −x/y(x), y(0) = −1}, y(x));**

gives the output

$$sol4 := y(x) = -\sqrt{-x^2 + 1}, \sqrt{-x^2 + 1}$$

suggesting that there are two solutions, in violation of uniqueness. However, it is easily seen that only the first function satisfies the initial condition. (Both functions satisfy the differential equation.)   This example shows that a good theoretical understanding is a valuable guide in interpreting computer-generated results, and therefore in identifying situations in which *Maple* has produced a misleading result.

The **dsolve** command currently (Version V.3) will not handle differential equations with decimal coefficients. For example, **dsolve** does not solve the equation $y' = 2.0$, but it does solve $y' = 2$. Thus all coefficients should be expressed as fractions when using **dsolve**.

Chapter 6

A Qualitative Approach to Differential Equations

In this chapter, we discuss a qualitative approach to the study of differential equations. With this approach, we obtain qualitative information about the solutions directly from the differential equation, without the use of a solution formula.

Consider the general first order differential equation

$$\frac{dx}{dt} = f(t, x). \tag{1}$$

We can obtain qualitative information about the solutions $x(t)$ by viewing (1) geometrically. Specifically, we can obtain this information from the direction field of (1). Recall that the direction field is obtained by drawing through each point (t, x) in the (t, x)-plane a short line segment with slope $f(t, x)$. Solutions, or integral curves, of (1) have the property that at each of their points they are tangent to the direction field at that point, and therefore the general *qualitative* nature of the solutions can be determined from the direction field. Direction fields can be drawn by hand for some simple differential equations, but *Maple* can draw them for any first order equation. We illustrate the qualitative approach with two examples.

EXAMPLE 1. Consider the equation

$$\frac{dx}{dt} = e^{-t} - 2x. \tag{2}$$

Maple's command for plotting direction fields is **dfieldplot**, in the **DEtools** package. To load this package, type **with(DEtools)**. You can then plot the direction field of (2) on the rectangle $-2 \le t \le 3$, $-1 \le x \le 2$ by typing

```
dfieldplot(exp(−t) − 2*x, [t, x], t = −2..3, x = −1..2,
    arrows = LINE, axes = BOXED);
```

The options are explained in the *Maple* online help. The resulting direction field is shown in Figure 1.

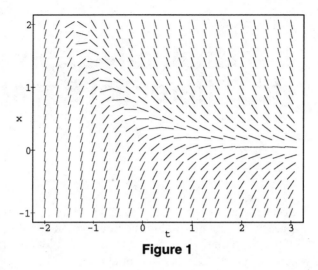

Figure 1

The direction field strongly suggests that if a solution is negative at some point, then it is increasing at that point, and that all solutions approach zero as $t \to \infty$. The general solution of equation (2) is $e^{-t} + ce^{-2t}$. Figure 2 shows the direction field together with several of these solutions.

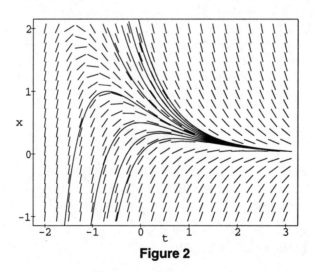

Figure 2

We can also deduce from the differential equation itself that the maximum points on the solution curves depicted in Figure 2 will occur along the curve $2x = e^{-t}$, since that is where $x' = 0$.

EXERCISE. Pursue this idea further by differentiating (2) and showing that the inflection points on the solution curves lie along the curve $4x = 3e^{-t}$.

Equation (2) can be solved explicitly because it is linear. Now let us consider an example that cannot be solved explicitly by any of the standard solution methods.

EXAMPLE 2. Consider the equation

$$\frac{dx}{dt} = x^2 + t. \tag{3}$$

Its direction field is obtained with the *Maple* command

**dfieldplot(x^2 + t, [t, x], t = −2..2, x = −2..2,
arrows = LINE, axes = BOXED);**

and is shown in Figure 3.

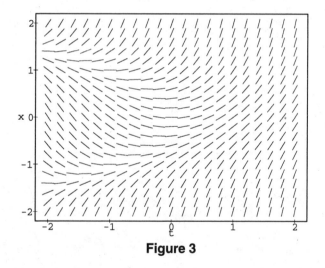

Figure 3

From the direction field, it appears that all solutions are increasing for $t > 0$, and that all solutions eventually become positive. Figure 3 also suggests that all solutions approach infinity. Does this happen at a finite value of t or only at $t = \infty$? It is not easy to decide on the basis of Figure 3, but in fact for each solution $x(t)$ there is a finite value t^* such that $\lim_{t \to t^*} x(t) = \infty$. Later, we will again encounter equations that cannot be solved explicitly by formula techniques. We will apply a combination of qualitative and numerical tools to analyze such equations, and in particular establish the fact just asserted about the solutions to equation (3) approaching infinity in finite time.

EXERCISE. Use the *Maple* command **dfieldplot** to duplicate some of the direction fields in your textbook.

Autonomous Equations

Equations of the form

$$\frac{dx}{dt} = f(x), \tag{4}$$

which do not involve t in the right-hand side, are called *autonomous* equations. Autonomous equations represent physical systems whose rules of evolution do not change with time, and are particularly susceptible to qualitative analysis.

Consider equation (4); to be concrete, suppose $f(x)$ has two zeros x_1 and x_2, called *critical points* of the differential equation. Furthermore, suppose the graph of $f(x)$ is as shown in Figure 4.

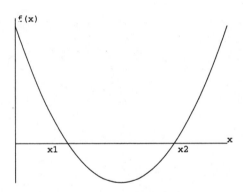

Figure 4

Then by considering the properties of $f(x)$, the direction field of (4) can be easily understood and drawn by hand. At the points $(0, x_1)$ and $(0, x_2)$ the slope is zero; at points $(0, x)$ with $x < x_1$, the slope is positive and increases from 0 to ∞ as x decreases from x_1 to $-\infty$; at points $(0, x)$ with $x_1 < x < x_2$, the slope is negative, and first decreases and then increases as x increases from x_1 to x_2; at points $(0, x)$ with $x > x_2$ the slope is positive and increases from 0 to ∞ as x increases from x_2 to ∞; finally, the slopes along any horizontal line are constant (since f does not depend on t). The direction field thus has the general appearance shown in Figure 5. Note that Figure 4 depicts $f(x)$ vs. x, while Figure 5 shows x vs. t.

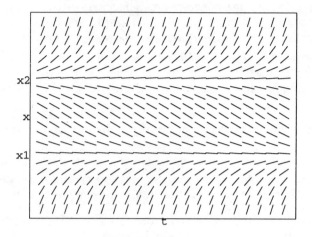

Figure 5

Several facts are suggested by the direction field, namely, that: (i) there are two constant solutions $x = x_1$ and $x = x_2$; (ii) solutions starting above x_2 tend to ∞; and (iii) all other solutions tend to x_1 as $t \to \infty$. In fact, we can derive these properties of the solutions $x(t)$ directly from the graph of $f(x)$ as follows.

(a) The constant functions $x(t) = x_1$ and $x(t) = x_2$ are solutions, called the *equilibrium solutions*. They are the unique solutions that satisfy the initial conditions $x(0) = x_1$ and $x(0) = x_2$, respectively.

(b) Consider a solution $x(t)$ with $x(0) < x_1$. Then, because of the uniqueness of solutions, it must be that $x(t) < x_1$ for all t and

$$x'(t) = f(x(t)) > 0.$$

Hence $x(t)$ is an increasing function. Since it is also bounded, it has a limit at infinity

$$\lim_{t \to \infty} x(t) = b \le x_1. \tag{5}$$

Could it happen that $b < x_1$? The answer is no, because if $b < x_1$, then

$$x'(t) = f(x(t)) \to f(b) > 0. \tag{6}$$

But equations (5) and (6) say that $x(t)$ approaches a horizontal asymptote at the same time that its slope is "permanently" bigger than a positive number. The resulting contradiction guarantees that

$$\lim_{t \to \infty} x(t) = x_1.$$

(c) If $x(t)$ is a solution with $x(0) > x_2$, then $x(t) > x_2$ for all t. Also

$$x'(t) = f(x(t)) > 0.$$

Hence $x(t)$ is once again increasing. In fact $x(t) \to \infty$. This can be shown by an argument similar to that used in part (b). Sometimes, as we shall see from the example below, $x(t)$ actually reaches ∞ in finite time.

(d) Now consider $x_1 < x_0 < x_2$. Then if $x(t)$ is a solution with $x(0) = x_0$, we must have $x_1 < x(t) < x_2$ for all t. Also, $x'(t) = f(x(t)) < 0$. Hence $x(t)$ is a decreasing function. Exactly as in part (b), it is not difficult to show that $\lim_{t \to \infty} x(t) = x_1$.

Note that in this analysis the properties of $x(t)$ are determined solely from the sign of $f(x)$.

We call the critical point x_1 *asymptotically stable* and call the critical point x_2 *unstable*, since solutions that start near x_1 converge to x_1, and those that start near x_2 not only do not converge to x_2, but eventually move away from x_2.

EXERCISE. Let $\bar{x}$ be the value between x_1 and x_2 where f takes on its minimum. Show that if $\bar{x} < x(0) < x_2$, then $x(t)$ has an inflection point where $x(t) = \bar{x}$.

Now we examine a specific example.

EXAMPLE 3. Consider the equation

$$\frac{dx}{dt} = x^2 - x.$$

Its direction field has the general appearance of Figure 5, with $x_1 = 0$ and $x_2 = 1$. But we can actually derive an explicit formula solution. If $x \neq 0$ and $x \neq 1$, we can solve by separating variables:

$$t + C = \int dt = \int \frac{dx}{x^2 - x}$$
$$= \int \left(\frac{1}{x - 1} - \frac{1}{x} \right) dx$$
$$= \ln|x - 1| - \ln|x|$$
$$= \ln \left| \frac{x - 1}{x} \right|$$
$$= \ln \left| 1 - \frac{1}{x} \right|.$$

Exponentiating both sides, we obtain

$$1 - \frac{1}{x} = ke^t,$$

where $k = \pm e^C$. Solving for x, we find that $x(t) = 1/(1 - ke^t)$. Noting that $x_0 = x(0) = 1/(1 - k)$ we have

$$x(t) = \frac{x_0}{(1 - x_0)e^t + x_0}. \tag{7}$$

Although formula (7) was derived under the assumption that $x_0 \neq 0, 1$, it is easily seen to be valid for all values of x_0.

Figure 6 contains the actual solution curves for the differential equation—as drawn by *Maple*.

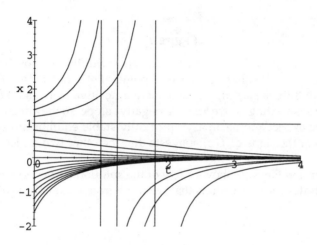

Figure 6

EXERCISES.

(a) Use formula (7) to verify the properties of $x(t)$ obtained above by the qualitative method. Determine where the solutions are increasing or decreasing, and whether there are limits as $t \to \infty$.

(b) Suppose $x_0 > 1$. Use formula (7) to show that $x(t) \to \infty$ in finite time. Find the time t^* at which this happens.

(c) Show that $x(t) = 0$ and $x(t) = 1$ are the equilibrium solutions. Does formula (7) yield these solutions?

Here is another example of an autonomous equation.

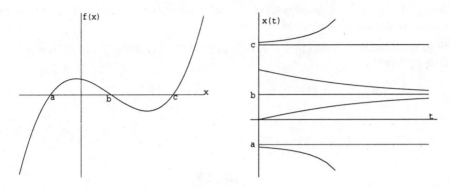

Figure 7

The left graph in Figure 7 shows a function $f(x)$ with three zeros; thus, the differential equation $x' = f(x)$ has three critical points. Let's look at the critical point in the middle. Solutions starting below b have a positive slope, so they increase toward b. Solutions starting above b have a negative slope, so they decrease toward b. Therefore, we expect b to be an asymptotically stable equilibrium solution. A similar analysis of the signs of $f(x)$ suggests that the other two critical points are unstable.

The right graph in Figure 7 shows a few of the solution curves. As you can see, this graph illustrates the conclusions that we drew from our analysis of the graph of $f(x)$.

Problem Set B

First Order Equations

1. The initial value problem

$$xy' + 2y = \sin x, \qquad y(\pi/2) = 1$$

has the solution

$$y(x) = x^{-2} \left(\frac{\pi^2}{4} - 1 - x \cos x + \sin x \right).$$

Define this function in *Maple* and then:

(a) Make a list of the values of $y(x)$ at $x = 0.5, 1, 1.5, 2, \ldots, 5$. (This can be done with the sequence operator. For more information, type **?dollar** in a *Maple* session. Also, recall the use of **evalf** to evaluate algebraic expressions numerically.)

(b) Graph $y(x)$ on the intervals $0 < x \le 2$, $1 \le x \le 10$, and $10 \le x \le 100$. Describe the behavior of the solution near $x = 0$ and for large values of x.

(c) Find the solutions $y_j(x)$ of the differential equation corresponding to the initial conditions

$$y_j(\pi/2) = 0.2j, \qquad j = 1, \ldots, 5.$$

Plot the functions $y_j(x)$, $j = 1, \ldots, 5$, on the same graph.

(d) What do the solutions have in common near $x = 0$? for large values of x? Can you find a solution to the differential equation that has no singularity at $x = 0$? If so, graph it.

2. Consider the initial value problem

$$xy' + y = 2x, \qquad y(1) = c.$$

(a) Solve it using *Maple*.

(b) Use *Maple* to graph the solutions for $c = 0.8, 0.9, 1, 1.1, 1.2$ on the interval $(0.75, 1.25)$.

(c) Evaluate these solutions at $x = 0.01, 0.1, 1, 10$.

(d) Now plot all five solutions together on the interval $(0, 2.5)$. How do changes in the initial data affect the solution as $x \to \infty$? as $x \to 0^+$?

(The sample solution for Problem 1 in the back of the book shows how to construct a sequence of values with nonintegral increments. See also the section *More about Sequences, Sets and Lists* in Chapter 8.)

3. Solve the initial value problem

$$y' - y = \cos x, \qquad y(0) = c.$$

Use *Maple* to graph solutions for $c = -0.9, -0.8, \ldots, -0.1, 0$. Display all the solutions on the same interval between $x = 0$ and an appropriately chosen right endpoint. Explain what happens to the solution curves for large values of x. (*Hint*: You should identify three distinct types of behavior.) Now, based on this problem, and the material in Chapters 5 and 6, discuss what effect small changes in initial data can have on the global behavior of solution curves. (See the note at the end of Problem 2.)

4. Consider the differential equation

$$\frac{dy}{dx} = \frac{x - e^{-x}}{y + e^y}$$

(*cf.* Problem 7, Section 2.3 in Boyce & DiPrima).

(a) Solve it using *Maple*. Observe that the solution is given implicitly in the form

$$f(x, y) = c.$$

(b) Use **contourplot** (see the online help) to see what the solution curves look like. For your x and y ranges, you might use **x = -1..3** and **y = -2..2**.

(c) Use **implicitplot** to plot the solution satisfying the initial condition $y(1.5) = 0.5$. Your plot should show two curves. Indicate which one corresponds to the solution.

(d) Given a value x_1, to find $y(x_1)$ you need to find the solution of

$$f(x_1, y) = f(1.5, 0.5)$$

(viewed as an equation in y) near $y = 0.5$. This can be done with the **fsolve** command. Find $y(0), y(1), y(1.8), y(2.1)$. Mark these values on your plot.

5. Consider the differential equation

$$(e^x \sin y - 2y \sin x)\, dx + (e^x \cos y + 2 \cos x)\, dy = 0,$$

(*cf.* Problem 7, Section 2.8 in Boyce & DiPrima).

(a) Solve it using *Maple*. Observe that the solution is given implicitly in the form

$$f(x, y) = c.$$

(b) Use **contourplot** to see what the solution curves look like. For your x and y ranges, you might use **x = −3..3** and **y = −3..3**.

(c) Use **implicitplot** to plot the solution satisfying the initial condition $y(0) = 0.5$. Your plot may show several curves. Indicate which one corresponds to the solution.

(d) Given a value x_1, to find $y(x_1)$ you need to find the solution of

$$f(x_1, y) = f(0, 0.5)$$

(viewed as an equation in y) near $y = 0.5$. This can be done with the **fsolve** command. Find $y(-1), y(1), y(2)$. Mark these values on your plot.

6. In this problem, we study continuous dependence of solutions on initial data.

(a) Solve the initial value problem

$$y' = y/(1 + x^2), \qquad y(0) = c.$$

(b) Let y_c denote the solution in part (a). Use *Maple* to plot the solutions y_c for $c = -10, -9, \ldots, -1, 0, 1, \ldots, 10$ on one graph. Display all the solutions on the interval $-20 \le x \le 20$.

(c) Compute $\lim_{x \to \pm\infty} y_1(x)$.

(d) Now find a single constant L such that for all real x, we have

$$|y_a(x) - y_b(x)| \le L|a - b|,$$

for any pair of numbers a and b. Show that $L = 1$ will work if we consider only negative values of x.

7. Use **dsolve** to solve the following differential equations or initial value problems from Boyce & DiPrima. In some cases, *Maple* will not be able to solve the equation (but before moving on to the next equation, make sure you haven't mistyped something). In other cases, *Maple* may give extraneous solutions (sometimes these correspond to imaginary roots of the equation it solves to get y in terms of x). If so, you should indicate which solution or solutions are valid. You also might try entering alternative forms of an equation, for example, $M + Ny' = 0$ instead of $y' = -M/N$, or vice versa.

(a) $x^3 y' + 4x^2 y = e^{-x}, y(-1) = 0$ (Sect. 2.1, Prob. 15)

(b) $y' = ry - ky^2, r > 0$ and $k > 0$ (Sect. 2.2, Prob. 29)

(c) $y' = x(x^2 + 1)/4y^3, y(0) = -1/\sqrt{2}$ (Sect. 2.3, Prob. 14)

(d) $(e^x \sin y + 3y) \, dx - (3x - e^x \sin y) \, dy = 0$ (Sect. 2.8, Prob. 8)

(e) $dy/dx = (2y - x)/(2x - y)$ (Sect. 2.9, Prob. 9(a))

(f) $dy/dx = (2x + y)/(3 + 3y^2 - x), y(0) = 0$ (Sect. 2.10, Prob. 3).

8. Use **dsolve** to solve the following differential equations or initial value problems from Boyce & DiPrima. See Problem 7 for additional instructions.

(a) $xy' + (x + 1)y = x, y(\ln 2) = 1$ (Sect. 2.1, Prob. 16)

(b) $y' - (1/x)y = x^{1/2}$ (Sect. 2.2, Prob. 15)

(c) $y' = 2(1 + x)(1 + y^2), y(0) = 0$ (Sect. 2.3, Prob. 16)

(d) $(x \ln y + xy) \, dx + (y \ln x + xy) \, dy = 0; x > 0, y > 0$ (Sect. 2.8, Prob. 11)

(e) $(x^2 + 3xy + y^2) \, dx - x^2 dy = 0$ (Sect. 2.9, Prob. 8)

(f) $dy/dx = -(2xy + y^2 + 1)/(x^2 + 2xy)$ (Sect. 2.10, Prob. 5).

9. Chapter 6 describes how to plot the direction field for a first order equation. For each equation below, plot the direction field on a rectangle large enough (but not too large) to show clearly all of its equilibrium points. Find the equilibria and state whether each is stable or unstable. If you cannot determine the precise value of an equilibrium point from the direction field, use **fsolve**.

(a) $y' = -y(y - 2)(y - 4)/10$

(b) $y' = y^2 - 3y + 1$.

(c) $y' = 0.1y - \sin y$.

10. In this problem, we use the direction field capabilities of *Maple* to study two nonlinear equations, one autonomous and one nonautonomous.

(a) Plot the direction field for the equation

$$\frac{dy}{dx} = 3 \sin y + y - 2$$

on a rectangle large enough (but not too large) to show all possible limiting behaviors of solutions as $x \to \infty$. Find approximate values for all the equilibria of the system (you should be able to do this with **fsolve** using guesses based on the direction field picture), and state whether each is stable or unstable.

(b) Plot the direction field for the equation

$$\frac{dy}{dx} = y^2 - xy,$$

again using a rectangle large enough to show the possible limiting behaviors. Identify the unique constant solution. Why is this solution evident from the differential equation? If a solution curve is ever below the constant solution, what must its limiting behavior be as $x \to +\infty$? For solutions lying above the constant solution, describe two possible limiting behaviors as $x \to +\infty$.

There is a solution curve which lies along the boundary of the two limiting behaviors. Explain (from the differential equation) why that solution curve cannot be bounded. Can you guess how its limiting behavior might differ from that of the two limiting behaviors you have identified?

11. The solution of the differential equation

$$y' = \frac{2y - x}{2x - y}$$

is given implicitly by $|x - y| = c|x + y|^3$ (Boyce & DiPrima, Problem 9, Section 2.9). (Take that as given; you need not try to verify it with **dsolve**.) However, it is difficult to understand the solutions directly from this algebraic information.

(a) Use **dfieldplot** to plot the direction field in several different rectangles.

(b) Use **implicitplot** to plot the solutions with initial conditions $y(2) = 1$ and $y(0) = -3$. (Note that **abs** is the absolute value function in *Maple*.) Use the **display** command to put these plots and the vector field plot together on the same graph. (Two plots named **r** and **s** can be combined with the command **display({r, s})** after loading the *Maple* **plots** package. See Chapter 8 and the online help for additional information.)

(c) For the two different initial conditions in part (b), use your pictures to estimate the largest interval on which the unique solution function is defined.

12. Consider the differential equation

$$x' = -tx^2.$$

(a) Use *Maple* to plot the direction field of the differential equation. Is there a constant solution? If $x(0) > 0$, what happens as t increases? If $x(0) < 0$, what happens as t increases?

(b) Use **dsolve** to solve the differential equation, thereby obtaining a solution of the form

$$x(t) = \frac{2}{t^2 + 2c}.$$

Note that $x(0) = 1/c$. In graphing $x(t)$, it helps to consider three separate cases: (i) $c > 0$, (ii) $c = 0$, and (iii) $c < 0$. In each case, graph the solution for several specific values of c, and identify important features of the curves. In particular, in case (iii), compute the location of the asymptotes in terms of c.

(c) Identify five different types of solution curves for the differential equation. In each case, specify the t-interval of existence, whether the solution is increasing or decreasing, and the limiting (asymptotic) behavior at the ends of the interval.

(d) Use the **display** command to combine the direction field plotted in (a) with the plot of a solution in case (iii). (Two plots named **r** and **s** can be combined with the command **display({r, s})** after loading the *Maple* **plots** package. See Chapter 8 and the online help for additional information.)

13. Consider the following logistic-with-threshold model for population growth:

$$x' = x(1 - x)(x - 3).$$

(a) Find the equilibrium solutions of the differential equation. Now draw the direction field, and use it to decide which equilibrium solutions are stable and which are unstable.

(b) Next replace the logistic law by the Gompertz model, but retain the threshold feature. The equation becomes

$$x' = x(1 - \ln x)(x - 3).$$

Once again, find the equilibrium solutions and draw the direction field. You will have difficulty "reading the field" between 2.5 and 3. There appears to be a continuum of equilibrium solutions.

(c) Plot the function $f(x) = x(1 - \ln x)(x - 3)$ on the interval $0.01 \leq x \leq 4$, and then use *Maple*'s **limit** command to evaluate $\lim_{x \to 0} f(x)$.

(d) Use these plots and the discussion in Chapter 6 to decide which equilibrium solutions are stable and which are unstable. Now use the last plot to explain why the direction field (for $2.5 \leq x \leq 3$) appears so inconclusive regarding the stability of the equilibrium solutions.

14. This problem is based on Example 3 in Section 2.5 of Boyce & DiPrima: "A tank contains Q_0 lb of salt dissolved in 100 gal of water. Water containing $\frac{1}{4}$ lb of salt per gallon enters the tank at a rate of 3 gal/min, and the well-stirred solution leaves the tank at the same rate. Find an expression for the amount of salt $Q(t)$ in the tank at time t."

The differential equation

$$Q'(t) = 0.75 - 0.03Q(t)$$

models the problem (*cf.* equation (17) in Section 2.5).

(a) Plot the right-hand side of the differential equation as a function of Q, and identify the critical point.

(b) Analyze the long-term behavior of the solution curves by examining the sign of the right-hand side of the differential equation, in a similar fashion to the discussion in Chapter 6.

(c) Use *Maple* to plot the direction field of the differential equation. In choosing the rectangle for the direction field be sure to include the point $(0,0)$ and the critical value of Q.

(d) Use **dsolve** to find the solution $Q(t)$ and plot it for several specific values of Q_0. Do the solutions behave as indicated in parts (b) and (d)? (You might try combining a direction field plot with that of the solution curves.)

15. A 10-gallon tank contains a mixture consisting of 1 gallon of water and an undetermined number $S(0)$ of pounds of salt in the solution. Water containing 1 lb/gal of salt begins flowing into the tank at the rate of 2 gal/min. The well-mixed solution flows out at a rate of 1 gal/min. Derive the differential equation for $S(t)$, the number of pounds of salt in the tank after t minutes, that models this physical situation. (Note: At time $t = 0$ there is 1 gallon of solution, but the volume increases with time.) Now draw the direction field of the differential equation on the rectangle $0 \le t \le 10$, $0 \le S \le 10$. From your plot,

(a) find the value A of $S(0)$ below which the amount of salt is a constantly increasing function; but above which, the amount of salt will temporarily decrease before increasing;

(b) indicate how the nature of the solution function in case $S(0) = 1$ differs from all other solutions.

Now use **dsolve** to solve the differential equation. Reinforce your conclusions above by

(c) algebraically computing the value of A;

(d) giving the formula for the solution function when $S(0) = 1$;

(e) giving the amount of salt in the tank (in terms of $S(0)$) when it is at the point of overflowing;

(f) computing, for $S(0) > A$, the minimum amount of salt in the tank, and the time it occurs;

(g) explaining what principle guarantees the truth of the following statement: If two solutions S_1, S_2 correspond to initial data $S_1(0)$, $S_2(0)$ with $S_1(0) < S_2(0)$, then for any $t \ge 0$, it must be that $S_1(t) < S_2(t)$.

16. In this problem, we use **fsolve** and **dsolve** to model some population data. The procedure will be:

   (i) Assume a model differential equation involving unknown parameters.
   (ii) Use **dsolve** to find the solution of the differential equation in terms of the parameters.
   (iii) Use **fsolve** to find the values of the parameters that fit the given data.
   (iv) Make predictions based on the results of the previous steps.

(a) Let's use the model

$$\frac{dp}{dt} = ap + b, \quad p(0) = c,$$

where p represents the population at time t. Check to see that **dsolve** can solve this initial value problem in terms of the unknown constants a, b, c. Then define a function that expresses the solution at time t in terms of a, b, c, and t.

(b) Next, let's try to model the population of Nevada, currently the fastest growing state in the U.S. Here is a table of census data:

Year	Population in thousands
1950	160.1
1960	285.3
1970	488.7
1980	800.5
1990	1201.8

We would like to find the values of a, b, and c that fit the data. However, with three unknown constants we will not be able to fit five data points. Use **fsolve** to find the values of a, b, and c that give the correct population for the years 1960, 1970, and 1980. We will later use the data from 1950 and 1990 to check the accuracy of the model. *Important:* In this part let t represent the time in years since 1950, because *Maple* may get stuck if you ask it to fit the data at such high values of t as 1960–1980. You will also need to specify ranges when you use **fsolve** so that the algorithm converges. You might specify **a = 0..1**, for example. You could also figure out a reasonable range for c and specify that as well.

(c) Now define a function of t that expresses the predicted population in year t using the values of a, b, c found in part (b). Find the population this model gives for 1950 and 1990, and compare with the values in the table above. Use the model to predict the population of Nevada in the year 2000, and to predict when the population will reach 3 million. How would you adjust these predictions based on the 1950 and 1990 data? Finally, graph the population the model gives from 1950 to 2050, and describe the predicted future of the population of Nevada, including the limiting population (if any) as $t \to \infty$.

17. Consider $x' = (\alpha - 1)x - x^3$.

(a) Use **solve** to find the roots of $(\alpha - 1)x - x^3$. Explain why $x = 0$ is the only real root when $\alpha \leq 1$, and why there are three distinct real roots when $\alpha > 1$.

(b) For $\alpha = -2, -1, 0$, draw a direction field for the differential equation and deduce that there is only one equilibrium solution. What is it? Is it stable?

(c) Do the same for $\alpha = 1$.

(d) For $\alpha = 1.5, 2$, draw the direction field. Identify all equilibrium solutions, and describe their stability.

(e) Explain the following statement: "As α increases through 1, the stable solution $x = 0$ *bifurcates* into two stable solutions."

Chapter 7

Numerical Methods

Even though many differential equations can be solved explicitly in terms of the elementary functions of calculus, many others cannot. Consider, for example, the equation

$$\frac{dy}{dx} = e^{-x^2}.$$

Its solutions are the integrals, or antiderivatives, of e^{-x^2},

$$y(x) = \int e^{-x^2}\, dx + C,$$

but it is known that these integrals cannot be expressed in terms of the elementary functions of calculus. Similarly, the solution to the associated initial value problem

$$\frac{dy}{dx} = e^{-x^2}, \qquad y(x_0) = y_0$$

can be written as

$$y(x) = y_0 + \int_{x_0}^{x} e^{-s^2}\, ds,$$

but this formula cannot be simplified further; specifically, it is not an elementary function. (An *elementary function* is defined to be a polynomial, power, trigonometric, inverse trigonometric, exponential, or logarithmic function, or any combination of them via the processes of algebra and of composition and inversion.) More dramatic is the "simple" equation

$$\frac{dy}{dx} = x + y^2.$$

The solutions to this equation cannot be written in terms of elementary functions, or even in terms of repeated integrals of elementary functions!

Just as we turn to numerical methods (*e.g.*, the trapezoidal or Simpson's rule) to evaluate definite integrals when we cannot find an antiderivative in terms of elementary functions, we also turn to numerical methods to solve initial value problems for differential equations that cannot be solved explicitly in terms of elementary functions. Even if the differential equation can be solved, the resulting formula may be so complicated (*e.g.*, it may be implicit) that a numerical method is preferable.

Numerical Solutions Using *Maple*

In this section we explain **dsolve(..., numeric)**, *Maple*'s main numerical differential equation solver, and **odeplot**, which is used to plot numerical solutions produced by **dsolve(..., numeric)**. In a later section we discuss **DEplot**, a less sophisticated command that only plots numerical solutions.

Suppose we are interested in finding the solution to the initial value problem

$$\frac{dy}{dx} = f(x,y), \qquad y(x_0) = y_0,$$

and suppose that we have no formula for $y(x)$. Then we have no obvious way to calculate $y(x)$ for particular values of x. In such a situation, our strategy will be to produce a function $y_a(x)$ that both is a good approximation to $y(x)$ and can be calculated. The subscript a on y_a stands for *approximate solution*.

An approximate solution can be found with the *Maple* command **dsolve(..., numeric)**. To illustrate, we consider the initial value problem

$$\frac{dy}{dx} = \frac{x}{y}, \qquad y(0) = 1. \tag{1}$$

Its exact solution is easily found to be

$$y(x) = \sqrt{x^2 + 1}.$$

Since we have an explicit formula for this solution, we will be able to compare the approximate solution $y_a(x)$ and the exact solution $y(x)$. To obtain $y_a(x)$, type

ivp := {diff(y(x), x) = x/y(x), y(0) = 1};
sol := dsolve(ivp, y(x), numeric, maxfun = 1000);

The first argument to **dsolve** is a set that specifies the differential equation and the initial condition. The second argument specifies the dependent variable y and the independent variable x. The third argument tells *Maple* to use the numerical solver instead of the symbolic one. The final argument, **maxfun = 1000**, is an option limiting the number of computations *Maple* will do to produce a numerical solution. This important option is explained in detail later.

The preceding commands produce the output

```
sol := proc(rkf45_x) ... end
```

The output means that **sol** is a *Maple* procedure that computes an approximate solution to our initial value problem. The expression "rkf45" refers to the particular numerical method used by **dsolve(..., numeric)**. To get the value of the approximate solution at a particular point, say at $x = 1.5$, type **sol(1.5)**, which produces $[x = 1.5, y(x) = 1.802775648877327]$. Note that $y(1.5) = \sqrt{13}/2 = 1.802775637...$, so that the approximate value is correct to eight digits.

To extract a standard function that just returns the *y*-value, we type

ya := u –> subs(sol(u), y(x));

Now **ya(1.5)** produces 1.802775648877327. We have obtained **ya** in two steps: we first defined **sol** and then defined **ya**. For a reason explained later (see the section *A Further Remark on dsolve(...,numeric)*), it is better to combine the two steps:

ya1 := u –> subs(dsolve(ivp, y(x), numeric, maxfun = 1000)(u), y(x));

Now we can make a table of values to compare the numerical solution with the actual solution. The commands

onerow := x –> [x, evalf(ya1(x)), evalf(sqrt(x^2 + 1))];
rowlist := map(onerow, [0.2*j $ j = 1..10]);
map(print, rowlist):

produce a table of numerical solution values and exact solution values at the points 0, 0.2, . . . , 1.8, 2. The result is shown in Table 1. (See Chapter 8 for more information about lists and the **map** command.)

x	**ya1(x)**	$y(x)$
0.2	1.019803907	1.019803903
0.4	1.077032964	1.077032961
0.6	1.166190383	1.166190379
0.8	1.280624855	1.280624847
1.0	1.414213571	1.414213562
1.2	1.562049944	1.562049935
1.4	1.720465063	1.720465053
1.6	1.886796237	1.886796226
1.8	2.059126041	2.059126028
2.0	2.236067990	2.236067978

Table 1

We see that we have at least eight correct digits in all cases. So **ya1(x)** is indeed a very good approximation to $y(x)$.

To plot a numerical solution, we use the *Maple* command **odeplot**. This command is in the **plots** package. For the same reason referred to above, we combine the computation of the numerical solution with the plotting command. So, to plot the solution on the interval [0, 2], type

with(plots):
odeplot(dsolve(ivp, y(x), numeric, maxfun = 1000), [x, y(x)], 0..2);

The result is shown in Figure 1.

EXERCISE. Display both **ya1(x)** and the exact solution $y(x) = \sqrt{x^2 + 1}$ on the same graph. Can you distinguish between the two curves?

Figure 1

We have illustrated **dsolve(..., numeric)** on the initial value problem (1), which can easily be solved explicitly. We can just as readily apply **dsolve(..., numeric)** to any first order initial value problem. Consider, for example,

$$\frac{dy}{dx} = x + y^2, \qquad y(0) = 1, \tag{2}$$

which cannot be solved in terms of elementary functions. The commands

ivp2 := {diff(y(x), x) = x + y(x)^2, y(0) = 1};
ya2 := u -> subs(dsolve(ivp2, y(x), numeric, maxfun = 1000)(u), y(x));

will produce an approximate solution.

EXERCISE. The solution $y(x)$ to (2) is increasing for x positive, and there is a finite value x^* such that $\lim_{x \to x^*} y(x) = \infty$; the interval of existence of the solution is $(-\infty, x^*)$. Graph the numerical solution. Does **odeplot** reveal the value of x^*?

When **dsolve(..., numeric)** computes a numerical solution at a point x, it marches from the initial point x_0 to x in a sequence of steps. If the exact solution is changing very rapidly, then **dsolve(..., numeric)** will take very small steps in order to stay close to the solution. This will be the case, for example, when the solution is oscillatory or singular (*i.e.*, has a vertical asymptote).

Each step involves several function evaluations. By default, the maximum number of function evaluations allowed is 30,000. Such a large number of steps may take a long time, even on a computer; moreover, when there is an asymptote, following the solution for 30,000 steps can lead to such large solution values that the numerical procedure fails. It is thus useful to limit the maximum number of steps allowed by **dsolve(..., numeric)** to a smaller number. This can be done with the **maxfun** option. For many problems, **maxfun = 1000** is an appropriate setting. On rare occasions, as when computing an oscillatory or singular solution, you may have to increase the value of **maxfun**.

EXERCISE. Use **dsolve(..., numeric)** with **maxfun = 1000** to calculate a numerical solution to

$$\frac{dy}{dx} = y \sin(x^2), \qquad y(0) = 1.$$

Now try to evaluate the numerical solution at $x = 5$ and $x = 10$. Can you explain why the numerical procedure generated by **dsolve(..., numeric)** fails at $x = 10$? Now compute a new numerical solution with **maxfun = 3000**, and evaluate this solution at $x = 10$. What happens? How far to the right can you go before **dsolve(..., numeric)** uses up its allotted 3000 steps? Reset **maxfun = 1000**, and then use **odeplot** to plot the solution on the interval $[0, 10]$. (Use the option **numpoints = 100** in **odeplot** to get a smoother graph.) Even though **maxfun** is set at 1000, **odeplot** plots the solution over the entire interval $[0, 10]$. Whenever 1000 function evaluations have been used, it starts over. Note that the gap in the graph corresponds to the place where **dsolve(..., numeric)** used up the maximum number of steps and started over.

REMARK. Although we have focused on first order equations in this chapter, **dsolve(..., numeric)** also works on higher order equations and systems of equations. See the section *Using dsolve(...,numeric) on Higher Order Equations* in Chapter 8, Chapter 12 and the Sample Worksheet Solutions for examples.

Some Elementary Numerical Methods

In order to explain how **dsolve(..., numeric)** calculates approximate values, we now discuss three elementary numerical methods. Each method will be applied to problem (1). The three methods provide better and better approximations.

We want to approximate the solution of the initial value problem

$$\frac{dy}{dx} = f(x, y), \qquad y(x_0) = y_0$$

on an interval $x_0 \le x \le b$. For n a positive integer, we divide the interval into n equal parts using points

$$x_0 < x_1 < x_2 < \cdots < x_n = b.$$

Each part has the same width, or *step size*, $h = x_{i+1} - x_i = (b - x_0)/n$; therefore $x_i = x_0 + ih$. At each point x_i we seek an approximation, which we call y_i, to the true solution $y(x_i)$ at x_i:

$$y_i \approx y(x_i).$$

The Euler Method. The simplest numerical solution method is due to Euler, and is based on the tangent line approximation to a function. Given the initial value y_0, we define y_i recursively by

$$y_{i+1} = y_i + h\, f(x_i, y_i), \qquad i = 0, 1, \ldots, n - 1.$$

This formula is derived as follows:

$$y(x_{i+1}) \approx y(x_i) + hy'(x_i), \qquad \text{by the tangent line approximation}$$
$$= y(x_i) + hf(x_i, y(x_i)), \qquad \text{using the differential equation}$$
$$\approx y_i + hf(x_i, y_i), \qquad \text{since } y_i \approx y(x_i)$$
$$= y_{i+1}.$$

The approximations $y(x_i) \approx y_i$ should become better and better as h is taken smaller and smaller.

EXAMPLE. Consider the initial value problem

$$\frac{dy}{dx} = \frac{x}{y}, \qquad y(0) = 1.$$

We wish to approximate $y(0.3)$ using the Euler Method with step size $h = 0.1$ and three steps. We find

$$x_0 = 0, \quad x_1 = 0.1, \quad x_2 = 0.2, \quad x_3 = 0.3$$
$$y_0 = 1$$
$$y_1 = y_0 + hf(x_0, y_0) = y_0 + hx_0/y_0 = 1$$
$$y_2 = y_1 + hx_1/y_1 = 1.01$$
$$y_3 = 1.0298.$$

Thus

$$y(0.3) = \sqrt{1.09} = 1.044030... \approx y_3 = 1.0298$$

$$\text{Error} = |y(0.3) - y_3| = 0.0142....$$

Next use $h = 0.05$ and 6 steps:

$$y_0 = 1$$
$$y_1 = 1$$
$$y_2 = 1.0025$$
$$y_3 = 1.0075$$
$$y_4 = 1.0149$$
$$y_5 = 1.0248$$
$$y_6 = 1.0370$$

$$\text{Error} = |y(0.3) - y_6| = 0.0070....$$

Note that cutting the step size in half has the effect of cutting the error approximately in half. One can prove that the Euler Method is a *first order method*, which means that at each point in the interval $[x_0, b]$,

$$\text{Error} \leq Ch$$

for some constant C (depending on $f(x, y)$, the initial condition, and the interval, but not on h). Thus, to gain an additional digit of accuracy, one would reduce the step size by a factor of $1/10$.

The Euler Method can be implemented using *Maple* as follows:

EulerMethod := proc(f, x0, y0, h, n) local a, i, x, y;
       x := evalf(x0); y := evalf(y0); a := [[x, y]];
       for i from 1 to n do
           y := y + h*f(x, y); x := x + h; a := [op(a), [x, y]];
       od; end;

To apply this program to the initial value problem (1), we first define the function $f(x, y) = x/y$, and then run the routine. So,

    f := (x, y) -> x/y;
    em := EulerMethod(f, 0, 1, 0.1, 10);

will produce a list of approximate solution values at $x = 0, 0.1, 0.2, \ldots, 1$. Note that **EulerMethod** uses a programming construct called a "for" loop. The program uses the local variable **a** to store the list of points; new points are added to the list using the *Maple* function **op** as soon as they are computed.

To evaluate the solution at a point x that is not an x_i, we must *interpolate* the approximate solution. The simplest way to do this is to "connect the dots" by drawing straight line segments from each point (x_i, y_i) to the next point (x_{i+1}, y_{i+1}); thus $y_a(x)$ would be the piecewise linear function connecting the computed points (x_i, y_i). To graph $y_a(x)$, we just use the *Maple* command

   plot(em);

The Improved Euler Method. We again start with the tangent line approximation, replacing the slope $y'(x_i)$ by the average of the two slopes $y'(x_i)$ and $y'(x_{i+1})$. This yields

$$y(x_{i+1}) \approx y(x_i) + h \, \frac{y'(x_i) + y'(x_{i+1})}{2}$$

$$= y(x_i) + h \, \frac{f(x_i, y(x_i)) + f(x_{i+1}, y(x_{i+1}))}{2}.$$

We now use the approximation $y(x_i) \approx y_i$ and the previous Euler approximation $y(x_{i+1}) \approx y_i + hf(x_i, y_i)$, to get

$$y(x_{i+1}) \approx y_i + h \, \frac{f(x_i, y_i) + f(x_{i+1}, y_i + hf(x_i, y_i))}{2}$$

$$= y_i + h \, \frac{y_i' + f(x_{i+1}, y_i + hy_i')}{2}$$

$$= y_{i+1},$$

where $y_i' = f(x_i, y_i)$. Given the initial value y_0, this analysis leads to the recursive formula

$$y_{i+1} = y_i + h \frac{y_i' + f(x_{i+1}, y_i + hy_i')}{2}, \qquad i = 0, 1, \ldots, n - 1.$$

EXAMPLE. We again consider problem (1) and find an approximation to $y(0.3)$ with $h = 0.1$. We obtain

$$y_1 = y_0 + h \frac{y_0' + f(x_1, y_0 + hy_0')}{2}$$

$$= y_0 + \frac{h}{2} \left(\frac{x_0}{y_0} + \frac{x_1}{y_0 + hx_0/y_0} \right)$$

$$= 1.005$$

$$y_2 = 1.019828$$

$$y_3 = 1.044064.$$

So Error $= |y(0.3) - y_3| = 0.000033\ldots$. Note that the error in the Improved Euler Method with $h = 0.1$ is considerably less than the error in the Euler Method with $h = 0.05$.

The Improved Euler Method is a *second order method*, which means that

$$\text{Error} \leq Ch^2.$$

Thus, to gain one more digit of accuracy in the approximation, one would reduce the step size by a factor of $1/\sqrt{10} \approx 0.32$. Equivalently, reducing the step size by a factor of $1/10$ will produce two more digits of accuracy.

The Runge-Kutta Method. Given the initial value y_0, this method is defined recursively by

$$y_{i+1} = y_i + \frac{h}{6}(k_1 + 2k_2 + 2k_3 + k_4),$$

where

$$k_1 = f(x_i, y_i)$$

$$k_2 = f(x_i + \frac{h}{2}, y_i + \frac{h}{2}k_1)$$

$$k_3 = f(x_i + \frac{h}{2}, y_i + \frac{h}{2}k_2)$$

$$k_4 = f(x_{i+1}, y_i + hk_3).$$

Note that a weighted average of the "slopes" k_1, k_2, k_3, k_4 is used in the formula for y_{i+1}.

EXAMPLE. Consider problem (1) and again find an approximation to $y(0.3)$, but now let $h = 0.3$ and take just one step. Then

$$k_1 = f(0,1) = 0$$
$$k_2 = f(0 + 0.15, 1 + 0.15(0)) = 0.15$$
$$k_3 = f(0.15, 1 + 0.15(0.15)) = 0.146699$$
$$k_4 = f(0.3, 1 + 0.3(0.146699)) = 0.287354$$
$$y_1 = 1 + \frac{0.3}{6}(0 + 2(0.15 + 0.146699) + 0.287354)$$
$$= 1.044038 \approx y(0.3).$$

So Error $= |y(0.3) - y_1| = 0.000007....$ We see that the error in the Runge-Kutta Method with $h = 0.3$ is less than the error in the Improved Euler Method with $h = 0.1$.

The Runge-Kutta Method is a *fourth order method*, which means that

$$\text{Error} \le Ch^4.$$

Reducing the step size by a factor of $1/10$ will produce four more digits of accuracy.

There are many numerical methods for differential equations in addition to the ones we have presented here. The method used in **dsolve(..., numeric)** is called "rkf45". It combines a fourth order method and a fifth order method, both similar to the fourth order Runge-Kutta Method discussed above, which were developed by Fehlberg (see L. Shampine and R. Allen, Jr., **Numerical Computing**, W. B. Saunders Company, 1973). It uses *variable step sizes*, choosing the step size at each step to try to ensure that the desired accuracy is achieved.

The type of error we have mentioned here is called *truncation error*. In addition, there is *round-off error*, which arises because the computer uses a fixed, finite number of digits. Letting $\tilde{y}_a(x)$ denote the actual computed approximate solution, which includes round-off error, the total error can be written

$$y(x) - \tilde{y}_a(x) = (y(x) - y_a(x)) + (y_a(x) - \tilde{y}_a(x))$$
$$= \text{Truncation Error} + \text{Round-off Error}.$$

Since most computers that run *Maple* carry 16 digits, the major portion of the error will be the truncation error. Thus, for most problems, round-off error can be safely ignored. For this reason we will not distinguish between $y_a(x)$ and $\tilde{y}_a(x)$.

REMARK. With numerical methods as with qualitative methods, we obtain information on the solution—quantitative in the one case and qualitative in the other—without the use of a solution formula.

The DEplot Command

Earlier, we explained how to use **dsolve(..., numeric)** and **odeplot** to obtain and plot numerical solutions of initial value problems. In this section, we describe an alternative method for plotting numerical solutions. The *Maple* command **DEplot** uses the elementary methods described in the previous section. Since they are less sophisticated than the method used by **dsolve(. . ., numeric)**, **DEplot** may produce less accurate results. For problems where the elementary methods are adequate, **DEplot** is easier to use.

Consider the initial value problem

$$y' = x - 1 + \cos y, \quad y(0) = 1. \tag{3}$$

To plot a numerical solution of this initial value problem on the interval $[0, 2]$, we type

> with(DEtools):
> DEplot(diff(y(x), x) = x − 1 + cos(y(x)), [x, y], 0..2, {[0, 1]});

The result is shown in Figure 2.

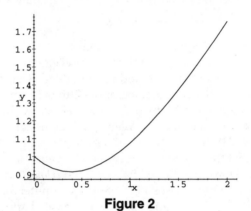

Figure 2

The first argument to **DEplot** specifies the differential equation; the second argument is a list consisting of the independent variable and the dependent variable (in that order); the third argument specifies the interval on which to plot the solution; and the fourth argument is a set of initial conditions. Here, we have specified a set $\{[0, 1]\}$ containing only one initial condition, $y(0) = 1$.

EXERCISE. Solve the initial value problem (3) with **dsolve(. . ., numeric)**, and graph the solution on the interval $[0, 2]$ using **odeplot**. Display the graphs produced by **odeplot** and **DEplot** on the same plot. Are the two graphs distinguishable?

It is possible to specify several initial conditions to get a simultaneous plot of several solution curves. For example, the command

> DEplot(diff(y(x), x) = x − 1 + cos(y(x)), [x, y], 0..2, {[0, 1], [0, 3], [1, 4], [2, 5]});

plots the four solutions of (3) satisfying the initial conditions $y(0) = 1$, $y(0) = 3$, $y(1) = 4$, and $y(2) = 5$. The result is shown in Figure 3.

Figure 3

The numerical method used by **DEplot** is the fourth order Runge-Kutta method with fixed step size. The default step size is the interval length divided by 20. In the preceding examples, we used **DEplot** on the interval $[0, 2]$, so the step size was $2/20$, or 0.1. If we were to plot the solution over a longer interval, say $[0, 20]$, the step size would be $20/20 = 1$, which is too large to give an accurate result. You can specify the step size with the **stepsize** option. For example, the option **stepsize = 0.1** sets the step size to 0.1. You should usually use a small step size.

In addition, you can choose a different numerical method. The available methods include the Euler Method and the Improved Euler Method. For example, to use the Euler Method on (1), you would type

> **DEplot(diff(y(x), x) = x/y(x), [x, y], 0..2, {[0, 1]}, method = `Euler`);**

(Note that the online documentation for **DEtools[options]** incorrectly lists the Euler Method option as **method = `euler`**.) As you know, selecting one method over another involves a tradeoff between computional effort and accuracy.

Controlling the Error in dsolve(..., numeric)

The numerical solver **dsolve(..., numeric)** attempts to produce an approximate solution $y_a(x)$ satisfying the accuracy requirement

$$\text{Error} = |y(x) - y_a(x)| \text{ is approximately} \leq 10^{-8}.$$

More accurate approximate solutions can be obtained by using certain options to **dsolve(..., numeric)**. For example,

> **Digits := 17;**

and

> **ya3 := u -> subs(dsolve(ivp, y(x), numeric, maxfun = 2000, abserr = Float(1, -15), relerr = Float(1, -15))(u), y(x));**

produce a more accurate approximation to the solution of (1): **ya3(1.5)** equals 1.8027756377319964, which is a 15-digit approximation to the exact value $\sqrt{13}/2$. (Note that the desired accuracy cannot be achieved with **maxfun** = 1000.)

The option **abserr = Float(1, −d)**, where **d** is a positive integer, attempts to control the absolute error, *i.e.*, to ensure that

$$\text{Absolute Error } = |y(x) - y_a(x)| \text{ is approximately } \le 10^{-d}.$$

The option **relerr = Float(1, −p)**, where **p** is a positive integer, attempts to control the relative error, *i.e.*, to ensure that

$$\text{Relative Error } = \frac{|y(x) - y_a(x)|}{|y(x)|} \text{ is approximately } \le 10^{-p}.$$

Actually, **dsolve(..., numeric)** only tries to satisfy the easier of these two goals. For this reason both d and p may have to be increased to get the desired accuracy.

The value of **Digits** determines the number of digits **dsolve(..., numeric)** uses in its calculations. Without these options, *Maple* uses the default settings 10 for **Digits** and **Float(1, 2 − Digits)** for **abserr** and **relerr**. Note that **abserr** and **relerr** must be at least two orders of magnitude less than the value of **Digits**, which is why we set **Digits := 17** in the preceding example. Since **Digits** is a *global* variable, changing the value of **Digits** affects the number of digits carried along in every floating point computation, including the results of **evalf**. In any event, the default options lead to approximately 8-digit accuracy. This will be satisfactory for most of the calculations in this course; but see the next section.

Reliability of Numerical Methods

We have claimed that **dsolve(..., numeric)**, when used with the default options, leads to approximately 8-digit accuracy. More precisely, the default options ensure that the *local error*, *i.e.*, the error made in a step of length h, is approximately $10^{-8} \times h$. One is generally more interested in the *global error*, *i.e.*, the cumulative error committed in taking the necessary number of steps to get from the initial point x_0 to some target point x. This error cannot be controlled completely by the numerical method because it depends on the differential equation as well as on the numerical method. The key issue is whether the differential equation is stable or unstable; these terms were defined in Chapter 5.

We have seen equations for which **dsolve(..., numeric)** gives very accurate results. Now we look at an example where **dsolve(..., numeric)** gives very poor results.

EXAMPLE. Consider the initial value problem

$$\frac{dy}{dx} - y = -3e^{-2x}, \qquad y(0) = 1.$$

The exact solution is $y(x) = e^{-2x}$; we plot it in Figure 4.

Figure 4

Next we find the numerical solution using **dsolve(..., numeric)**, and plot it together with the exact solution:

```
exact4 := plot(exp(−2*x), x = 0..12):
ivp4 := {diff(y(x), x) − y(x) = −3*exp(−2*x), y(0) = 1};
appr4 := odeplot(dsolve(ivp4, y(x), numeric, maxfun = 1000), [x, y(x)], 0..12):
display({appr4, exact4});
```

Figure 5

We see from Figure 5 that the graphs are indistinguishable from 0 to about 8, but then the curves separate sharply. By clicking on the graphics window (as described on p. 37), we see that $y_a(12) = 0.1388\ldots$, which is very different from the exact value $y(12) = e^{-24} \approx 3.78 \times 10^{-11}$.

How can this failure be explained? The solution to our differential equation with initial condition $y(0) = 1 + \epsilon$ is $y(x) = e^{-2x} + \epsilon e^x$. Figure 6 shows a plot of the solutions corresponding to initial values $1 - (0.5 \times 10^{-5}), 1 - (0.25 \times 10^{-5}), 1, 1 + (0.25 \times 10^{-5}), 1 + (0.5 \times 10^{-5})$.

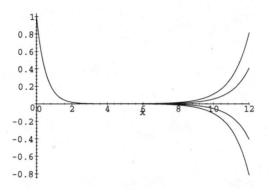

Figure 6

We see that solutions with initial values slightly different from 1 separate very sharply from the solution with initial value exactly 1 after about 8; those with initial values greater than 1 approach $+\infty$, and those with initial values less than 1 approach $-\infty$. Now **dsolve(. . ., numeric)**, like any numerical method, introduces errors. These errors—whether truncation errors or round-off errors—have caused the numerical solution to jump to a solution that started just above 1. Once on such a solution, the numerical solution will follow it or another such solution. Since these solutions approach $+\infty$, the numerical solution does likewise.

Could we have anticipated this failure? Recall the discussion of stable and unstable differential equations in Chapter 5. The solutions of unstable equations are very sensitive to their initial values, and hence a numerical method will have trouble following the solution it is attempting to calculate. Recall also that an equation $dy/dx = f(x,y)$ is unstable if $\partial f/\partial y > 0$, and stable if $\partial f/\partial y \leq 0$. For our example, $f(x,y) = y - 3e^{-2x}$ and $\partial f/\partial y = 1 > 0$. So we are trying to approximate the solution of an unstable differential equation, and we should not be surprised that we have trouble, especially over long intervals (beyond about 8 for this example). By contrast, note that for the initial value problem (1) above, $\partial f/\partial y = -x/y^2 < 0$ for $x > 0$. All this suggests caution when dealing with unstable equations. In fact, caution is always recommended when modeling physical problems with unstable equations, especially over long intervals (*cf.* the discussion in Chapter 5).

In assessing the reliability of a numerically computed solution there is another test one can make. Suppose we have made a calculation using the default options, as we have done with our example. Then one can do another calculation, using more stringent accuracy requirements, and compare the results. If they are nearly the same, one can have confidence that they are both fairly accurate; but if they differ substantially, then one should suspect that the first calculation is not accurate.

Let's do this with our example:

Digits := 12;
appr5 := odeplot(dsolve(ivp4, y(x), numeric, maxfun = 1000,
    abserr = Float(1, −10), relerr = Float(1, −10)), [x, y(x)], 0..16):

Next we plot both numerical solutions together with the exact solution:

display({exact4, appr4, appr5});

Figure 7

We see from Figure 7 that the second numerical solution is accurate over a longer interval, out to about 13, whereas the first was accurate out to about 8. In particular, the two numerical solutions differ after about 8. Even if we didn't know the exact solution, we could have concluded that the first numerical solution is accurate out to, but not beyond, about 8.

In summary, we have learned that local accuracy—the accuracy that a numerical method can control—leads to reasonable global accuracy if the differential equation is stable, and that the reliability of a numerical solution can also be checked by computing another numerical solution with more stringent accuracy requirements.

We have discussed the reliability of **dsolve(. . ., numeric)**, focusing on the effect of instability of the differential equation on its accuracy. Now we turn to a discussion of the reliability of **DEplot**. Instability of the differential equation has a similar effect on the accuracy of **DEplot**. But **DEplot** is subject to another form of instability because it uses a fixed step size. To illustrate this difficulty, consider the initial value problem

$$\frac{dy}{dx} = -\pi xy, \qquad y(0) = 1,$$

whose exact solution is $y(x) = e^{-\pi x^2/2}$. In Figure 8, we have plotted the exact solution on $[0, 15]$ together with the solution produced by **DEplot** with the Euler Method and **stepsize = 0.1**.

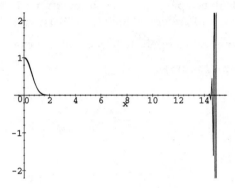

Figure 8

We see that the numerical solution is fairly accurate for x less than about 14, but then becomes wildly inaccurate. How can this inaccuracy be explained? Since the differential equation is stable, the problem is not caused by its instability. For the Euler Method with fixed step size h, it is known that the global error at each step is multiplied by a factor depending on h and $\partial f/\partial y$. To be precise,

Global Error at $x_{k+1} = (1 + hJ) \cdot$ Global Error at x_k + Local Error at x_{k+1},

where $J = (\partial f/\partial y)(x_k, \eta_k)$, for some η_k. (See D. Kahaner, C. Moler, and S. Nash, **Numerical Methods and Software**, Prentice Hall, Inc., 1989.) If $|1 + hJ| < 1$, then the error does not grow, but if $|1 + hJ| > 1$, it does grow, and the method is called unstable. In our example, the *amplification factor* $1 + hJ$ is equal to $1 - 0.1\pi x_k$, and $|1 + hJ| > 1$ if $x_k > 20/\pi \approx 6.4$. So for $x_k > 6.4$ the error begins to grow, and eventually becomes large. This is confirmed by Figure 8. If we had used a smaller step size, the approximate solution would have been more accurate for small x, but would have eventually become unstable and inaccurate. The situation is similar for the Improved Euler Method and the Runge-Kutta Method: for any fixed step size, the method may eventually become unstable and inaccurate.

A Further Remark on dsolve(...,numeric)

Earlier, we recommended extracting functions from the procedure returned by **dsolve(..., numeric)** in a single step rather than in two steps. In this section we explain why this is necessary. Consider the initial value problem

$$\frac{dy}{dx} = 1 - 2xy, \quad y(0) = 0. \tag{4}$$

We can extract a function from the numerical solution in two steps:

```
ivp6 := {diff(y(x), x) = 1 − 2*x*y(x), y(0) = 0};
sol6 := dsolve(ivp6, y(x), numeric, maxfun = 2000);
ya6 := u −> subs(sol6(u), y(x));
```

If we evaluate **ya6** at some point, say $x = 0.1$, the procedure **sol6** produced by **dsolve(..., numeric)** starts at $x = 0.0$, employs the initial condition $y(0) = 0$, and steps from $x = 0.0$ to $x = 0.1$ to compute the approximate value $0.993\ldots$ for **ya6(0.1)**. Next suppose we evaluate **ya6** at $x = 0.2$. Then **dsolve(..., numeric)** starts at the point $x = 0.1$, employs the newly computed initial condition $y(0.1) = 0.993\ldots$, and steps from $x = 0.1$ to $x = 0.2$. By starting at $x = 0.1$ and using as initial value the final value from the previous calculation, **dsolve(..., numeric)** sensibly avoids repeating the calculation from $x = 0.0$ to $x = 0.1$. The value of this feature is best appreciated when calculating solution values at an increasing sequence of positive points, such as $x = 0.1, 0.2, \ldots, 0.9, 1.0$. One steps from $x = 0.0$ to $x = 0.1$, then from 0.1 to $x = 0.2$, *etc.*, without repeating any of the previous calculations. A similar benefit accrues when computing solution values at a decreasing sequence of negative points.

One must beware, however, that computing solution values at a sequence of points that is neither increasing nor decreasing from the initial data point can lead to inaccurate results. To see this, repeat the *Maple* command defining **sol6**. Evaluate **ya6** first at $x = 4.5$, and then at $x = 0.0$. You will find that $ya6(4.5) = 0.114\ldots$ and $ya6(0.0) = -3.865\ldots$. This is in sharp conflict with the initial value $y(0) = 0$ specified in the original call to **dsolve(..., numeric)**. How can this discrepancy be explained? When $ya6(4.5) = 0.114\ldots$ is computed, **dsolve(..., numeric)** starts at the point $x = 0.0$, and steps across to $x = 4.5$. Then, to calculate $ya6(0.0)$, **dsolve(..., numeric)** starts at the point $x = 4.5$, employs the initial condition $y(4.5) = 0.114\ldots$, and steps back from $x = 4.5$ to $x = 0.0$. If our numerical method tracked the solution exactly, we would have gotten the value 0. Of course, the method is not exact; it includes truncation and round-off errors. Since our differential equation is unstable to the left, these errors are severe. (When going to the left, the Theorem on p. 49 of Chapter 5 applies with the roles of K and L reversed. In particular, an equation is unstable to the left if $\partial f / \partial y < 0$. In the case at hand, $\partial(1 - 2xy)/\partial y = -2x < 0$. Thus the numerical calculation from 4.5 to 0.0 is highly inaccurate.)

If you follow our recommendation and always combine the two steps (calling **dsolve(..., numeric)** and using **subs** to extract a function) into a single command, then you ensure that each calculation starts at the original initial data point. If **ya6** is defined this way, and if you calculate $ya6(4.5)$, and then $ya6(0.0)$, you will get the correct value 0.

A similar issue arises when using **odeplot**. For example, suppose you were told that the initial value problem $y' = y^2 + x$, $y(0) = 1$ has a solution that blows up somewhere in the interval $0 < x < 1$, and you were asked to find that value. The commands

```
ivp7 := {diff(y(x), x) = y(x)^2 + x, y(0) = 1};
sol7 := dsolve(ivp7, y(x), numeric, maxfun = 1000);
with(plots);
odeplot(sol7, [x, y(x)], 0..1);
```

produce a graph that reveals only that the vertical asymptote is somewhere in the interval $0.9 < x < 1.0$. A second try of the form

```
odeplot(sol7, [x, y(x)], 0.9..1);
```

will produce slightly inaccurate results. This happens because the initial value in **dsolve(. . ., numeric)** has been reset to the last value computed in the first try, and therefore graphing on the interval $(0.9, 1)$ causes you to solve to the left after solving to the right. In this example the discrepancy is minor, but in other examples it can be more dramatic. To avoid this problem, it is best to reinitialize each time **odeplot** is called. This can be achieved by the command recommended in the section *Numerical Solutions Using Maple*. An alternative approach is to define a function that produces a new graph as a function of the plotting interval:

```
curve := range -> odeplot(dsolve(ivp7, y(x), numeric, maxfun = 1000),
    [x, y(x)], range);
```

The command **curve(0..1)** will plot the solution on the interval $(0, 1)$, and then the command **curve(0.9..1)** will plot it accurately on the smaller interval.

Comparison of dsolve(...,numeric) and DEplot

Except for the dangers highlighted in the previous section, **dsolve(. . ., numeric)** is an accurate, robust numerical solver. Its variable step feature makes it especially valuable for calculating solutions that oscillate or are singular. We recommend using **dsolve(. . ., numeric)** as the primary numerical differential equation solver in *Maple*. However, for many problems **DEplot** produces satisfactory results.

There is one exception to this recommendation. The procedure in **odeplot**, even when used as recommended, is unreliable when plotting to the left of the initial point, *e.g.*, plotting a solution with initial value at $x = 0$ on an interval of the form $(-a, a)$. For **odeplot** evaluates the solution at an increasing sequence of points starting at $x = -a$. To calculate these values, **dsolve(. . ., numeric)** first solves to the left from $x = 0.0$ to $x = -a$, and then solves back to the right from $x = -a$. **DEplot** does not have this problem, and it is thus best to use it in such situations. **DEplot** is generally not as accurate as **dsolve(. . ., numeric)**, unless the constant step size is chosen to be very small.

Chapter 8

Features of *Maple*

This chapter is a continuation of Chapter 3, *Doing Mathematics with Maple*. We describe some of the more advanced features of *Maple*, focusing on the *Maple* commands and techniques most useful for studying differential equations. We also describe some aspects of *Maple*'s internal structure that should help in working with complicated expressions and commands.

Names and Values.   A *Maple* object usually has both a *name* and a *value*. For example, the symbol x has the name "x". Initially, its value is also its name, "x". However, if you type

> x := 2;

$$x := 2$$

the situation changes. The name of x is still "x", but its value is now 2.

When you enter an input statement in a *Maple* session, *Maple* generally tries to find values for all of the variables in the statement. *Maple* substitutes the value of a variable for its name when it processes the input. If the value of a variable is another variable, then *Maple* will in turn substitute the value of that variable, and so on. This is called *full evaluation*.

Note that once a value has been assigned to a variable it ceases to be a variable in the true sense of the word, and becomes instead just a name for its value. In certain situations, you may want to insist that *Maple* treat something as a variable. You can do this by enclosing the variable name in right quotes ('). For example:

> 'x'^2;

$$x^2$$

Compare this with the unquoted version.

> x^2;

$$4$$

The effect of evaluation on a quoted name is to strip away one set of right quotes. No further evaluation is performed. We will see several examples below where right quotes are useful to prevent full evaluation.

Clearing Values.   One of the most common sources of errors in using *Maple* is the failure to keep track of variable or function definitions. For example, suppose that early in a session you type
> i := 3;

$$i := 3$$

You keep working and twenty minutes later you want to evaluate the sum $1 + 1/2 + \ldots + 1/9$. So, you type
> sum(1/i, i = 1..9);
```
   Error, (in sum) summation variable previously assigned,
      second argument evaluates to, 3 = 1 ..  9
```
Because *i* already had a value, *Maple* saw this command as **sum(1/3, 3 = 1..9)**, and objected to it.

One way to avoid this kind of error is by using right quotes to suppress evaluation. For example,
> sum(1/'i', 'i' = 1..9);

$$\frac{7129}{2520}$$

A simpler way to avoid the error is to clear the value of *i* before you use it.

Maple provides a way to find out which variables have already been assigned. The command **anames( )** produces a list of all names that have been assigned some value. If you have been working for a long time, this list may be overwhelming. So, you can also check to see whether a specific variable has been assigned by using the command **assigned**.
> assigned(i);

true

> i := 'i':
> assigned(i);

false

Recall that the **restart** command will clear all the values in a *Maple* session.

Functions and Expressions.   *Maple* distinguishes between a *function* and an *expression*. In order to use *Maple* effectively, you must learn to make the same distinction. You should review the section *User-defined Functions and Expressions* in Chapter 3 if you've forgotten the difference between functions and expressions.

There are several ways to define a function in *Maple*. The simplest way is to use *Maple*'s arrow notation.
> restart;

> **f := x -> x^2 - 1;**

$$f := x \rightarrow x^2 - 1$$

> **f(2);**

$$3$$

Functions of several variables can also be defined.

> **phi := (x, y) -> x^2 + y^2;**

$$\phi := (x, y) \rightarrow x^2 + y^2$$

Note that the list of arguments must be enclosed in parentheses.

A function can be evaluated with a symbolic argument as well as a numeric argument:

> **f(y);**

$$y^2 - 1$$

The result of this evaluation is the expression $y^2 - 1$. This is a subtle point: the symbol **f** is the name of a *function*; the symbol **f(x)** is the name of an *expression* involving **x**.

To remove the definition of a function you must unassign the name of the function.

> **f := 'f':**
> **f(y);**

$$f(y)$$

The command **unapply** can be used to turn an expression into a function. For example, suppose we define

> **expr1 := sin(x) + cos(x);**

$$expr1 := \sin(x) + \cos(x)$$

We then type

> **g := unapply(expr1, x);**

$$g := x \rightarrow \sin(x) + \cos(x)$$

The command **unapply** takes the first argument, which must be an expression (or a name of an expression) containing one or more variables, evaluates this expression, and then makes it into a function of the specified variables. To make a function of two variables, you could type, for example,

> **expr2 := x^2 + y^2;**

$$expr2 := x^2 + y^2$$

> **h := unapply(expr2, x, y);**

$$h := (x, y) \rightarrow x^2 + y^2$$

> **h(2, 3);**

$$13$$

There is a subtle difference between using **unapply** and the arrow notation to define a function. Note that in the examples of **unapply**, the names *expr*1 and *expr*2 were evaluated and replaced with their values. This does not happen if you define the function with an arrow.

> **g := x –> expr1;**

$$g := x \rightarrow expr1$$

> **g(0);**

$$\sin(x) + \cos(x)$$

What happens here is that when *Maple* evaluates a function defined with the arrow notation, it *first* substitutes the argument (in this case x) into the expression on the right-hand side, and *then* evaluates the right-hand side. Since x does not appear as a variable on the right-hand side in this example, the function we define this way is actually independent of x. Thus g has been defined to be a function that returns as its *constant* value the expression *expr*1. The point of this discussion is that the arrow notation can only be used when the argument (in this case, x) appears explicitly on the right-hand side of the arrow. The command **unapply** should be used when you want to build a function using the name of a previously defined expression.

A third way of defining a function is by creating a *Maple procedure* using the command **proc**. This involves some understanding of programming. For an introduction to *Maple* programming, see B. Char, *et al.*, **First Leaves: A Tutorial Introduction to Maple V**, Springer-Verlag, 1992. An example of a simple *Maple* program is given in the glossary of this book.

It is possible in *Maple* to define values of functions at particular points. Suppose, for example, that we want to define the function $f(x) = \sin(x)/x$. We know from elementary calculus that the limit of this function as x approaches 0 is 1, but if we evaluate the function at $x = 0$, *Maple* gives an error. We could circumvent this problem by doing the following:

> **f := x –> sin(x)/x;**

$$f := x \rightarrow sin(x)/x$$

> **f(0) := 1;**

$$f(0) := 1$$

What we have done here is merely to specify that at the point $x = 0$, *Maple* should ignore the general definition $f := x \to \sin(x)/x$, and instead just set $f(0) = 1$. This feature is occasionally useful when working with functions that have expressions in the denominator that might take on zero values. However this syntax should NEVER be used to define a general function because no evaluation takes place when this syntax is used. For example,

> **f := 'f':**
> **f(x) := sin(x)/x;**

$$f(x) := \frac{sin(x)}{x}$$

> **f(x);**

$$\frac{sin(x)}{x}$$

> **f(1);**

$$f(1);$$

As far as *Maple* is concerned we have not defined a general function, but rather a specific instance of a function. Thus $f(x)$ is merely a name for the expression $\sin(x)/x$. There is no substitution, and no evaluation. The symbol $f(1)$ has *not* been defined, so *Maple* just echoes what we've typed.

If you accidentally type a definition like **f(x) := sin(x)/x**, you can clear it by reassigning the name of the function.

> **f := 'f';**

$$f := f$$

Substitution. We have seen that a function can be evaluated at various values of the argument. A similar effect can be accomplished with expressions using the substitution command **subs**.

> **subs(x = 5, x^2 − 1);**

$$24$$

The **subs** command is extremely useful and versatile. What it does is to use one or more equations to substitute for variables in an expression (the last argument of the command). Here is another example:

> **subs(x = a, y = b, z = c, (x^2 − 3*y)/z);**

$$\frac{a^2 - 3b}{c}$$

When you use the **subs** command with more than one equation (as in the preceding example), the substitution is done from left to right. Thus in the preceding example a is first substituted for x, then b for y, then c for z. If you want the substitutions to occur simultaneously, you must enclose the equations in braces. Here is an example in which we switch x and y in an expression.

> **subs({x = y, y = x}, x/y);**

$$\frac{y}{x}$$

You can test your understanding of the **subs** command by predicting what the output of the preceding statement would be if the braces were omitted.

The most common use of **subs** is to manipulate expressions that have been previously typed in by the user or generated by *Maple*. Here is an example in which we find the solution of the differential equation $y' = xy$ with initial condition $y(0) = 1$.

> **soln := dsolve(diff(y(x), x) = x*y(x), y(x));**

$$soln := y(x) = e^{\frac{1}{2}x^2}\_C1$$

By inspecting the solution, we see that the undetermined constant _C1 must be 1 in order for the solution to satisfy the initial condition. Thus the solution is obtained by substituting 1 for _C1.

> **subs(_C1 = 1, soln);**

$$y(x) = e^{\frac{1}{2}x^2}$$

Equations vs. Assignments.   In *Maple*, an *equation* is different from an *assignment*. For example, $x = 2$ is an equation, whereas $x := 2$ is an assignment. Compare the effects of entering an equation and an assignment.

> **x = 2;**

$$x = 2$$

> **x;**

$$x$$

> **x := 2;**

$$x := 2$$

> **x;**

$$2$$

Note that an equation has no effect on the value of the variables in the equation.

Equations can even be assigned names.

> **nice_eqn := E = m*c^2;**

$$nice\_eqn := E = m c^2$$

The right- and left-hand sides of an equation can be extracted using the functions **rhs** and **lhs**.

> lhs(nice_eqn) − rhs(nice_eqn);

$$E - m\,c^2$$

Differentiation. The distinction between functions and expressions becomes important when differentiating. *Maple* has two commands for differentiation. The **diff** command operates on expressions.

> f := t −> t^2:
> diff(f(t), t);

$$2t$$

Notice that the output of **diff** is another expression.

The **D** operator differentiates functions, and returns a function as its output.

> D(f);

$$t \to 2t$$

When you differentiate an expression, you must state explicitly which variable should be used. When you differentiate a function, you must not mention the name of the variable.

One place where you must use the **D** command is to specify initial values for derivatives. In order to solve the second order initial value problem

$$y'' = 9y + 2x, \qquad y(0) = 1, \qquad y'(0) = 0,$$

you could type

> de := diff(y(x), x$2) = 9*y(x) + 2*x;

$$de := \frac{\partial^2}{\partial x^2} y(x) = 9y(x) + 2x$$

> initial := y(0) = 1, D(y)(0) = 0;

$$initial := y(0) = 1, D(y)(0) = 0$$

> dsolve({de, initial}, y(x));

$$y(x) = -\frac{2}{9}x + \frac{29}{54}e^{3x} + \frac{25}{54}e^{-3x}$$

If you want to refer to the value of a higher derivative, then the notation is more complex. For example, suppose you want to specify the initial value $y'''(0) = 1$. One way to write this condition is

> D(D(D(y)))(0) = 1;

$$(D^{(3)})(y)(0) = 1$$

As you might imagine, all those layers of **D**'s and parentheses can become confusing. *Maple* offers an alternative:

> **(D@@3)(y)(0) = 1;**

$$(D^{(3)})(y)(0) = 1$$

Type **?@** for more information about this operator.

Sequences, Sets, and Lists.   The three most common data structures in *Maple* are *sequences*, *sets*, and *lists*. A *sequence* is a collection of *Maple* objects separated by commas, as in $1, 2, 3$ or a, b, c. A *list* is a sequence surrounded by square brackets, as in $[1, 2, 3]$ or $[a, b, c]$. A *set* is a collection of *Maple* objects separated by commas and surrounded by braces, as in $\{1, 2, 3\}$ or $\{a, b, c\}$. These three data types are similar except for one important difference: In a set, order and repetition are irrelevant. Thus the sets $\{c, b, a\}$ and $\{a, a, b, c\}$ are identical to $\{a, b, c\}$. On the other hand, the lists $[c, b, a]$, $[a, a, b, c]$, and $[a, b, c]$ are all different. They are also different as sequences.

Of these three types of objects, the fundamental one is the sequence. A list is simply a sequence surrounded by brackets, and a set is a sequence surrounded by braces in which order and repetition are ignored.

You can create and name a sequence very easily:

> **s := b, c, d;**

$$s := b, c, d$$

You can also add items to the beginning or end of a sequence:

> **s := a, s, e;**

$$s := a, b, c, d, e$$

You can recover the individual elements of a sequence using brackets. Inside the brackets you put a number or range indicating the positions of the elements you wish to extract.

> **s[2];**

$$b$$

> **s[2..4];**

$$b, c, d$$

Lists and sets are constructed by wrapping brackets or braces around sequences.

> **list1 := [s];**

$$list1 := [a, b, c, d, e]$$

> **set1 := {s};**

$$set1 := \{c, b, a, d, e\}$$

Note that the order of elements is not preserved when we define a set. To extract the elements of a set or list we use the command **op** (for "operand"). The output is in the form of a sequence.

> **op(list1);**

$$a, b, c, d, e$$

> **op(set1);**

$$c, b, a, d, e$$

Using **op**, we can build new lists out of old lists.

> **list2 := [op(list1), 1, 2, 3];**

$$[a, b, c, d, e, 1, 2, 3]$$

For sets, we can use the more natural command **union**.

> **set1 union {1, 2, 3};**

$$\{1, 2, 3, c, b, a, d, e\}$$

Particular elements of lists can be extracted using the same procedure as for sequences.

> **list2[5];**

$$e$$

> **list2[4..7];**

$$d, e, 1, 2$$

In fact, the same procedure also works for sets, but is not recommended since sets are arbitrarily ordered.

Although it is easy to define a sequence, list, or set by simply typing in the elements, it is often convenient to automate this process. This can be done using either the **seq** command or the **$** (dollar sign) operator. To illustrate these facilities, we'll build a sequence in two different ways by evaluating a function $f(x)$ at the integers $0, \ldots, 4$.

> **f := x -> x^2 - 1:**
> **f(i) $ i = 0..4;**

$$-1, 0, 3, 8, 15$$

The symbol **$** is called the *sequence operator*. When you use the sequence operator, the index variable (in this case, i) remains unchanged.

> **i;**

$$i$$

We can also define this sequence using the **seq** command.

```
> seq(f(i), i = 0..4);
```

$$-1, 0, 3, 8, 15$$

When you use the **seq** command, the index variable acquires a value.

```
> i;
```

$$5$$

It is important to remember that the **seq** command has a residual effect on the indexing variable. You should also know that the sequence operator fails if the indexing variable has previously been assigned a value (failure can be avoided by quoting the indexing variable). But the **seq** command works even if the indexing variable has previously been assigned. Because of these effects, it is good practice to reserve certain variables (such as i and j) for use as index variables, and to avoid using them in other constructions.

Another important difference between the sequence operator and **seq** command is the order of evaluation. The sequence operator first evaluates the expression to the left of the dollar sign, and then substitutes the value of the index into the expression. The **seq** command first substitutes the value of the index and then evaluates the expression. This is a rather subtle difference, but it can have serious consequences. Consider the following sequence of commands.

```
> i := 'i':
> solve(x^2 = i, x) $ i = 1..2;
Error, wrong number (or type) of parameters in function $;
> seq(solve(x^2 = i, x), i = 1..2);
```

$$1, -1, \sqrt{2}, -\sqrt{2}$$

In both input lines, we've attempted to create a sequence consisting of the square roots of the integers 1 and 2. The first attempt using the sequence operator fails because of premature evaluation; *Maple* tries to solve the equation $x^2 = i$ *before* it assigns a value to i. The second attempt works because *Maple* first assigns values to i and then evaluates the **solve** command. You could rectify the problem with the sequence operator by enclosing the expression to the left-hand side of the dollar sign in right quotes to delay evaluation. Problems with premature evaluation are likely to occur when you use the sequence operator to construct sequences out of complex expressions. In these situations the **seq** command is preferred.

There are two other reasons you might prefer the **seq** command. First, it is more flexible. Its second argument need not be a range of values; it can be a list or a set. For example, if you want to evaluate the function f (defined earlier) at the points 0.13, 2, 3, and 7.4, you could type

```
> seq(f(x), x = [0.13, 2, 3, 7.4]);
```

$$-.9831, 3, 8, 53.76$$

```
> x := 'x':
```

Note that in this example we have used a *list* of parameters. Note also that we have unassigned the index x after using it in the **seq** command (can you guess what value x had before we cleared it?). You can also use a *set* of parameters, as in x = {0.13, 2, 3, 7.4} (but not a sequence of parameters). Since sets are unordered, the sequence that *Maple* returns may not be in the same order as the set of parameters.

The second reason to use **seq** is that it is better suited for constructing expression sequences that depend on two or more parameters. We describe this in more detail in the next section.

More about Sequences, Sets, and Lists. Sequences, sets, and lists are useful when you want to do many things with a single command. For example, to plot the expressions $x^2 + c$ for values of c ranging from -5 to 5, you could type **plot({x^2 + c $ c = −5..5}, x = 0..5)**. The syntax {x^2 + c $ c = −5..5} creates a *set* of functions, which are then plotted by the **plot** command.

Both the sequence operator and the **seq** command increment the index by 1. More specifically, when you specify a range for the index, *Maple* initially sets the index equal to the first value in the range, and then increments it successively by 1 until the index becomes greater than the second value in the range, at which point *Maple* stops.

```
> i := 'i':
> {i $ i = 2.1..4};
```

$$\{2.1, 3.1\}$$

```
> [seq(i, i = −9..(2.1))];
```

$$[-9, -8, -7, -6, -5, -4, -3, -2, -1, 0, 1, 2]$$

```
> i := 'i':
```

You may want to build a sequence with a parameter in increments other than 1. To do this you just "rescale" the parameter. Here is a list of values of the exponential function at the points $0, 0.2, 0.4, \ldots, 1.0$.

```
> expvalues := [exp(0.2*i) $ i = 0..5];
```

$$expvalues :=$$
$$[1, 1.221402758, 1.491824698, 1.822118800, 2.225540928, 2.718281828]$$

Note that the parameter varies from 0 to 5 in increments of 1, but the argument of the exponential function, which is 0.2 times the parameter, varies from 0 to 1 in increments of 0.2.

The *Maple* command **map** can be used to apply a function to the elements of a list.

```
> map(log, expvalues);
```

$$[0, .1999999999, .4000000002, .5999999998, .7999999998, .9999999998]$$

The logarithm is the inverse of the exponential function, so if *Maple* were doing exact arithmetic the result of the preceding command would be $[0, 0.2, 0.4, 0.6, 0.8, 1]$.

Round-off errors account for the slight difference in the actual output.

The **map** command provides a way to print a *Maple* list in tabular form. In the following example, we create a "list of lists" and then print it in tabular form.

> **t := [[x = j, y = sin(j)] $ j = 0..4];**

$$t := [[x = 1, y = sin(1)], [x = 2, y = sin(2)], [x = 3, y = sin(3)],$$
$$[x = 4, y = sin(4)]]$$

We'd really like to see decimal approximations of these values, so we'll use **evalf** to get decimal approximations to 4 places.

> **t := evalf(t, 4);**

$$t := [[x = 1., y = .8415], [x = 2., y = .9093], [x = 3., y = .1411],$$
$$[x = 4., y = -.7568]]$$

> **map(print, t):**

$$[x = 1., y = .8415]$$

$$[x = 2., y = .9093]$$

$$[x = 3., y = .1411]$$

$$[x = 4., y = -.7568]$$

The colon at the end of the **map** command prevents *Maple* from printing an extra line containing an empty list. You could actually combine the three steps above into the single complex command **map(print, evalf([[x = j, y = sin(j)] $ j = 1..4]))**. A similar effect can be obtained with the **array** command.

> **array(t);**

$$\begin{bmatrix} x = 1., & y = .8415 \\ x = 2., & y = .9093 \\ x = 3., & y = .1411 \\ x = 4., & y = -.7568 \end{bmatrix}$$

In certain situations you may want to construct sequences or lists that depend on two or more parameters. You might do this, for example, if you're solving a second order differential equation in y, and want to study the solutions for various values of the initial conditions $y(x_0) = y_0$, $y'(x_0) = y'_0$. To construct a list depending on several parameters, you can use nested calls to the **seq** command or sequence operator. Here is an example in which we construct the set of all fractions with numerator and denominator between 1 and 4.

> **{seq(seq(a/b, b = 1..4), a = 1..4)};**

$$\{1, 2, 3, 4, 1/2, 1/3, 1/4, 2/3, 3/2, 3/4, 4/3\}$$

To do this with the sequence operator, it is necessary to use right quotes to prevent premature evaluation.

> **a := 'a':**
> **b := 'b':**
> **{'a/b $ b = 1..4' $ a = 1..4};**

$$\{1, 2, 3, 4, 1/2, 1/3, 1/4, 2/3, 3/2, 3/4, 4/3\}$$

Because of problems with premature evaluation, the **seq** command is generally preferred for nested constructions.

We showed above how to use **op** to strip brackets or braces off a list or set. This command can also be used together with the **map** command to strip off extra brackets or braces inside a list or set.

> **nestedlist := [[a, b], [c, d]];**

$$nestedlist := [[a, b], [c, d]]$$

> **map(op, nestedlist);**

$$[a, b, c, d]$$

Compare this with the effect of the command **op(nestedlist)**.

Graphics. We will encounter at least eight plotting commands in this course, including **plot, contourplot, implicitplot, textplot, display, dfieldplot, DEplot,** and **odeplot**. We briefly describe most of these in this section.

The most important thing to keep in mind with various plotting commands is the type of *Maple* object the command is designed to plot. For example, the **plot** command plots functions, expressions, lists of points, or parametric functions, and nothing else. On the other hand, **implicitplot** is designed to plot equations (although it will plot an expression or function by turning it into an equation of the form *expression* $= 0$). Moreover, the distinction between functions and expressions is important in all the plotting commands. If *Maple* gives you an error message or an implausible plot when you enter a plot command, the first thing you should check is whether you are plotting the right kind of object for that particular command, and whether you are using precisely the right syntax for that object and that command.

The simplest and most versatile plotting command is **plot**. We explained in Chapter 3 how to use it to plot a single function or expression. To plot multiple functions or expressions, the collection must be specified in the form of a *set*, as opposed to a list or sequence. The vertical range of the plot may be specified as an option. For example, to plot the two functions $e^x \cos x$ and $x^3 - 3x + 2$ on the interval $[-3, 3]$ with range $[-10, 10]$, we type

> **plot({exp(x)*cos(x), x^3 − 3*x + 2}, x = −3..3, y = −10..10);**

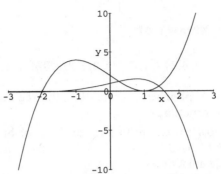

In this construction the **y** in **y** = −**10..10** is really just a place holder. It appears in the plot as a label on the vertical axis. Any string could appear in its place. Thus if the functions in the previous input represented voltage, you might enter the command as **plot({exp(x)*cos(x), x^3 − 3*x + 2}, x = −3..3, voltage = −10..10)**. You could also omit the label altogether and simply enter the range of the dependent variable as −**10..10**.

Plots can be assigned names and later recalled. For example,

> **plot1 := plot({exp(x)*cos(x), x^3 − 3*x + 2}, x = −3..3, y = −10..10):**

Because of the colon at the end of the command, *Maple* does not print any output. In particular, it does not display the graph. If you use a semicolon in this construction, then it *still* doesn't display the graph; instead, it prints a very long list of points in your Worksheet. (This list is the underlying data structure of the plot.) To view the named plot, you simply type its name (in this case, **plot1**), followed by a semicolon.

The **plot** command can be used to plot curves defined by parametric equations.

> **plot([exp(−t/100)*cos(t), exp(−t/100)*sin(t), t = 0..200]);**

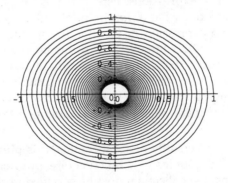

The **plot** command can also be used to plot a list of points. The list may be given explicitly or it may be generated by another command. By default, *Maple* connects the points with straight line segments.

> **plot2 := plot([[−3, 1], [−1, 2], [0.5, 8], [2, 3], [3, 2]]):**
> **plot2;**

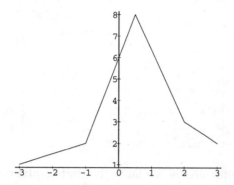

Several previously named plots can be displayed on a single graph using the command **display**. This command is in the **plots** package and must be explicitly loaded. For example, the command **display({plot1, plot2})** displays *plot1* and *plot2* on the same graph. Note that the names of the plots may appear as a set or a list, but not a sequence. One use for the **display** command is to add textual annotations to a graph. After creating and naming a plot, you can add labels with the **textplot** command (also in the **plots** package). The argument to **textplot** is a list or set of items, each of the form [x0, y0, `label`]. The label is placed at coordinates $(x0, y0)$. Note that the label must be enclosed in left quotes (type **?`** for more information). For example, you could type

> **with(plots):**
> **plot3 := textplot([[1, 8, `f(x)`], [2.6, 7, `g(x)`], [1.8, −5, `h(x)`]]):**
> **display({plot1, plot2, plot3});**

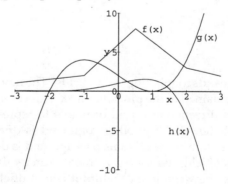

The **contourplot** command plots level curves of a function or expression, *i.e.*, sets of points on which the function or expression is constant. There are four different calling sequences for **contourplot**, but the most common usage is with an expression involving exactly two variables. For example,

> **contourplot(x^2 + y^2, x = −5..5, y = −5..5, axes = BOXED);**

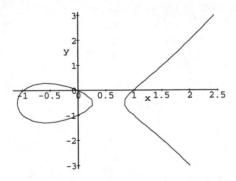

The **implicitplot** command is similar to the **contourplot** command in that it is used to plot a *single* level set of a function or expression. It is most commonly used to study functions that are defined implicitly by an equation. The important thing to remember about this command is that it takes for its argument an *equation* involving exactly two variables (the argument can also be an expression involving two variables, in which case *Maple* uses the equation "expression=0"). You must explicitly specify the range of each of these variables. For example, you could type

> **implicitplot(y^2 + y = x^3 − x, x = −2..3, y = −3..3);**

Maple has two commands for plotting vector fields. The more general command is **fieldplot**, which is contained in the **plots** package. This command places arrows of different length and direction at a grid of points to represent the changes in a vector field (see Chapter 13). The other command is **dfieldplot**, which was introduced in Chapter 6. It is in the **DEtools** package, and is designed specifically for plotting the direction fields associated with an ordinary differential equation. The principal difference between it and **fieldplot** is that **dfieldplot** plots vectors (or line segments) of fixed length, while **fieldplot** plots vectors whose length is proportional to the magnitude of the functions defining the vector field.

Maple's support for graphing solutions to differential equations includes the commands **odeplot** (in the **plots** package) and **DEplot** (in the **DEtools** package).

These commands were introduced in Chapter 7.

All the plotting commands let you control the look of a plot by changing certain options. On some systems, some of these options can be changed interactively using the controls in a plot window. The other options must be set before the plot is created. Type **?plot[options]** for a list of options to the main plotting commands, and **?DEtools[options]** for the options to the **DEplot** and **dfieldplot** commands.

The **plot** command is an adaptive plotting routine; it starts by plotting a certain number of evenly spaced points, and in regions where the graph is changing rapidly, it goes back and tries to plot more points to get a better picture. The option **numpoints** tells *Maple* how many points to start with; the default value is 49. In certain situations you may need to set a higher value of numpoints to get a smoother plot.

Plotting Multiple Solutions with odeplot.   In Chapter 5, we showed how to create and plot a *family* of symbolic solutions of a differential equation depending on the initial value. It is possible to do the same kind of thing with numerical solutions. The process is different, however, because the output of the numerical solver is more complicated, and because the numerical solver only works with an actual numerical initial value. Here is an example. First, we define a function **curve1** whose value at c is the numerical solution with initial condition $y(1) = c$.

> **eqn1 := diff(y(x), x) = sqrt(y(x) + x);**

$$eqn1 := \frac{\partial}{\partial x} y(x) = \sqrt{y(x) + x}$$

> **curve1 := c –> dsolve({eqn1, y(1) = c}, y(x), numeric,**
> **maxfun = 1000);**

$$curve1 := c \rightarrow dsolve\left(\{eqn1, y(1) = c\}, y(x), numeric, maxfun = 1000\right)$$

When we used **dsolve**, we created a set of solution curves and then plotted the set with the **plot** command. But **odeplot** can only plot a single function at a time, so in order to make a plot of several numerical solutions we have to first make a set of plots using **odeplot**, and then use **display** to put all the plots on a single graph.

> **with(plots):**
> **graph1 := c –> odeplot(curve1(c), [x, y(x)], 0..5);**

$$graph1 := c \rightarrow odeplot(curve1(c), [x, y(x)], 0..5)$$

> **list1 := {seq(graph1(0.5*i), i = –2..2)}:**
> **display(list1);**

We could also use the function **curve1** to evaluate the numerical solution at a particular value of x for various values of the parameter c. For example, to find the value of the numerical solution at $x = 2$ of the solution with initial condition $y(1) = 5$, we type

> **curve1(5)(2);**

$$[x = 2.0000000007, y(x) = 7.793107536]$$

Note the syntax of this command: **curve1(5)** is the numerical solution with the specified initial condition; **curve1(5)(2)** is the value of this solution at $x = 2$.

Using dsolve(..., numeric) on Higher Order Equations.   In Chapter 7, we showed how to produce numerical solutions of first order initial value problems using **dsolve(..., numeric)**.   Higher order initial value problems can be solved using essentially the same procedure. Here is an example using **dsolve(..., numeric)** to solve a third order initial value problem.

> **eqn2 := diff(y(x), x$3) = cos(y(x)) + 2*x^2;**

$$eqn2 := \frac{\partial^3}{\partial x^3} y(x) = cos(y(x)) + 2x^2$$

> **iniconds := y(0) = 1, D(y)(0) = 0, (D@@2)(y)(0) = 1;**

$$iniconds := y(0) = 1, D(y)(0) = 0, D^{(2)}(y)(0) = 1$$

> **sol2 := dsolve({eqn2, iniconds}, y(x), numeric, maxfun = 2000):**
> **evalf(sol2(1), 4);**

$$\left[x = 1.0, y(x) = 1.615, \frac{d}{dx} y(x) = 1.395, \frac{d^2}{dx^2} y(x) = 2.030\right]$$

Notice that evaluating the numerical solution produced by **dsolve(..., numeric)** yields a list containing the value of the numerical solution, as well as its first and second derivatives.

More about DEplot.   We described the **DEplot** command in Chapter 7. In this section we give some examples of **DEplot** with second order equations. (See the

Differentiation section earlier in this chapter for an example of **dsolve(. . ., numeric)** on second order equations.) We also show how to use **DEplot** on equations with singular solutions.

For a second order equation we must specify two initial conditions. In the following example, we use $y(0) = 0.5, y'(0) = 2$.

> **eqn3 := diff(y(x), x$2) = x^3*y(x) + 1;**

$$eqn3 := \frac{\partial^2}{\partial x^2} y(x) = x^3 y(x) + 1$$

> **with(DEtools):**
> **DEplot(eqn3, [x, y], x = −3..2, {[0, 0.5, 2]});**

Now consider the differential equation

> **eqn4 := diff(x(t), t$2) = −x(t);**

$$eqn4 := \frac{\partial^2}{\partial t^2} x(t) = -x(t)$$

We know that a fundamental set of solutions of this equation is $\{\cos t, \; \sin t\}$. Here is what **DEplot** does with this equation.

> **DEplot(eqn4, [t, x], 0..40, {[0, 1, 4]});**

Notice how jagged the graph is. This is an indication that the step size used by **DEplot** is too large to capture the detailed behavior of the solution. The default step size used by *Maple* is the length of the specified interval divided by 20. Thus in the preceding example, the step size is $40/20 = 2$. We specify the step size manually with the option **stepsize**. For example,

> **DEplot(eqn4, [t, x], 0..40, {[0, 1, 4]}, stepsize = 0.2);**

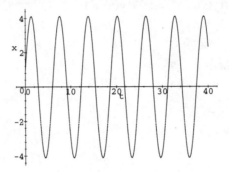

Much better!

Now consider the first order equation $y' = y^2$. The solution of this equation with initial condition $y(0) = y_0$ is

$$y(x) = -\frac{1}{x - \frac{1}{y_0}}.$$

Thus every solution (except the trivial one $y(x) = 0$), has a vertical asymptote at $x = 1/y_0$. If we try to plot a solution of this equation using **DEplot**, we get an error message, as well as an empty plot.

> **eqn5 := diff(y(x), x) = y(x)^2;**

$$eqn5 := \frac{d}{dx}y(x) = (y(x))^2$$

> **DEplot(eqn5, [x, y], x =0..2, {[0, 1]});**

```
Over or underflow in conversion to doubleOver or
underflow in conversion to doubleOver or ...
```

In this example, we have used the initial condition $y(0) = 1$, so the solution has a singularity at $x = 1$. To prevent the error message, we specify a y-range for the plot, and then use the option **limitrange = true** to tell **DEplot** to stop computing once the solution goes outside the specified range. Here's an example:

> **DEplot(eqn5, [x, y], x = 0..2, {[0, 1]}, y = 0..100,**
>   **limitrange = true, stepsize = 0.01);**

Note that we have also decreased the step size to help *Maple* track the solution near the singularity.

In a "real-life" situation, you might not know in advance whether the solution of the differential equation has a singularity. An error of the type mentioned above would tip you off to the existence of a singularity, in which case you could use the aforementioned options to **DEplot** to get a reasonable plot.

One final note about **DEplot**: although this command is used primarily for plotting numerical solutions, it can be used to obtain actual values of the numerical solution. To do this, we exploit the fact that a *Maple* plot structure consists primarily of a list of points to be plotted. You can see this list by assigning a name to the output of the plot command and then using **op** to see the elements of the list. For example,

> **plot5 := DEplot(eqn5, [x, y], x = 0..1, {[0, 1]}):**
> **op(1, plot5);**

CURVES([[0, 1.0], [0.05000000000, 1.052631563], [0.1000000000, 1.111111072],
    [0.1500000000, 1.176470514], [0.2000000000, 1.249999873],
    [0.2500000000, 1.333333125], [0.3000000000, 1.428571094],
    [0.3500000000, 1.538461003], [0.4000000000, 1.666665804],
    [0.4500000000, 1.818180402], [0.5000000000, 1.999997610],
    [0.5500000000, 2.222218030], [0.6000000000, 2.499992250],
    [0.6500000000, 2.857127496], [0.7000000000, 3.333299877],
    [0.7500000000, 3.999916961], [0.8000000000, 4.999750838],
    [0.8500000000, 6.665661751], [0.9000000000, 9.993196688],
    [0.9500000000, 19.85801620], [1.0, 163.9834074]],
    STYLE(*LINE*),COLOUR(*RGB*, 1.0, 1.0, 1.0))

The elements of this list, starting with [0, 1.0], are the x-y coordinates of the points of the numerical solution. You could also display this list by simply ending the first input statement with a semicolon instead of a colon.

Troubleshooting

In this section, we collect some advice for avoiding mistakes that users of *Maple* commonly make. We also discuss the warning messages that *Maple* produces, and describe some techniques for recovering from errors.

The Most Common Mistakes. Here is a list of some of the most common mistakes in using *Maple*.

1. Failure to clear values. See the section *Clearing Values* above.
2. Missing semicolons at the end of input statements. *Maple* will not respond until you type a colon or semicolon.
3. Syntax errors, including mismatched braces, brackets, or parentheses. *Maple* usually catches these mistakes.
4. Failure to distinguish between objects such as functions, expressions, and equations. In particular, attempting to plot the wrong type of object.
5. Using a command from a *Maple* package without loading it. For example, typing **DEplot** without first typing **with(DEtools)**.
6. Typing the wrong kind of "=" sign. A plain "=" sign indicates an equation, while ":=" indicates an assignment, as in **x := 1**.
7. Improperly concatenating variables. For example, **xy** is a variable named xy and not x times y. The product of x and y must be written **x*y**.
8. Improper use of special functions. For example, to use the natural logarithm function in *Maple* you type **log(x)** and not **log x**. The exponential funtion is **exp(x)**.
9. Mistakes arising from the use of quotation marks (") to refer to the output of the previous command. The previous command is the one most recently executed, not necessarily the preceding command in the Worksheet.
10. Incorrectly defining a function using the syntax **f(x) := ....** See the section *Functions and Expressions* in this chapter.
11. Typing **y** instead of **y(x)** in **dsolve** and **dsolve(..., numeric)**.

Error and Warning Messages. Pay close attention to the error and warning messages that *Maple* generates. Although these messages may seem cryptic, they sometimes give valuable clues to locating mistakes. For example, suppose that we execute the following command without first defining a function $u(x)$.

```
> plot(u(x), x = 0..1);
Warning in iris-plot:  empty plot
```

This strange error message is *Maple*'s way of telling you that you haven't really given it anything to plot. In this case, we tried to plot a function that hadn't been defined. "Iris" is the internal name for the interface part of the *Maple* program; the message shows that the warning is coming from "iris-plot".

Occasionally, an error message tells you exactly what's wrong. For example,

```
> eqn := diff(y(x), x) = y^2;
```

$$eqn := \frac{d}{dx}y(x) = y^2$$

> **dsolve(eqn);**

```
Error, (in dsolve) dsolve uses a 2nd argument,vars,
which is missing
```

In this case, we've forgotten to specify the second argument. The correct syntax is **dsolve(eqn, y(x))**. Frequently, error messages are:

> **dsolve(eqn, y(x), numeric);**

```
Error, (in dsolve/numeric) improper op or
subscript selector
```

In this example, we've neglected to specify the initial condition, though the error message gives no hint of that. The proper syntax is **dsolve({eqn, y(0) = 1}, y(x), numeric)**.

In many cases, error messages are due to errors made by the user. In other cases, these messages occur because *Maple* is being asked to do something that is either mathematically impossible, or exceeds the mathematical capabilities of the software. Here's a simple example.

> **1/0;**

```
Error, division by zero
```

Here's a more complicated example.

> **sol := dsolve({eqn, y(0) = 1}, y(x), numeric, maxfun = 3000);**

$$sol := proc(rkf45\_x)...end$$

> **sol(1);**

```
Error, (in dsolve/numeric_solnall)
rkf45 is unable to achieve requested accuracy
```

In this example, the solution of the initial value problem has a singularity at $x = 1$. When we enter **sol(1)**, we ask *Maple* to go beyond the singularity. It correctly refuses to do so, because it cannot maintain the desired degree of accuracy as it approaches the vertical asymptote.

Problem Set C

Numerical Solutions of Differential Equations

In this problem set you will use **dsolve(. . ., numeric)**, **odeplot**, and **DEplot**, *Maple*'s numerical solvers for ordinary differential equations. These commands are explained in Chapters 7 and 8.

1. We are interested in the solution $y = \phi(x)$ to the initial value problem (IVP)
$$y' = x^2 + y^2, \qquad y(0) = 1. \qquad (i)$$
Observe that on the interval $0 \le x \le 1$, we have the inequalities
$$y^2 \le x^2 + y^2 \le 1 + y^2.$$
Therefore we must have $\phi_0(x) \le \phi(x) \le \phi_1(x)$, where ϕ_0, ϕ_1 are the solutions to the respective IVPs
$$\begin{cases} y' = y^2 \\ y(0) = 1, \end{cases} \qquad \begin{cases} y' = 1 + y^2 \\ y(0) = 1. \end{cases}$$
Solve these two IVPs explicitly and conclude that $\phi(x) \to \infty$ as $x \to x_*$, for some $x_* \in [\pi/4, 1]$. Then use *Maple* to compute a numerical solution of (i), and find an approximate value of x_* using **odeplot**.

2. We are interested in the solution $y = \phi(x)$ to the initial value problem (IVP)
$$y' = y^2 - x, \qquad y(0) = 2. \qquad (i)$$
Observe that on the interval $0 \le x \le 1$, we have the inequalities
$$y^2 \ge y^2 - x \ge y^2 - 1.$$
Therefore we must have $\phi_0(x) \ge \phi(x) \ge \phi_1(x)$, where ϕ_0, ϕ_1 are the solutions to the respective IVPs
$$\begin{cases} y' = y^2 \\ y(0) = 2, \end{cases} \qquad \begin{cases} y' = y^2 - 1 \\ y(0) = 2. \end{cases}$$
Solve these two IVPs explicitly and conclude that $\phi(x) \to \infty$ as $x \to x_*$, for some $x_* \in [0.5, 0.5 \ln 3]$. Then use *Maple* to compute a numerical solution of (i), and find an approximate value of x_* using **odeplot**.

3. We shall study solutions $y = \phi_b(x)$ to the IVP

$$y' = (y - x)(1 - y^3), \qquad y(0) = b$$

for nonnegative values of x.

(a) Plot numerical solutions $\phi_b(x)$ for several values of b. Make sure to include values of b that are less than or equal to 0, between 0 and 1, equal to 1, and greater than 1.

(b) Now, on the basis of these plots, describe the behavior of the solution curves $\phi_b(x)$ for positive x, when $b \leq 0, 0 < b < 1, b = 1$, and $b > 1$. Identify limiting behavior and indicate where the solutions are increasing or decreasing.

(c) Finally, by combining your plots with a plot of the line $y = x$, show that the solution curves for $b > 1$ are asymptotic to this line. Explain from the differential equation why that is plausible. Plot the direction field of the differential equation to confirm your analysis.

4. We shall study solutions $y = \phi_b(x)$ to the IVP

$$y' = (y - x^2)(1 - y^2), \qquad y(0) = b$$

for nonnegative values of x.

(a) Plot numerical solutions $\phi_b(x)$ for several values of b. Make sure to include values of b that are less than -1, equal to -1, between -1 and 1, equal to 1, and greater than 1.

(b) Now, based on these plots, describe the behavior of the solution curves $\phi_b(x)$ for positive x, when $b < -1$, $b = -1$, $-1 < b < 1$, $b = 1$, and $b > 1$. Identify limiting behavior and indicate where the solutions are increasing or decreasing.

(c) Finally, by combining your plots with a plot of the parabola $y = x^2$, show that the solution curves for $b > 1$ are asymptotic to this parabola. Explain from the differential equation why that is plausible. Plot the direction field of the differential equation to confirm your analysis.

5. In this problem, we analyze the Gompertz-threshold model from Problem 13 of Problem Set B. That is, consider the differential equation

$$y' = y(1 - \ln y)(y - 3).$$

Using various nonnegative values of $y(0)$, find and plot several numerical solutions on the interval $0 \leq t \leq 10$. (Changing the range of the plot may be helpful here.) By examining the differential equation and analyzing your plots, identify all equilibrium solutions and discuss their stability.

6. Consider the IVP

$$\frac{dy}{dx} = \frac{x - e^{-x}}{y + e^y}, \qquad y(1.5) = 0.5.$$

(a) Use **dsolve(..., numeric)** to find approximate values of the solution at $x = 0, 1, 1.8$, and 2.1. Then plot the solution.

(b) If you did Problem 4 in Problem Set B, enter those results into this worksheet. Compare the values of the actual solution and the numerical solution at the four specified points. Plot the actual solution and the numerical solution on the same graph.

(c) Now plot the numerical solution on several large intervals (*e.g.*, $0 \le x \le 10$ or $0 \le x \le 100$). Make a guess about the nature of the solution as $x \to \infty$. Try to justify your guess on the basis of the differential equation.

7. Consider the IVP

$$e^x \sin y - 2y \sin x + (e^x \cos y + 2 \cos x) \frac{dy}{dx} = 0, \qquad y(0) = 0.5.$$

(a) Use **dsolve(..., numeric)** to find approximate values of the solution at $x = -1, 1$, and 2. Then plot the solution.

(b) If you did Problem 5 in Problem Set B, enter those results into this worksheet. Compare the values of the actual solution and the numerical solution at the three specified points. Plot the actual solution and the numerical solution on the same graph.

(c) Now plot the numerical solution on several large intervals (*e.g.*, $0 \le x \le 10$ or $0 \le x \le 100$). Make a guess about the nature of the solution as $x \to \infty$. Try to justify your guess on the basis of the differential equation.

8. We know that the differential equation

$$y' = e^{-x^2}$$

cannot be solved in terms of elementary functions.

(a) Use **dsolve** to solve this equation.

(b) Note the occurrence of the built-in function **erf**. Mathematics texts refer to this function as the *error function*. Use the *Maple* differentiation operator **diff** to see that

$$\frac{d}{dx}(\mathrm{erf}(x)) = \frac{2}{\sqrt{\pi}} e^{-x^2}.$$

In fact,

$$\mathrm{erf}(x) = \frac{2}{\sqrt{\pi}} \int_0^x e^{-t^2}\, dt.$$

(c) Although one does not have elementary formulas for this function, the numerical capabilities of *Maple* mean that we "know" this function as well as we "know" elementary functions like $\tan x$. To illustrate this, evaluate $\mathrm{erf}(x)$ at $x = 0, 1$, and 10.5, and plot $\mathrm{erf}(x)$ on $-10 \le x \le 10$.

(d) Compute $\lim_{x \to \infty} \operatorname{erf}(x)$ and $\int_{-\infty}^{\infty} e^{-t^2}\, dt$.

(e) Next solve the IVP

$$y' = 1 - 2xy, \qquad y(0) = 0$$

using the *Maple* command **dsolve**. What does the solution do for large x? Find the value x at which the solution takes its maximum. What is the maximum value?

(f) Compute $\partial f / \partial y$ for the function $f(x, y) = 1 - 2xy$. Discuss stability of the equation in (e). Plot solutions on the intervals $[-3, 0]$ and $[0, 3]$, using several different initial conditions at the left endpoints of each interval. Explain how these plots illustrate your conclusions about stability.

9. Consider the IVP

$$xy' + (\sin x)y = 0, \qquad y(0) = 1.$$

(a) Use **dsolve** to solve the IVP.

(b) Note the occurrence of the built-in function **Si**, called the Sine Integral function. Check that this function is an antiderivative of $\sin x / x$ by differentiating it. Evaluate $\lim_{x \to \infty} \operatorname{Si}(x)$.

(c) Plot $\operatorname{Si}(x)$. Discuss the features of the graph.

(d) Do the same with the solution to the IVP.

(e) Now solve the IVP using **dsolve(..., numeric)**, and plot the computed solution using **odeplot**.

You may find that *Maple* fails to deal with $\sin x / x$ at $x = 0$, even though the singularity is removable. One way to get around this is to give the initial condition $y = 1$ at a value of x extremely close to, but not equal to, zero. Since we are only finding an approximate solution with **dsolve(..., numeric)** anyhow, there shouldn't be much harm done as long as the amount by which we move the initial condition is small compared with the error we expect from the numerical procedure. Alternatively, you could try redefining the differential equation to be $y' + f(x)y = 0$ with

$$f(x) = \begin{cases} \sin x / x, & x \neq 0 \\ 1, & x = 0. \end{cases}$$

Such an f can be defined with the command: **f := x -> sin(x)/x; f(0) := 1;** (see the section *Functions and Expressions* in Chapter 8).

(f) Discuss the stability of the differential equation. Illustrate your conclusions by graphing solutions with different initial values on the interval $[-10, 10]$.

10. Solve the following equations numerically, then plot the solutions. On the basis of your plots, predict what happens to each solution as x increases. In

particular, if there is a limiting value for y, either finite or infinite, then find it. If it is unclear from the plot you've made, try replotting on a larger interval. Another possibility is that the solution blows up in finite time. If so, estimate the time. If your solution curves appear jagged, use an option to adjust the number of points being plotted (**numpoints** for **odeplot** or **stepsize** for **DEplot**).

(a) $y' = e^{-2x} + \dfrac{1}{1 + y^2}, \quad y(0) = -1$

(b) $y' = e^{-2x} + y^2, \quad y(0) = -1$

(c) $y' = \cos x - y^3, \quad y(0) = 0$

(d) $y' = (\sin x)y - y^2, \quad y(0) = 1.$

11. Solve the following equations numerically, then plot the solutions. On the basis of your plots, predict what happens to each solution as x increases. See Problem 10 for more instructions.

(a) $y' = 5x - 3\sqrt{y}, \quad y(0) = 2$

(b) $y' = (x^2 - y^2) \sin y, \quad y(0) = -1$

(c) $y' = \dfrac{y^2 + 2xy}{x^2 + 3}, \quad y(1) = 2$

(d) $y' = -2x + e^{-xy}, \quad y(0) = 1.$

12. This problem illustrates one of the possible pitfalls of blindly applying numerical methods without paying attention to the theoretical aspects of the differential equation itself. Consider the equation

$$-4x^2 + 2y(x) + xy'(x) = 0.$$

(a) Use the *Maple* program in Chapter 7 to compute the Euler Method approximation to the solution with initial condition $y(-0.5) = 4.25$, using step size $h = 0.2$ and $n = 10$ steps. The program will generate a list of ordered pairs of numbers representing the (x, y) coordinates of points of the approximate solution. Use **plot** to obtain a piecewise linear graph of the approximate solution.

(b) Now modify the program to implement the Improved Euler Method. Repeat part (a) using the Improved Euler Method. Can you make sense of your answers?

(c) Next try to use **dsolve(..., numeric)** to find an approximate solution on the interval $(-0.5, 1.5)$, and plot it with **odeplot**. What is the interval on which the approximate solution has been defined?

(d) Solve the equation explicitly and graph the solutions for the initial conditions $y(0) = 0$, $y(-0.5) = 4.25$, $y(0.5) = 4.25$, $y(-0.5) = -3.75$, and $y(0.5) = -3.75$. Now explain your results in (a)–(c). Could we have known, without solving the equation, whether to expect meaningful results in parts (a) and (b)? Why? Can you explain how **odeplot** avoids making the same "mistake"?

13. Consider the IVP

$$\frac{dy}{dx} = e^{-x} - 2y, \qquad y(-1) = 0.$$

(a) Use the *Maple* program in Chapter 7 to compute the Euler Method approximation to $y(x)$ with step size $h = 0.5$ and $n = 4$ steps. The program will generate a list of ordered pairs (x_i, y_i). Use **plot** to display the piecewise linear function connecting the points (x_i, y_i). Repeat with $h = 0.2$ and $n = 10$.

(b) Now modify the program to implement the Improved Euler Method, and repeat part (a) using the Improved Euler Method.

(c) Find the exact solution of the IVP and plot the solution, the two Euler approximations, and the two Improved Euler approximations on the same graph. Label the five curves.

(d) Now use the Euler Method program with $h = 0.5$ to approximate the solution on the interval $[-1, 9]$. Plot both the approximate and exact solutions on this interval. How close is the approximation to the exact solution as x increases? In light of the discussion of stability in Chapters 5 and 7, explain your results in parts (a)–(c).

14. Consider the IVP

$$\frac{dy}{dx} = y - 4e^{-3x}, \qquad y(0) = 1.$$

(a) Use the *Maple* program in Chapter 7 to compute the Euler Method approximation to $y(x)$ with step size $h = 0.5$ and $n = 6$ steps. The program will generate a list of ordered pairs (x_i, y_i). Use **plot** to display the piecewise linear function connecting the points (x_i, y_i). What appears to be happening to y as x increases?

(b) Repeat part (a) with $h = 0.2$ and $n = 15$, and then with $h = 0.1$ and $n = 30$. How are the approximate solutions changing as the step size decreases? Can you make a reliable prediction about the long-term behavior of the solution?

(c) Use **dsolve(..., numeric)** to find an approximate solution and plot it on the interval $[0, 3]$. Now what does it look like y is doing as x increases? Next plot the solution from **dsolve(..., numeric)** on a larger interval (going at least to $x = 20$). Again, what is happening to y as x increases?

(d) Solve the IVP explicitly and compare the exact solution to the approximations found above. In light of the discussion of stability in Chapters 5 and 7, explain your results in parts (a)–(c).

15. Consider the IVP

$$\frac{dy}{dx} = 2y - 2 + 3e^{-x}, \qquad y(0) = 0.$$

(a) Use the *Maple* program in Chapter 7 to compute the Euler Method approximation to $y(x)$ with step size $h = 0.2$ and $n = 10$ steps. The program will generate a list of ordered pairs (x_i, y_i). Use **plot** to display the piecewise linear function connecting the points (x_i, y_i) What appears to be happening to y as x increases?

(b) Repeat part (a) with $h = 0.1$ and $n = 20$, and then with $h = 0.05$ and $n = 40$. How are the approximate solutions changing as the step size decreases? Can you make a reliable prediction about the long-term behavior of the solution?

(c) Use **dsolve(..., numeric)** to find an approximate solution and plot it on the interval $[0, 2]$. Now what does it look like y is doing as x increases? Next plot the solution from **dsolve(..., numeric)** on a larger interval (going at least to $x = 10$). Again, what is happening to y as x increases?

(d) Solve the IVP explicitly and compare the exact solution to the approximations found above. In light of the discussion of stability in Chapters 5 and 7, explain your results in parts (a)–(c).

16. We know that e^x is the solution to the IVP

$$\frac{dy}{dx} = y, \qquad y(0) = 1,$$

so if we solve this IVP numerically we get approximate values for e^x. Use **dsolve(..., numeric)**, employing the accuracy options discussed in Chapter 7, to calculate values for $e^{0.1}, e^{0.2}, \ldots, e$ that have 15 correct digits. Present your results in a table. In a second column print the values of e^x for $x = 0.1, 0.2, \ldots, 1$, obtained by using the built-in function **exp**. Show at least 15 digits. Compare the two columns of values.

Chapter 9

Qualitative Theory of
Second Order Linear Equations

In an introductory course, one spends a great deal of time studying second order linear differential equations with *constant coefficients*:

$$ay'' + by' + cy = g(x).$$

This is in part because such equations model a wide variety of physical situations. It is also because we usually cannot find solution formulas for more general second order equations. Nevertheless, general second order equations are important in many applications.

In this chapter, we study second order linear differential equations with *variable coefficients*. The general form of such an equation is:

$$y'' + p(x)y' + q(x)y = g(x).$$

Airy's equation,

$$y'' - xy = 0, \tag{1}$$

and Bessel's equation,

$$y'' + \frac{1}{x}y' + y = 0, \tag{2}$$

are examples of variable coefficient equations. Both equations have important applications in physics. For example, Airy's equation arises in diffraction problems in optics, and Bessel's equation occurs in the study of vibrations of a circular membrane and of water waves with circular symmetry.

In this chapter, we introduce comparison methods and a geometric method for analyzing second order linear equations with variable coefficients. These qualitative methods are important because they do not require explicit solution formulas.

Comparison methods provide information on the solutions of a variable coefficient equation by comparing the equation with an appropriate constant coefficient equation. This possibility is suggested by the following example. For large x, the coefficient $1/x$ in Bessel's equation (2) is close to 0. So, Bessel's equation is close to the equation $y'' + y = 0$, whose general solution can be written as $y = R\cos(x - \delta)$. Thus, one might expect solutions to Bessel's equation to oscillate and look roughly

117

like sine waves for large x. We present a result that validates this type of comparison.

The geometric method is based on direction fields, which are not directly applicable to a second order equation. We show, however, how to construct a related first order equation whose direction field yields information about the solutions of the second order equation.

Why should we take such an indirect approach to analyzing a differential equation when we could simply examine the plot of a numerical solution produced by *Maple*? We can, of course, get much information from numerical methods and graphics. There is other information, however, that qualitative methods yield more effectively: properties shared by all solutions of a differential equation, the oscillatory nature of solutions of an equation, or the precise rate of decay or growth of solutions.

Comparison Methods

In this section, we discuss the Sturm Comparison Theorem and the relation between the zeros of two linearly independent solutions of a second order linear equation.

The Sturm Comparison Theorem.   This theorem, whose proof will be given later, validates the type of comparison mentioned at the beginning of this chapter.

STURM COMPARISON THEOREM. *Let $u(x)$ be a solution to the equation*

$$y'' + q(x)y = 0,$$

and suppose $u(a) = u(b) = 0$ for some $a < b$ (but u is not identically zero). Let $v(x)$ be a solution to the equation

$$y'' + r(x)y = 0,$$

where $r(x) \geq q(x)$ for all $a \leq x \leq b$. Then $v(x) = 0$ for some x in $[a, b]$.

We typically use this result to compare a variable coefficient equation with an appropriate constant coefficient equation. Consider, for example, the equation

$$y'' + \frac{1}{x}y = 0. \tag{3}$$

Let K be a positive number. If $0 < x \leq K$, then $1/x \geq 1/K$. We now apply the above theorem with $q(x) = 1/K$ and $r(x) = 1/x$. Thus, we compare equation (3) to the constant coefficient equation $y'' + (1/K)y = 0$, whose general solution is $u(x) = R\cos(\sqrt{1/K}x - \delta)$. Given any interval in $(0, K]$ of length $\pi\sqrt{K}$, the value of δ can be chosen so that $u(x) = 0$ at the endpoints of the interval. Then the Sturm Comparison Theorem implies that every solution of (3) has a zero on this interval. This argument implies that on $(0, K]$, the zeros of (3) cannot be farther apart than $\pi\sqrt{K}$.

In particular, solutions of (3) must oscillate as $x \to \infty$, though the oscillations may become less frequent as x increases. Indeed, by turning the above comparison around, one concludes that the zeros of solutions of (3) in $[K, \infty)$ must be at least $\pi\sqrt{K}$ apart.

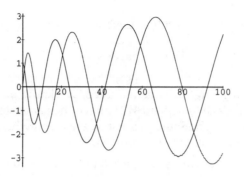

Figure 1

Figure 1 shows two representative solutions of (3) computed with **dsolve(...,**
numeric). As you can see, the predictions of the previous paragraph are confirmed
by the graph.

The Sturm Comparison Theorem can also be used to study the zeros of Airy's
equation and of Bessel's equation. In the latter case, a substitution is made to
eliminate the y' term. See Problems 15 and 16 in Problem Set D.

The Interlacing of Zeros. You may have noticed that the curves in Figure 1 take
turns crossing the horizontal axis. We say that the zeros of the two solutions are
interlaced: between any two zeros of one solution there is a zero of the other. This
is a common phenomenon—the property of interlaced zeros holds for any pair of
linearly independent solutions of a homogeneous second order linear differential
equation

$$y'' + p(x)y' + q(x)y = 0. \tag{4}$$

If $p(x) = 0$, as is the case in equation (1), the proof of the interlacing result
follows from an application of the Sturm Comparison Theorem by comparing the
equation with itself. For the more general equation (4), the proof is based on the
Wronskian. Let $y_1(x)$ and $y_2(x)$ be any two linearly independent solutions of (4).
Recall that the Wronskian of $y_1(x)$ and $y_2(x)$ is

$$W(x) = y_1(x)y_2'(x) - y_1'(x)y_2(x).$$

Since y_1 and y_2 are solutions of (4), it follows that W satisfies the differential
equation

$$W' = -p(x)W,$$

whose general solution is

$$W(x) = Ce^{-\int p(x)dx}.$$

This formula shows that $W(x)$ does not change sign—it always has the same sign as the constant C, which must be nonzero (or else y_1 and y_2 would be linearly dependent).

Assume $y_1(a) = y_1(b) = 0$, and that there are no zeros of y_1 between a and b. Then

$$W(a) = -y_1'(a)y_2(a),$$
$$W(b) = -y_1'(b)y_2(b).$$

Since y_1 does not change sign between a and b, we know $y_1'(a)$ and $y_1'(b)$ have opposite signs. Then, since $W(a)$ and $W(b)$ have the same sign, $y_2(a)$ and $y_2(b)$ must have opposite signs. Therefore y_2 must be zero somewhere between a and b. Similarly, y_1 must have a zero between any two zeros of y_2.

EXERCISE. The solutions to Airy's equation and Bessel's equation are considered so important that they have been given names in *Maple*. The Airy functions Ai(x) and Bi(x) are a fundamental set of solutions for (1), and the Bessel functions $J_0(x)$ and $Y_0(x)$ are a fundamental set of solutions for (2). These functions are built into *Maple* as **Ai(x)**, **Bi(x)**, **BesselJ(0, x)**, and **BesselY(0, x)**. Use *Maple* to check that the zeros of the two solutions **Ai(x)** and **Bi(x)** to Airy's equation are interlaced, and do the same for the Bessel functions **BesselJ(0, x)** and **BesselY(0, x)**.

Proof of the Sturm Comparison Theorem. The proof is based on the Wronskian, as was the proof of the interlacing result. Recall the hypotheses: $u'' + q(x)u = 0$ and $v'' + r(x)v = 0$, with $q(x) \leq r(x)$ between two zeros a and b of u. Since u is not identically zero, we can assume u does not change sign between a and b. (If it did it would have a zero between a and b, and we could look at a smaller interval.) Assume, for instance, that $u > 0$ between a and b. Since $u = 0$ at a and b, it follows that $u'(a) > 0$ and $u'(b) < 0$. (Notice that these derivatives cannot be zero because then by the uniqueness theorem u would be identically zero.) We want to prove that v is zero somewhere in $[a, b]$; we suppose it is not, say $v(x) > 0$ throughout $[a, b]$, and argue to obtain a contradiction.

Let $W(x)$ be the Wronskian of u and v,

$$W(x) = u(x)v'(x) - u'(x)v(x);$$

then

$$W(a) = -u'(a)v(a) < 0,$$
$$W(b) = -u'(b)v(b) > 0.$$

Also, since $q(x) \leq r(x)$,

$$W' = uv'' - u''v = u(-r(x)v) - (-q(x)u)v = (q(x) - r(x))uv \leq 0.$$

But this is impossible—the last inequality implies W does not increase between a and b, yet $W(a) < 0 < W(b)$. This contradiction means that v cannot have the same sign throughout $[a, b]$, and therefore v must be zero somewhere in the interval.

A Geometric Method

As mentioned above, direction fields are not directly applicable to second order equations. We now show, however, that with a given second order homogeneous equation, we can associate a first order equation whose direction field yields information about the solutions of the second order equation. (Our approach is similar to the classical method of associating a first order Riccati equation to a second order linear equation. The substitution we use is akin to the Prüfer substitution for Sturm-Liouville systems; see G. Birkhoff and G.-C. Rota, **Ordinary Differential Equations**, 3rd ed., J. Wiley and Sons, Inc., 1978.)

Consider the homogeneous equation

$$y'' + p(x)y' + q(x)y = 0. \tag{5}$$

Let

$$z = \arctan\left(\frac{y}{y'}\right);$$

then

$$z' = \left(1 + \left(\frac{y}{y'}\right)^2\right)^{-1} \frac{d}{dx}\left(\frac{y}{y'}\right) = \frac{y'^2}{y'^2 + y^2} \frac{y'^2 - yy''}{y'^2} = \frac{y'^2 - yy''}{y'^2 + y^2}.$$

Also, since $\tan z = y/y'$, notice that

$$\sin z = \frac{y}{\sqrt{y'^2 + y^2}}, \quad \cos z = \frac{y'}{\sqrt{y'^2 + y^2}}.$$

Then if y satisfies (5), and y is not identically zero, it follows that

$$z' = \frac{y'^2 - yy''}{y'^2 + y^2} = \frac{y'^2 - y(-p(x)y' - q(x)y)}{y'^2 + y^2} = \frac{y'^2 + p(x)yy' + q(x)y^2}{y'^2 + y^2}.$$

In other words,

$$z' = \cos^2 z + p(x)\sin z \cos z + q(x)\sin^2 z. \tag{6}$$

We have shown that for every solution y of (5) that is not identically zero, there is a corresponding solution z of (6). (This is not a one-to-one correspondence—every constant multiple of a solution y corresponds to the same solution z.) Although the solution curves of (6) will be different from the solution curves of (5), we now show that we can learn about the solutions of (5) by studying the solutions of (6); specifically, by considering the direction field of (6).

The Constant Coefficient Case. We begin by considering the equation

$$y'' - y = 0,$$

whose general solution is

$$y = c_1 e^x + c_2 e^{-x}.$$

The corresponding first order equation is

$$z' = \cos^2 z - \sin^2 z.$$

In Figure 2, we show the direction field of this equation, which we produced with the *Maple* command

dfieldplot(cos(z)^2 − sin(z)^2, z(x), x = 0..10, z = −Pi/2..Pi/2,
    arrows = LINE, axes = BOXED);

(Recall that we must first type **with(DEtools)** to load the *Maple* package **DEtools**.)

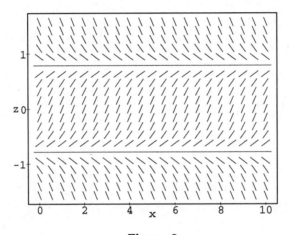

Figure 2

Notice that we plot z from $-\pi/2$ to $\pi/2$; this is the range of values taken on by the arctan function. You may wonder what happens if z goes off the bottom of the graph. The answer is that z "wraps around" to the top of the graph. Recall that $z = \arctan(y/y')$; the points $z = \pm\pi/2$ correspond to $y' = 0$, and when y' changes sign, then so does z by passing from $-\pi/2$ to $\pi/2$ (or vice versa).

Next, observe that there is an unstable equilibrium at $z = -\pi/4$, which corresponds to $y/y' = \tan(-\pi/4) = -1$; this represents solutions of the form $y = ce^{-x}$. Similarly, the stable equilibrium $z = \pi/4$ corresponds to $y/y' = \tan(\pi/4) = 1$, which represents the solutions $y = ce^x$. The fact that most solutions of the equation satisfied by z (those with initial condition other than $-\pi/4$) approach the stable equilibrium $z = \pi/4$ corresponds to the fact that most solutions $y = c_1 e^x + c_2 e^{-x}$ (those with $c_1 \neq 0$) grow like e^x as x increases.

Another basic example is

$$y'' + y = 0,$$

for which the corresponding first order equation is

$$z' = \cos^2 z + \sin^2 z = 1.$$

That is, z simply increases linearly, though every time it reaches $\pi/2$ it wraps around to $-\pi/2$. This corresponds to the oscillation of solutions y; for every time $z = \arctan(y/y')$ passes through zero, then so must y, and vice versa.

EXERCISE. Consider the general second order linear homogeneous equation with constant coefficients:

$$ay'' + by' + c = 0.$$

Investigate how the roots of the characteristic equation, if real, correspond to equilibrium solutions for z. Show that if the roots of the characteristic equation are complex, then z' is always positive.

The Variable Coefficient Case. The examples above suggest ways to draw parallels between solutions z of (6) and solutions y of (5). First of all, if z is positive, then y and y' have the same sign. This implies that y is moving away from zero as x increases. We say in this case that y is *growing*, meaning that $|y|$ is increasing. Similarly, if z is negative then y and y' have opposite signs, which implies that y is moving toward zero as x increases—we say in this case that y is *decaying*, meaning that $|y|$ is decreasing. If z changes sign by passing through zero, then so does y, and if z passes through $\pm\pi/2$, then y' changes sign, showing that y has passed through a local maximum or minimum.

In light of these observations, let us summarize what we can predict about the *long-term behavior* of a solution y of (5) in terms of the corresponding solution z of (6).

- If z remains positive as x increases, then y grows away from zero.
- If z remains negative as x increases, then y decays toward zero.
- If z continues to increase from $-\pi/2$ to $\pi/2$ and wraps around to $-\pi/2$ again, then y *oscillates* as x increases.

Notice from (6) that $z' = 1$ whenever $z = 0$, so it is not possible for z to decrease through zero. Thus the long-term behavior of z will usually fall into one of the three categories above.

We can be more precise about the growth or decay rate of y in cases where z approaches a limiting value. If the limiting value is θ, then y/y' approaches $\tan \theta$ as x increases. In other words, $y' \approx (\cot \theta)y$ for large x. Thus

$$y \approx ce^{(\cot \theta)x}$$

for large x, and $\cot \theta$ is the asymptotic exponential growth (or decay) rate of y. If z approaches zero as x increases, then y/y' approaches zero as well. One can show that y grows (if $z > 0$) or decays (if $z < 0$) faster than any exponential function. Similarly, if z approaches $\pi/2$, then y grows slower than exponentially, and if z

approaches $-\pi/2$, then y decays slower than exponentially. Since y'/y approaches zero in these cases, y could grow or decay toward a finite, nonzero value.

Let us now see what the direction field of (6) tells us about solutions of Airy's and Bessel's equations.

Airy's Equation.   For Airy's equation,

$$y'' - xy = 0, \tag{7}$$

the corresponding first order equation is

$$z' = \cos^2 z - x \sin^2 z.$$

Figure 3 shows the direction field of this equation, plotted by a *Maple* command similar to the one used for Figure 2.

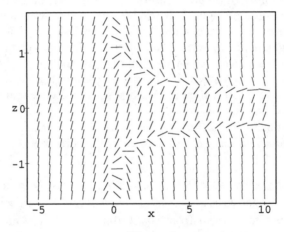

Figure 3

Notice that z is increasing steadily for negative x, so solutions of (7) must oscillate for negative x. For positive x, it is evident that solutions of (7) cannot oscillate; z passes through zero at most once, after which it remains positive. Hence the corresponding solution of (7) grows away from zero as x increases. It appears that once z becomes positive, it decreases to zero, indicating that most solutions of (7) grow faster than exponentially.

We now know there are solutions of (7) that grow very fast as x increases, and there are no oscillating solutions for positive x. Is it possible to have a decaying solution of (7)? Equivalently, is it possible for z to remain negative as x increases? Figure 3 strongly suggests that there is such a solution z, and hence that there is a solution y to (7) that decays toward zero at a rate faster than exponential.

The Airy function Ai(x) is, by definition, the unique (up to a constant multiple) solution of (7) that decays as x increases. As expected, the other Airy function Bi(x) grows as x increases. You can see what these functions look like by plotting **Ai(x)** and **Bi(x)** in *Maple*. The general solution of (7) is a linear combination of Ai(x) and Bi(x).

Bessel's Equation. For Bessel's equation

$$y'' + \frac{1}{x}y' + y = 0, \tag{8}$$

the corresponding first order equation is

$$z' = \cos^2 z + \frac{1}{x}\sin z \cos z + \sin^2 z.$$

Figure 4 shows the direction field of this equation.

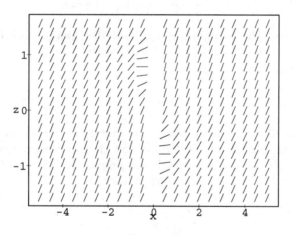

Figure 4

The picture is simpler than the one for Airy's equation. When x is away from zero, z is increasing steadily. So, solutions of (8) oscillate for both positive and negative x. Near $x = 0$, the direction field is irregular because of the $1/x$ term in the differential equation. We can't tell what happens from this picture, but there is reason to expect solutions of (8) will not behave nicely near this singularity in the differential equation.

One question this approach cannot answer easily is whether the amplitude of oscillating solutions grows, decays, or remains steady as x increases. Since the coefficient of the y' term in (8) is positive, we can expect solutions of (8) to behave like a physical oscillator with damping—the amplitude of oscillations should decrease as x increases. Since the damping coefficient goes to zero as x increases, we cannot be sure (without a more refined analysis) whether the amplitude of solutions of (8) must decrease to zero. In fact it does, as you can check by plotting the Bessel functions **BesselJ(0, x)** and **BesselY(0, x)** in *Maple*.

Other Equations. Here are some other differential equations for which you can try this method.

- Bessel's equation of order n,

$$y'' + \frac{1}{x}y' + \left(1 - \frac{n^2}{x^2}\right)y = 0,$$

for various n (above we studied the case $n = 0$). You can check your predictions using the *Maple* functions **BesselJ(n, x)** and **BesselY(n, x)**. These functions are considered in Problem 18 of Problem Set D.

- The modified Bessel equation of order n,

$$y'' + \frac{1}{x}y' - \left(1 + \frac{n^2}{x^2}\right)y = 0,$$

for various n. The *Maple* functions **BesselI(n, x)** and **BesselK(n, x)** are a fundamental set of solutions for this equation.

- The parabolic cylinder equation

$$y'' + \left(n + \frac{1}{2} - \frac{1}{4}x^2\right)y = 0$$

for various n. This equation arises in quantum mechanics, but its solutions are not built into *Maple*; you can check your predictions against approximate solutions from **dsolve(..., numeric)** instead. This equation is considered in Problem 17 of Problem Set D.

Problem Set D

Second Order Equations

1. Airy's equation is the linear second order homogeneous equation $y'' = xy$. Although it arises in a number of applications, including quantum mechanics, optics and waves, it cannot be solved exactly by the standard symbolic methods. In order to analyze the solution curves, let us reason as follows.

   (a) For x close to zero, the equation resembles $y'' = 0$, which has general solution $y = c_1x + c_2$. We refer to this as a "facsimile" solution. Using **DEplot**, graph a numerical solution to Airy's equation with initial conditions $y(0) = 0, y'(0) = 1$, and the facsimile solution (with the same initial data) on the interval $(-2, 2)$. How well do they match?

   (b) For $x \approx -K^2 << 0$, the equation resembles $y'' = -K^2y$, and the corresponding facsimile solution is given by $y = c_1 \sin(Kx + c_2)$. Again using the initial conditions $y(0) = 0, y'(0) = 1$, use **DEplot** to plot a numerical solution of Airy's equation over the interval $(-18, -14)$. Using the value $K = 4$, try to find values of c_1 and c_2 so that the facsimile solution matches well with the actual solution. Why shouldn't we expect the initial conditions for Airy's equation to be the appropriate initial conditions for the facsimile solution?

   (c) For $x \approx K^2 >> 0$, Airy's equation resembles $y'' = K^2y$, which has solution $y = c_1 \sinh(Kx + c_2)$. (The hyperbolic sine function is called **sinh(x)** in *Maple*.) Plot a numerical solution of Airy's equation together with a facsimile solution (with $K = 4$) on the interval $(14, 18)$. In analogy with part (b), you have to choose values for c_1 and c_2 in the facsimile solution. (Try $c_1 = 1, c_2 = 0$.)

   (d) Plot the numerical solution of Airy's equation on the interval $(-20, 2)$. What does the graph suggest about the frequency and amplitude of oscillations as $x \to -\infty$? Could any of that information have been predicted from the facsimile analysis?

2. Consider Bessel's equation of order zero

$$x^2y'' + xy' + x^2y = 0 \qquad (i)$$

with initial data $y(0) = 1$, $y'(0) = 0$. The solution $J_0(x)$ is usually called the Bessel function of order zero of the first kind. Strictly speaking, this equation has a singularity at $x = 0$. However, this is one instance of a solution to a linear equation that exists outside the expected domain of definition. Still, as you will see below, the presence of the singularity can affect your computations.

(a) For x close to 0, x^2 is very small compared to x. The equation (i) is therefore approximately $xy' = 0$. Solve this equation with the preceding initial data. What does this "facsimile" solution to the original problem suggest to you about the behavior of J_0 near the origin?

(b) For x large and positive, x is small compared to x^2; and so we may approximate (i) by the equation $x^2(y'' + y) = 0$. Solve this equation with the same initial data. What does this suggest about the nature of the function J_0 for large x?

(c) Still thinking of x as large and positive, rewrite (i) in the form

$$y'' + \frac{1}{x}y' + y = 0.$$

If $x \approx K \gg 0$, we might approximate the equation by the constant coefficient equation

$$y'' + \frac{1}{K}y' + y = 0.$$

Solve that equation and see what further information you obtain about J_0. (If need be, choose a specific value for K, say $K = 100$, and examine the solution in order to refine your conclusion from (b).) Now explain why J_0 must be an even function, and so make the same deduction for large negative x.

(d) Throw caution to the winds and try **dsolve** on the original problem. You may be surprised to learn that *Maple* can handle it. Graph the solution function and see how well it manifests the qualitative properties you inferred in parts (a)–(c).

(e) Have a crack at the IVP with **dsolve(..., numeric)**. Can you find the value of the solution at $x = 1$? Explain your results.

3. This and some of the following problems concern models for the motion of a pendulum, which consists of a weight attached to a rigid arm of length L that is free to pivot in a complete circle. Neglecting friction and air resistance, we see that the angle $\theta(t)$ that the arm makes with the vertical direction satisfies the differential equation

$$\theta''(t) + \frac{g}{L}\sin(\theta(t)) = 0, \tag{i}$$

where $g = 32.2$ ft/sec^2 is the gravitational acceleration constant. We will assume the arm has length 32.2 ft and so replace (i) by the simpler form

$$\theta'' + \sin\theta = 0. \tag{ii}$$

(Alternatively, one can rescale time, replacing t by $\sqrt{g/L}\,t$, to convert (i) to (ii).) For motions with small displacements (θ small), $\sin\theta \approx \theta$, and (ii) can be approximated by the linear equation

$$\theta'' + \theta = 0. \tag{iii}$$

This equation has general solution $\theta(t) = A\cos(t-\delta)$, with *amplitude A* and *phase shift δ*. Since all the solutions to the linear approximation (iii) have period 2π, we expect that, for small displacements, the solutions to the true pendulum (ii) should have period close to 2π. One can investigate how the period depends on the amplitude A by plotting a numerical solution of equation (ii) using initial conditions $\theta(0) = A, \theta'(0) = 0$ on an appropriate interval for various A. Estimate, to within 0.1, the period of the pendulum for the amplitudes $A = 0.1$, 0.7, 1.5, and 3.0. What is happening to the accuracy of the linear approximation as the initial displacement increases?

4. In this problem, we'll look at what the pendulum does for various initial velocities (*cf.* Problem 3). Define a *Maple* function of v that will numerically solve the differential equation $(3.ii)$ using initial conditions $\theta(0) = 0, \theta'(0) = v$. Do likewise for equation $(3.iii)$. Plot the solutions to both the nonlinear equation $(3.ii)$ and the linear equation $(3.iii)$ for each of the following values of the initial velocity v: 1, 1.99, 2, 2.01. Use a time interval from $t = 0$ to $t = 40$. Clearly mark which is the nonlinear solution and which is the linear solution on each plot. Compare the linear and nonlinear behavior in each case. For the nonlinear equation, interpret what the graph indicates the pendulum is doing physically. Speculate as to the true motion.

5. In this problem, we'll investigate the effect of damping on the pendulum, using the model

$$\theta'' + b\theta' + \sin\theta = 0$$

(*cf.* Problem 3). Define a *Maple* function of b that will find a numerical solution of this differential equation with initial conditions $\theta(0) = 0, \theta'(0) = 4$. Then plot the solution from $t = 0$ to $t = 20$ for the values $b = 0.5$, 1, and 2. Interpret what is happening *physically* in each case, *i.e.*, describe explicitly what the graph says the pendulum is doing. Now do the same for the linear approximation

$$\theta'' + b\theta' + \theta = 0,$$

for the same values of b. Compare the linear and nonlinear behavior in each case.

6. In this problem, we'll look at the effect of a periodic external force on the pendulum, using the model

$$\theta'' + 0.05\theta' + \sin\theta = 0.3\cos\omega t$$

(*cf.* Problems 3–5). We have chosen a value for the damping coefficient that is more typical of air resistance than the values in the previous problem. Write a

Maple function of ω that numerically solves this equation with initial conditions $\theta(0) = 0, \theta'(0) = 0$. Then plot the result from $t = 0$ to $t = 60$ for the following values of the frequency ω: $0.6, 0.8, 1, 1.2$. (Note: You may need to increase **numpoints** to get a reasonable picture.) Which frequency moves the pendulum farthest away from its equilibrium position? Do the same analysis for the linear approximation

$$\theta'' + 0.05\theta' + \theta = 0.3 \cos \omega t$$

and answer the same question. For which frequencies do the linear and nonlinear equations have widely different behaviors? Which forcing frequency seems to induce resonance-type behavior in the pendulum? Graph that solution on a longer interval and decide whether the amplitude goes to infinity.

7. In many applications, second order equations come with *boundary conditions* rather than *initial conditions*. For example, consider a cable that is attached at each end to a post, with both ends at the same height (let us call this height $y = 0$). If the posts are located at $x = 0$ and $x = 1$, the height y of the cable as a function of x satisfies the differential equation

$$y'' = c\sqrt{1 + (y')^2}$$

with boundary conditions $y(0) = 0, y(1) = 0$. The constant c depends on the length of the cable; for this problem we'll use $c = 1$. *Maple* can't solve this boundary problem directly. Nonetheless, we can approximate the solution of the differential equation that satisfies the boundary value conditions as follows. For a given value of s, find a solution to the above equation (using $c = 1$) with initial conditions $y(0) = 0, y'(0) = s$. Find the value of s that leads to a solution satisfying the condition $y(1) = 0$. Graph the solution on $[0, 1]$ and determine the maximum dip in the cable.

8. The problem of finding the function $u(x)$ satisfying

$$\begin{cases} a(x)u''(x) + a'(x)u'(x) = f(x), 0 \le x \le 1 \\ \qquad\qquad u(0) = u(1) = 0 \end{cases}$$

arises in studying the longitudinal displacements in a longitudinally loaded elastic bar. The bar is of length 1, its left end is at $x = 0$, and its right end at $x = 1$. In the differential equation above, $f(x)$ represents the external force on the bar (which is assumed to be longitudinal, *i.e.*, directed along the bar), $a(x)$ represents both the elastic properties and the cross-sectional area of the bar, and $u(x)$ is the longitudinal displacement of the bar at the point x. This problem is an example of a *boundary value problem*; the conditions $u(0) = u(1) = 0$, which specify that the ends of the bar are fixed, are called boundary conditions. The function $a(x)$ may be constant; this is the case if neither the elastic properties nor the cross-sectional area depends on the position x in the rod, *i.e.*, if the rod is uniform. But if the rod is not uniform, then $a(x)$ is not constant, and the equation has variable coefficients. Similarly, $f(x)$ will be constant only if the external force is applied uniformly along the rod.

Now suppose $a(x) = \pi(2+\cos^2(2\pi x))$ and $f(x) = 1500x^4$. Find and plot the corresponding solution $u(x)$. Since the equation has variable coefficients, constant coefficient methods are not applicable, so we will use a numerical method. We cannot apply **dsolve(..., numeric)** directly, since it requires initial conditions. Nonetheless, we can use **dsolve(..., numeric)** as follows to approximate the solution. Write a function that, for a given value of s, finds a numerical solution to the equation with the initial conditions $u(0) = 0, u'(0) = s$ and plots this solution for $0 \leq x \leq 1$. Note that the first boundary condition is one of our initial conditions. Then by evaluating this function for various values of s you should be able to get a fairly accurate value for the s that leads to a solution satisfying the second boundary condition $u(1) = 0$. Next define a second function (of s) that finds a numerical solution of the equation with the initial conditions $u(0) = 0, u'(0) = s$, and then numerically evaluates $u(1)$. Using this function, you should be able to get an accurate approximation for the desired s. Plot the final (accurate) solution to the boundary value problem. What is the maximum displacement, and where does it occur?

9. In this problem, we study the effects of air resistance.

(a) A paratrooper steps out of an airplane at a height of 1000 ft, and after 5 seconds opens her parachute. Her weight, with equipment, is 195 lbs. Let $y(t)$ denote her height above the ground after t seconds. Assume that the air resistance is $0.005y'(t)^2$ lbs in free fall and $0.6y'(t)^2$ lbs with the chute open. At what height does the chute open? How long does it take to reach the ground? At what velocity does she hit the ground? (This model assumes that air resistance is proportional to the *square* of the velocity, and that the parachute opens instantaneously.)

(*Hint*: Pay attention to units. Recall that the mass of the paratrooper is $195/32$, measured in lb sec^2/ft. Here, 32 is the acceleration due to gravity, measured in ft/sec^2.)

(b) Let $v = y'$ be the velocity during the second phase of the fall (while the chute is open). One can view the equation of motion as an autonomous first order ODE in the velocity:

$$v' = -32 + \frac{192}{1950}v^2.$$

Make a qualitative analysis of this first order equation, finding in particular the critical or equilibrium velocity. This velocity is called the terminal velocity. How does the terminal velocity compare with the velocity at the time the chute opens and with the velocity at impact?

(c) Assume the paratrooper is safe if she strikes the ground at a velocity within 5% of the terminal velocity in (b). Except for the initial height, use the parameters in (a). What is the lowest height from which she may parachute safely? (*Please do not try this at home!*)

10. This problem is based on Problems 26 and 27 in Boyce & DiPrima, Section 3.8. Consider the IVP

$$u'' + cu' + u = 0, \quad u(0) = 2, \quad u'(0) = 0.$$

(a) Find the solution. For $c = 0.25$, graph the solution. Determine an approximate time τ at which the solution becomes "negligible." Interpret negligible to mean that no meaningful difference between the curve and the x-axis can be discerned on your plot. Repeat this process for the values $c = 0.25, 0.5, \ldots, 1.75, 2$. Make a list of values (c, τ) corresponding to the eight values of c. Plot the resulting points. How does τ depend on c? What does the theory of damped vibrations predict about the relationship between τ and c?

(b) Now plot the solution curves for the values $c = 1.75, 1.8, \ldots, 2.2, 2.25$. The issue we would like to resolve is: at what point does the transition from oscillatory to nonoscillatory behavior occur. The characteristic equation tells you it is $c = 2$. Why? By adjusting your domain and range, try to verify that. If you cannot, explain what prevents you from doing so. (*Hint:* For $c = 1.9$, for example, compute where the curve first crosses the x-axis. What is the magnitude at nearby points?)

11. This problem is based on Problems 19 and 20 in Boyce & DiPrima, Section 3.9. Consider the IVP

$$u'' + u = 3\cos(\omega t), \quad u(0) = 0, \quad u'(0) = 0.$$

(a) Find the solution (using **dsolve**). For $\omega = 0.5, 0.6, 0.7, 0.8, 0.9$, plot the solution curves on the interval $0 \le x \le 10$. Note that $\omega_0 = 1$ is the natural frequency of the homogeneous equation. Describe how the solution curves behave as ω gets closer to 1.

(b) Notice that the formula in (a) is invalid when $\omega = 1$. Find and plot a numerical solution curve for $\omega = 1$. What phenomenon is exhibited? Corroborate your conclusion by plotting on a longer interval.

(c) Compare the plots for $\omega = 1$ and $\omega = 0.9$ on a longer interval to see that the behavior for $\omega = 0.9$ is different from that in (b). What phenomenon is exhibited by the curve for $\omega = 0.9$?

12. In this problem we study how solutions of the initial value problem

$$\frac{d^2y}{dt^2} + 0.15\frac{dy}{dt} - y + y^3 = 0, \quad y(0) = a, \quad y'(0) = 0$$

depend on the initial value a.

Plot a numerical solution of this equation from $t = 0$ to $t = 40$ for each of the initial values $a = 0.5, 1, 1.5, 2, 2.5$. You may have to increase **maxfun** and **numpoints** in order to make some of these plots.

Describe how increasing the initial value of y affects the solutions, both in terms of their limiting behavior and their general appearance. (In making comparisons, pay careful attention to the scale on the y-axis.)

Finally, plot all five solutions on one graph. Would such a picture be possible for solutions of a first order differential equation? Why or why not?

13. In this problem, we consider the long-term behavior of solutions of the initial value problem

$$\frac{d^2y}{dt^2} + 0.15\frac{dy}{dt} - y + y^3 = 0.3\cos(\omega t), \quad y(0) = 0, \quad y'(0) = 0$$

for various frequencies ω in the forcing term.

Plot a numerical solution of this equation from $t = 0$ to $t = 100$ for each of the eight frequencies $\omega = 0.8, 0.9, \ldots, 1.4, 1.5$. You may have to increase **maxfun** and **numpoints** in order to make these plots. You should also expect *Maple* to take more time than usual in making them.

Describe and compare the different long-term behaviors you see. Due to the forcing term, all solutions will oscillate, but pay particular attention to the magnitude of the oscillations, and to whether or not there is a periodic pattern to them. Are there any similarities between your results for this nonlinear system and the phenomenon of resonance for linear systems with periodic forcing?

14. In this problem, we study the zeros of solutions of the second order differential equation

$$y'' + (2 + \sin x)y = 0. \tag{i}$$

(a) Compute and plot several solutions of this equation with different initial conditions: $y(0) = c, y'(0) = d$. To be specific, choose three different values for the pair c, d and plot the corresponding solutions over $[0, 20]$. By inspecting your plots, find a number L that is an upper bound for the distance between successive zeros of the solutions. Then find a number l that is a lower bound for the distance between successive zeros.

(b) Information on the zeros of solutions of linear second order ODEs can be obtained from the Sturm Comparison Theorem (see Chapter 9). By comparing (i) with the equation $y'' + y = 0$, you should be able to get a value for L, and by comparing (i) with $y'' + 3y = 0$, you should be able to find l. How do these values compare with the values obtained in part (a)? (You will find it useful to note that the general solution of $y'' + ky = 0$, where k is a positive constant, can be written as $y = R\cos(\sqrt{k}x - \delta)$, with $R \geq 0, \delta$ arbitrary. R is called the *amplitude* and δ the *phase shift*.)

(c) Plot a solution of (i) and a solution of $y'' + y = 0$ on the same graph, and verify that between any two zeros of the latter solution, there is at least one zero of the solution of (i).

15. Consider Bessel's equation of order zero

$$x^2 y'' + xy' + x^2 y = 0.$$

(a) Compute and plot several solutions of this equation with different initial conditions: $y(1) = c, y'(1) = d$. To be specific, choose three different values for the pair c, d and plot the corresponding solutions over $[0.1, 20]$. (Why isn't it a good idea to use $x = 0$ in the initial conditions?) By inspecting your plots, find a number L that is an upper bound for the distance between successive zeros of the solutions. Then find a number l that is a lower bound for the distance between successive zeros.

(b) Now confirm your findings with the Sturm Comparison Theorem. It doesn't apply directly, but if we introduce the new function $z(x) = x^{1/2} y(x)$, Bessel's equation becomes

$$z'' + (1 + 1/(4x^2))z = 0,$$

which has the form of the equation in the Comparison Theorem. Since y will have a zero wherever z has a zero, we can study the zeros of y by studying the zeros of z. By comparing the equation for z with the equation $z'' + z = 0$, determine an upper bound L on the distance between successive zeros of any solution of Bessel's equation.

(c) Let a be a positive number. For $x \in [a, \infty)$, the quantity $1 + 1/(4x^2)$ is less than or equal to the constant $1 + 1/(4a^2)$. By making an appropriate comparison, determine a lower bound l on the distance between successive zeros of any solution of Bessel's equation (for $x > a$). What is the limiting value of l as a goes to ∞? Approximately how far apart are the zeros when x is large? Did your graphical study lead to comparable values for l and L?

16. A solution of a second order linear differential equation is called *oscillatory* if its graph crosses the x-axis infinitely many times, and *nonoscillatory* if it crosses only finitely many times. In this problem, we will be interested in determining the oscillatory nature of nonzero solutions to some second order linear ODEs. First consider the equation $y'' + ky = 0$, where k is a constant. If $k > 0$, it has the general solution $y = R\cos(\sqrt{k}x - \delta)$, with $R \geq 0, \delta$ arbitrary. R is called the *amplitude* and δ the *phase shift*. From this formula we see that any solution $y(x)$ has infinitely many zeros and hence crosses the axis infinitely many times, *i.e.*, is oscillatory. If $k < 0$, the general solution is $y(x) = c_1 e^{\sqrt{-k}x} + c_2 e^{-\sqrt{-k}x}$, so we see that solutions have at most one zero, *i.e.*, are nonoscillatory. If $k = 0$, the general solution is $y(x) = c_1 x + c_2$. These have at most one zero and so are nonoscillatory.

Next consider Airy's equation

$$y'' = xy, \tag{i}$$

which arises in various applications. Since (i) has a variable coefficient, we cannot study it by elementary methods; in particular, we cannot find the general solution as we did for the constant coefficient equation. We will instead first make a graphical study of the solutions of (i), and then study the solutions using the Sturm Comparison Theorem (see Chapter 9). Compute and plot several numerical solutions of (i) with different initial conditions $y(0) = c, y'(0) = d$. To be specific, choose three different values for the pair c, d, and graph the corresponding solutions over the interval $[-10, 5]$. What do you observe? Do solutions have zeros on the negative x-axis? A few? Many? Do they get closer together as x becomes more negative? Do solutions have zeros on the positive x-axis? Where are the solutions oscillatory?

Information on the zeros of solutions of linear second order ODEs, and hence information on their oscillatory nature, can also be obtained from the Sturm Comparison Theorem. By comparing (i) with the equation $y'' - by = 0$ for $x \le b < 0$, what do you learn about zeros on the negative x-axis and their spacing, and hence about the oscillatory nature of solutions of (i) for $x \le 0$? By comparing (i) with $y'' = 0$ for $0 < x$, what do you learn about the oscillatory nature of solutions for $x > 0$? How many zeros could a solution have on the positive x-axis? Do the graphs you plotted above confirm these results?

17. In this problem, we study solutions of the parabolic cylinder equation

$$y'' + \left(n + \frac{1}{2} - \frac{x^2}{4}\right) y = 0,$$

which arises in the study of quantum-mechanical vibrations. Since the equation is unchanged if x is replaced by $-x$, any solution function will be symmetric with respect to the y-axis. Therefore, we focus our attention on $x \ge 0$.

(a) Find the corresponding first order equation for $z = \arctan(y/y')$, as described in the *Geometric Method* section of Chapter 9.

(b) For $n = 1$, plot the direction field for the z equation from $x = 0$ to $x = 10$. (Remember to use $-\pi/2 \le z \le \pi/2$.) Based on the plot, predict what the solutions y to the parabolic cylinder equation look like near $x = 0$, and for larger x. Is there a value of x around which you expect their behavior to change?

(c) Now numerically solve the parabolic cylinder equation for $n = 1$ with two sets of initial conditions $y(0) = 1, y'(0) = 0$ and $y(0) = 0, y'(0) = 1$. Plot the two solutions on the same graph. (It will probably help to change the range on the plot.) Do the solutions behave as you expected?

(d) Repeat parts (b) and (c) for $n = 5$. Point out any differences from the case $n = 1$.

(e) Repeat parts (b) and (c) for $n = 15$. Discuss how the solutions are changing as n increases.

(f) Now consider the three solutions (for $n = 1, 5$, and 15) with $y(0) = 0$. Point out similarities and differences. By drawing an analogy with Airy's equation, argue from the direction fields that, for any n, exactly one solution function decays for large x while all others grow. Do you have enough graphical evidence from the numerical plots to conclude that the solution corresponding to the initial data $y(0) = 0$, $y'(0) = 1$ is that function? Why or why not? (*Hint*: Look to previous discussions of stability of solutions as a guide.)

18. In this problem, we study solutions of Bessel's equation of order n,

$$y'' + \frac{1}{x}y' + \left(1 - \frac{n^2}{x^2}\right)y = 0,$$

for $n > 0$. Solutions of this equation, called Bessel functions of order n, are used in the study of vibrations and waves with circular symmetry. Since the equation is unchanged if x is replaced by $-x$, we focus our attention on $x \geq 0$.

(a) Find the corresponding first order equation for $z = \arctan(y/y')$, as described in the *Geometric Method* section of Chapter 9.

(b) For $n = 1$, plot the direction field for the z equation from $x = 0$ to $x = 20$. (Remember to use $-\pi/2 \leq z \leq \pi/2$.) Based on the plot, predict what the Bessel functions of order 1 look like near $x = 0$, and for larger x. Is there a value of x around which you expect their behavior to change?

(c) Now plot the Bessel functions **BesselJ(n, x)** and **BesselY(n, x)** for $n = 1$ on the same graph. (It will probably help to change the range on the plot.) Do the solutions behave as you expected?

(d) Repeat parts (b) and (c) for $n = 5$. Point out any differences from the case $n = 1$.

(e) Repeat parts (b) and (c) for $n = 15$. Discuss how the solutions are changing as n increases.

Chapter 10

Series Solutions

A primary theme of this book is that numerical, geometric, and qualitative methods can be used to study solutions of differential equations, even when we cannot find an exact formula solution. Of course, exact solutions are extremely valuable, and there are many techniques for finding them. For instance, techniques for finding exact solutions of second order linear differential equations include:

- The exponential substitution, which leads to solutions of an arbitrary constant coefficient homogeneous equation;
- The method of *reduction of order,* which produces a second linearly independent solution of a homogeneous equation when one solution is already known;
- The method of *undetermined coefficients,* which solves special kinds of inhomogeneous equations with constant coefficients; and
- The method of *variation of parameters,* which yields the solution of a general inhomogeneous equation, given a fundamental set of solutions to the homogeneous equation.

Each of these techniques reduces the search for a formula solution to a simpler problem in algebra or calculus: finding the root of a polynomial, computing an antiderivative, or solving a pair of simultaneous linear equations.

The process of finding formulas for exact solutions of equations, either by hand or by computer, is called *symbolic computation.* The **dsolve** command incorporates some of the techniques listed above. It enables us to find exact solutions more rapidly and more reliably than we could by hand.

There are many differential equations that do not yield to the techniques listed above. By using more advanced ideas from calculus, however, we can find exact solutions for a wider class of differential equations. In this chapter and the next, we discuss two such calculus-based techniques for finding exact solutions of differential equations: *Series Solutions* and *Laplace Transforms.* The method of Series Solutions enables us to solve differential equations with variable coefficients. The theory of Laplace Transforms (discussed in the next chapter) enables us to solve constant coefficient linear differential equations with discontinuous inhomogeneous terms. These are sophisticated techniques, involving improper integrals, complex variables, and power series. Both techniques are computationally intensive, and both have been implemented as options to **dsolve**.

Series Solutions

Consider the second order homogeneous linear differential equation with variable coefficients

$$a(x)y''(x) + b(x)y'(x) + c(x)y(x) = 0. \tag{1}$$

Suppose the coefficient functions a, b, and c are *analytic* (i.e., have convergent power series representations) in a neighborhood of a point $x = x_0$. For simplicity, we shall assume that $x_0 = 0$, but everything we say remains valid for any point of analyticity. We begin by dividing by $a(x)$ to normalize the equation. This causes no problems as long as $a(0) \neq 0$. In this case, we refer to the origin as an *ordinary point* for the equation. Changing notation, we write

$$y''(x) + p(x)y'(x) + q(x)y(x) = 0. \tag{2}$$

Equations (1) and (2) have the same solutions. We will search for a power series solution of the form

$$y(x) = \sum_{n=0}^{\infty} a_n x^n. \tag{3}$$

If we can find such a solution, then $y(0) = a_0$ and $y'(0) = a_1$. Thus, if we are given initial values, then we can find the first two coefficients of the power series solution.

By substituting the infinite series (3) into equation (2), expanding p and q as power series, and combining terms of the same degree, we obtain a *recursion relation* for the coefficients a_n. In other words, we obtain algebraic equations for a_n that involve a_0, a_1, ..., a_{n-1} and known coefficients of the power series of p and q. Sometimes, we can solve the recursion relation in *closed form* by finding an algebraic formula for a_n. This formula would involve known functions of n (such as $n!$ or powers of n) and a_0 and a_1, but no other coefficients of lower degree. If no initial data are given, then a solution to the recursion relation produces a general solution of the differential equation with arbitrary constants a_0 and a_1.

Solving a recursion relation in closed form is like finding an exact formula solution for a differential equation. In many cases, we cannot solve the recursion relation. Nevertheless, we can still use the recursion relation to compute as many coefficients as we wish. As long as we stay close to the origin, the leading terms should give a good approximation to the full power series solution. One must be careful, however, because the power series solution will be valid only inside its radius of convergence. The radius of convergence will be at least as large as the distance from the origin to the nearest singularity of p or q. When the recursion relation is solvable in closed form, we can use a standard test from calculus to compute the radius of convergence precisely. In general, we can only make an educated guess.

We can use *Maple* to automate the process of finding power series solutions. In fact, the power series method is built into the **dsolve** command and is invoked with the option **type = series**.

EXAMPLE. Consider the initial value problem

$$y'' - xy' - y = 0, \qquad y(0) = 2, \qquad y'(0) = 1$$

from Problem 15 in Section 5.2 of Boyce & DiPrima. We can solve this with **dsolve** by typing

> **eqn1 := diff(y(x), x$2) − x*diff(y(x), x) − y(x) = 0;**
> **sol1 := dsolve({eqn1, y(0) = 2, D(y)(0) = 1}, y(x), type = series);**

The resulting power series is

$$y(x) = 2 + x + x^2 + \frac{1}{3}x^3 + \frac{1}{4}x^4 + \frac{1}{15}x^5 + O\left(x^6\right).$$

The symbol $O(x^6)$ includes all terms of at least order 6. If we drop the term $O(x^6)$ from this expression, we get a *Taylor polynomial*, which approximates the power series. In *Maple*, we can do this by typing **convert(rhs(sol1), polynom)**.

The order of the series solution is determined by the global variable **Order**, whose default value is 6. To see the series solution up to order 10, we set **Order :=** **11**. Thus

> **Order := 11;**
> **dsolve({eqn1, y(0) = 2, D(y)(0) = 1}, y(x), type = series);**

yields

$$y(x) = 2 + x + x^2 + \frac{1}{3}x^3 + \frac{1}{4}x^4 + \frac{1}{15}x^5 + \frac{1}{24}x^6 + \frac{1}{105}x^7$$
$$+ \frac{1}{192}x^8 + \frac{1}{945}x^9 + \frac{1}{1920}x^{10} + O\left(x^{11}\right).$$

The initial conditions tell *Maple* where to expand the power series. In the preceding examples, the initial conditions were given at $x = 0$, so the series solution was given as an expansion at $x = 0$. To expand at $x = 1$, for example, we could type

> **dsolve({eqn1, y(1) = 1, D(y)(1) = 0}, y(x), series);**

The result will be a power series expansion at $x = 1$ of the solution of the IVP; *i.e.*, a power series in $(x - 1)$.

The **dsolve** command without the **series** option will find exact solutions to many homogenous second order equations with polynomial coefficients. Often, these solutions involve special functions like **BesselJ** and **BesselY**. Equations with coefficients that are not polynomials generally require series methods.

Singular Points

In the discussion above, we considered equations of the form

$$a(x)y'' + b(x)y' + c(x)y = 0,$$

where $a(0) \neq 0$. We transformed the equation into the form

$$y'' + p(x)y' + q(x)y = 0$$

by dividing by $a(x)$. If $a(0) = 0$, then dividing by $a(x)$ may result in one or both of $p(x)$ and $q(x)$ being singular at $x = 0$. In this case, we say that the equation has a *singularity* at $x = 0$.

A prototype is the Euler equation:

$$x^2 y'' + bxy' + cy = 0,$$

where b and c are constants. Dividing by x^2 yields the equation

$$y'' + \frac{b}{x}y' + \frac{c}{x^2}y = 0,$$

so $p(x) = b/x$ and $q(x) = c/x^2$. Both $p(x)$ and $q(x)$ are singular at $x = 0$. Such isolated singularities, where the singularity of p is no worse than $1/x$ and the singularity of q is no worse than $1/x^2$, are called *regular singular points*. More precisely, we say that a function $f(x)$ has a *pole of order* n at x_0 if $\lim_{x \to x_0} f(x) = \infty$, and n is the smallest integer such that $\lim_{x \to x_0} (x - x_0)^n f(x)$ is finite. A homogeneous linear differential equation $y^{(n)} + p_1(x)y^{(n-1)} + \ldots + p_n(x)y = 0$ is said to have a regular singular point at x_0 if it is singular at x_0, and p_k has a pole of order at most k at x_0.

Here is a summary of the general approach to solving second order linear equations with regular singular points. We suppose, for simplicity, that the singular point is $x = 0$, and we look for solutions on the interval $(0, \infty)$. Let $p_0 = \lim_{x \to 0} xp(x)$ and $q_0 = \lim_{x \to 0} x^2 q(x)$. Let r_1 and r_2 be the roots of the *indicial equation* $r(r - 1) + p_0 r + q_0 = 0$. We look for a solution of the differential equation of the form

$$y_1(x) = x^{r_1} u(x),$$

where $u(0) = 1$. If $r_1 - r_2$ is not an integer, then we look for a second solution of the form

$$y_2(x) = x^{r_2} v(x),$$

where $v(0) = 1$. If $r_1 = r_2$, then we look for a second solution of the form

$$y_2(x) = y_1(x) \ln(x) + x^{r_1} v(x),$$

where $v(0) = 0$. If $r_1 - r_2$ is a positive integer, then we look for a solution of the form

$$y_2(x) = ay_1(x) \ln(x) + x^{r_1} v(x),$$

where a is a constant and $v(0) = 1$. The functions $u(x)$ and $v(x)$ will be analytic at 0, and therefore will have power series expansions at $x = 0$. These solutions are called *Frobenius series* solutions.

One could use *Maple* to apply these techniques by hand, but **dsolve(..., series)** already uses them to solve equations with regular singular points. When applying **dsolve** to singular equations, it is important to remember that the solutions may blow up at the singular point. Consequently, it often does not make sense to specify an initial condition at the singular point.

EXAMPLE. Consider the differential equation:

$$2xy'' + y' + xy = 0.$$

The origin is a regular singular point, and the indicial equation has roots $r = 0$ and $r = 1/2$. Hence, the differential equation should have a Frobenius series solution of the form

$$x^{1/2} \sum_{n=0}^{\infty} a_n x^n.$$

To solve this equation with **dsolve**, we type:

eqn2 := 2*x*diff(y(x), x\$2) + diff(y(x), x) + x*y(x) = 0;
dsolve(eqn2, y(x), type = series);

The solution is:

$$y(x) = \_C1\,\sqrt{x}\left(1 - \frac{1}{10}x^2 + \frac{1}{360}x^4 + O\left(x^6\right)\right)$$
$$+ \_C2\left(1 - \frac{1}{6}x^2 + \frac{1}{168}x^4 + O\left(x^6\right)\right).$$

Note that we did not specify an initial condition in this example, although we could have since the solutions are nonsingular at 0. In general, specifying an initial condition (at the singular point) for a singular differential equation will cause **dsolve** to fail.

EXERCISE. Use **dsolve** with the **series** option to solve the Euler equation

$$x^2 y'' + 3xy' + y = 0.$$

Are the solutions singular at 0? What happens if you specify an initial condition at $x = 0$ in the **dsolve** command?

It is important to note that for equations with regular singular points, the Frobenius series tells us how fast the solution blows up at the singularity, *e.g.*, the solution blows up like $1/x$, or $x^{-1/2}$, etc. This information is not easily gleaned from a numerical solution. For equations with an irregular singular point, we cannot expect a Frobenius series solution to be valid, and other techniques (numerical or qualitative) must be used. Some of those techniques are addressed in Problem Set E.

In this chapter, we have focused on linear homogeneous second order differential equations. The method of series solutions can also be used for inhomogeneous equations, higher order equations, and nonlinear equations. In fact, as we've noted before, most differential equations cannot be solved in terms of elementary functions. For many of these equations, a series solution is the only analytic solution available.

Chapter 11

Laplace Transforms

A *transform* is a mathematical operation that changes a given function into a new function. Transforms are often used in mathematics to change a difficult problem into a more tractable one. In this chapter, we introduce the *Laplace Transform*, which is particularly useful for solving linear differential equations with constant coefficients and discontinuous inhomogeneous term. The key feature of the Laplace Transform is that (roughly speaking) it changes the operation of differentiation into the operation of multiplication. Thus the Laplace Transform changes a differential equation into an algebraic equation. To solve a linear differential equation with constant coefficients, you apply the Laplace Transform to change the differential equation into an algebraic equation, solve the algebraic equation, and then apply the Inverse Laplace Transform to transform the solution of the algebraic equation back into a solution of the differential equation.

The Laplace Transform of a function f is a new function, denoted by F or by $\mathcal{L}(f)$, and defined as follows:

$$F(s) = \mathcal{L}(f)(s) = \int_0^\infty f(t)e^{-st}\, dt.$$

This transform is called an *integral transform* because it is obtained by integrating the function f against another function e^{-st}, called the *kernel* of the transform. The integral in question is an improper integral, so we have to make sure that it converges. Note that while the argument s of the function F appears in the integrand, the integration is with respect to the variable t. Note also that the integral is over the domain $[0, \infty)$, so we need only assume that the function f is defined for $t \geq 0$.

To get a feel for the Laplace Transform, we compute the Laplace Transform of the function e^{at}.

$$\mathcal{L}(e^{at})(s) = \int_0^\infty e^{at}e^{-st}\, dt = \lim_{c \to \infty} \int_0^c e^{at}e^{-st}\, dt$$

$$= \lim_{c \to \infty} \int_0^c e^{(a-s)t}\, dt = \lim_{c \to \infty} \frac{e^{(a-s)t}}{(a-s)}\bigg|_0^c =$$

$$= \lim_{c \to \infty} \left(\frac{e^{(a-s)c}}{(a-s)} - \frac{1}{a-s} \right)$$

$$= \begin{cases} 1/(s-a), & \text{if } s > a \\ +\infty, & \text{if } s \leq a. \end{cases}$$

Note that the Laplace Transform of e^{at} is defined for $s > a$. In fact, a straightforward argument shows that if f is any piecewise continuous function on $[0, \infty)$ with the property that $|f(t)| \leq Ke^{at}$, for some constant $K > 0$, then the improper integral defining the Laplace Transform converges for $s > a$, and therefore $\mathcal{L}(f)(s)$ is defined for $s > a$. We say that a function is *piecewise continuous* if it only has a discrete set of jump discontinuities. If f satisfies an inequality of the form $|f(t)| \leq Ke^{at}$, we say that f is of *exponential order*. Most functions one encounters in practice are of exponential order. From now on, we only consider piecewise continuous functions of exponential order. In particular, if f is a bounded function, then it satisfies the inequality $|f(t)| \leq K = Ke^{0t}$ for some $K > 0$, so $\mathcal{L}(f)(s)$ is defined for all $s > 0$. More generally, any function whose growth is of exponential order has a Laplace Transform which is defined for sufficiently large s.

EXERCISE. Compute the Laplace Transform of the functions $f(t) = 1$ and $\cos t$. (For $\cos t$, you must integrate by parts twice.)

We asserted that the Laplace Transform transforms differentiation into multiplication. This is a consequence of the integration by parts formula:

$$\begin{aligned} \mathcal{L}(f')(s) &= \int_0^\infty f'(t)e^{-st}\, dt = \lim_{c \to \infty} \int_0^c f'(t)e^{-st}\, dt \\ &= \lim_{c \to \infty} \left[f(t)e^{-st}\big|_0^c - \int_0^c f(t)(-se^{-st})\, dt \right] \\ &= -f(0) + s \lim_{c \to \infty} \int_0^c f(t)e^{-st}\, dt \\ &= s\mathcal{L}(f)(s) - f(0). \end{aligned} \tag{1}$$

To be precise, we must assume that f is continuous and f' is piecewise continuous for this formula to hold. We can summarize (1) as follows: If the Laplace Transform of f is $F(s)$, then the Laplace Transform of f' is $sF(s) - f(0)$. In other words, the Laplace Transform changes the operation of differentiation into the operation of multiplication (by the independent variable) plus a translation (by $-f(0)$). The formula in (1) has a straightforward generalization to higher derivatives. If the Laplace Transform of f is F, $f^{(k)}$ is continuous for $k = 0 \ldots n-1$, and $f^{(n)}$ is piecewise continuous, then

$$\mathcal{L}(f^{(n)})(s) = s^n F(s) - s^{n-1}f(0) - s^{n-2}f'(0) - \cdots - f^{(n-1)}(0).$$

The Laplace Transform has many other important properties, of which we mention two here. First, the Laplace Transform is linear, i.e., $\mathcal{L}(af+bg) = a\mathcal{L}(f)+b\mathcal{L}(g)$.

Linearity of the Laplace Transform follows easily from linearity of integration. Second, the Laplace Transform is invertible; the inverse is called the Inverse Laplace Transform, and is denoted by $\mathcal{L}^{-1}$. The Inverse Laplace Transform has the property that $\mathcal{L}^{-1}(\mathcal{L}(f)) = f$, *i.e.*, the Inverse Laplace Transform of the Laplace Transform of a function is the function itself. The Inverse Laplace Transform is also an integral transform, but it involves contour integrals in the complex plane, so we do not give the definition here.

Solving Differential Equations with Laplace Transforms

Let's see what happens when we apply the Laplace Transform to a second order linear differential equation with constant coefficients. Consider the initial value problem

$$ay''(t) + by'(t) + cy(t) = f(t), \qquad y(0) = y_0, \qquad y'(0) = y_0'. \tag{2}$$

When we apply the Laplace Transform to this equation, we get the algebraic equation

$$a(s^2 Y(s) - sy_0 - y_0') + b(sY(s) - y_0) + cY(s) = F(s),$$

where $Y(s)$ is the Laplace Transform of $y(t)$, and $F(s)$ is the Laplace Transform of $f(t)$. We solve this algebraic equation for $Y(s)$, to get

$$Y(s) = \frac{F(s) + asy_0 + ay_0' + by_0}{as^2 + bs + c},$$

and then compute the Inverse Laplace Transform of the right-hand side to get an expression for $y(t)$.

Traditionally, Laplace Transforms and Inverse Laplace Transforms were computed by reading tables. You can also use *Maple* to compute Laplace Transforms automatically. The Laplace Transform of a function $y(t)$ is computed by

laplace(y(t), t, s)

and the inverse transform of a function $Y(s)$ is computed by

invlaplace(Y(s), s, t)

For example, **laplace(cos(t), t, s)** yields $s/(1 + s^2)$.

You could use the **laplace** and **invlaplace** commands to solve differential equations in *Maple*; but *Maple* has already implemented the Laplace Transform method as an option to the **dsolve** command. Thus we could solve the initial value problem (2) by typing

eqn1 := a*diff(y(t), t$2) + b*diff(y(t), t) + c*y(t) = f(t);
dsolve({eqn1, y(0) = y0, D(y)(0) = yp0}, y(t), method = laplace);

Of course, without particular values for a, b, c, f, y_0 and y_0', the solution will be a complicated symbolic expression.

EXAMPLE. Consider the initial value problem:

$$y''(t) - 2y(t) = \sin 2t, \quad y(0) = 1, \quad y'(0) = 2.$$

Typing

```
eqn2 := diff(y(t), t$2) - 2*y(t) = sin(2*t);
dsolve({eqn2, y(0) = 1, D(y)(0) = 2}, y(t), method = laplace);
```

produces the solution

$$y(t) = \frac{7}{6}\sqrt{2}\sinh(\sqrt{2}t) + \cosh(\sqrt{2}t) - \frac{1}{6}\sin(2t).$$

The **method = laplace** option is not necessary to solve this initial value problem (although it makes the solution look nicer). In fact, without this option, **dsolve** uses the method of variation of parameters. If you were solving the IVP by hand, you could also use the method of undetermined coefficients. The full power of the Laplace Transform method comes into play when solving equations that involve discontinuous functions.

Discontinuous Functions

The Laplace Transform is especially useful for solving differential equations that involve piecewise continuous functions. The basic building block for piecewise continuous functions is the *unit step function u(t)*, defined by

$$u(t) = \begin{cases} 0, & \text{if } t < 0, \\ 1, & \text{if } t \geq 0. \end{cases}$$

In honor of the physicist and engineer Oliver Heaviside (1850-1925), who developed the Laplace Transform method to solve problems in electrical engineering, this function is sometimes called the Heaviside function. In *Maple*, this function has been implemented with the name **Heaviside**.

The unit step function is best thought of as a switch, which is off until time 0, and then on starting at time 0. The function $1 - u(t)$ is also a switch, on until 0, and then off. To make a switch that comes on at time c, we simply translate $u(t)$ by c; thus $u(t-c)$ is a switch that comes on at time c. Similarly, $1 - u(t-c)$ is a switch that goes off at time c. The unit step function translated by c is often written $u_c(t) = u(t-c)$. Note that $1 - u(t-c) = u(c-t)$, or equivalently, $1 - u_c(t) = u_{-c}(-t)$.

The unit step function can be used to build piecewise continuous functions by switching pieces of the function on and off at appropriate times. To turn a function on at time c, multiply it by $u_c(t)$, and to turn it off at time d, multiply it by $(1-u_d(t))$. Consider, for example, the function

$$f(t) = \begin{cases} 0, & t < 0, \\ 1, & 0 \leq t < 1, \\ t^2, & 1 \leq t < 3, \\ \sin 2t, & t \geq 3. \end{cases}$$

We can write this as

$$f(t) = u_0(t)(1 - u_1(t)) + u_1(t)(1 - u_3(t))\, t^2 + u_3(t)\sin 2t.$$

In *Maple*, we would enter this as

f := t –> Heaviside(t)*Heaviside(1 – t)
    + Heaviside(t – 1)*Heaviside(3 – t)*t^2
    + Heaviside(t – 3)*sin(2*t)

Here, we have used the identity **Heaviside(c – t) = (1 – Heaviside(t – c))**. Here is a plot of f.

Figure 1

In this plot, you can clearly see the three different "pieces" of the function. (The vertical segment in the graph is an artifact of *Maple*'s plotting routine, and is not part of the function.)

EXERCISE. Write down an expression for the following function in terms of the **Heaviside** function, and then plot it:

$$f(t) = \begin{cases} 0, & t < 1, \\ \cos t, & 1 \le t < 2, \\ \sin t, & t \ge 2. \end{cases}$$

Another important discontinuous function is the *Dirac delta function*, usually denoted $\delta(t)$ or $\delta_0(t)$, and sometimes called the *unit impulse function*. To understand this function, recall that the total impulse imparted by a varying force $F(t)$ is the integral of $F(t)$. If we consider a constant force of total impulse one and make this force act over a smaller and smaller time interval around 0, then in the limit we obtain the Dirac delta function. Thus, the delta function represents an idealized force of total impulse 1 concentrated at the instant $t = 0$. The delta function belongs to a class of mathematical objects called *generalized functions*. (It is not a true function since its value at 0 would be infinite.) The magnitude and timing of the delta function can be changed by multiplying the delta function by a constant and translating it. Thus, the function $10\delta(t - 8)$ represents a force of total impulse 10 concentrated at the instant $t = 8$. The function $\delta(t - c)$ is sometimes denoted $\delta_c(t)$. The Dirac delta function is implemented in *Maple*, under the name **Dirac**.

EXERCISE. The fact that **Dirac** is not a true function causes unusual behavior in *Maple*. Plot the Dirac function on the interval $[-1, 1]$ (you won't see anything). Evaluate the function at 0 and 1. Integrate the function over the interval $[-1, 1]$.

Both the unit step function and the Dirac delta function have Laplace Transforms. For example,

$$\mathcal{L}(u_c)(s) = \int_0^\infty u_c(t)e^{-st}\,dt = \int_c^\infty e^{-st}\,dt$$

$$= \frac{e^{-cs}}{s}, \quad s > 0.$$

To compute the Laplace Transform of $\delta(t)$, we must write $\delta(t)$ as a limit of *bona fide* functions. The easiest way to do this is to use step functions. We can write a function of total integral one, concentrated on the interval $[-\epsilon, \epsilon]$, as

$$\frac{1}{2\epsilon}(u_{-\epsilon}(t) - u_\epsilon(t)).$$

Thus

$$\delta(t) = \lim_{\epsilon \to 0^+} \frac{1}{2\epsilon}(u_{-\epsilon}(t) - u_\epsilon(t)),$$

and

$$\mathcal{L}(\delta_c)(s) = \lim_{\epsilon \to 0^+} \frac{1}{2\epsilon}(\mathcal{L}(u_{c-\epsilon})(s) - \mathcal{L}(u_{c+\epsilon})(s))$$

$$= \lim_{\epsilon \to 0^+} \frac{1}{2\epsilon}\left(\frac{e^{(\epsilon-c)s}}{s} - \frac{e^{-(\epsilon+c)s}}{s}\right)$$

$$= \lim_{\epsilon \to 0^+} (e^{-cs})\frac{e^{\epsilon s} - e^{-\epsilon s}}{2\epsilon s}$$

$$= (e^{-cs})\lim_{\epsilon \to 0^+} \frac{s(e^{\epsilon s} + e^{-\epsilon s})}{2s}$$

$$= (e^{-cs})\lim_{\epsilon \to 0^+} \cosh(\epsilon s)$$

$$= e^{-cs}.$$

(We used L'Hôpital's rule in passing from the third to the fourth line.) Thus $\mathcal{L}(\delta_c)(s) = e^{-cs}$. In particular, setting $c = 0$, we get that $\mathcal{L}(\delta)(s) = 1$.

Additional properties of the Laplace Transform are explored in Problems 10 and 11 of Problem Set E.

Differential Equations with Discontinuous Forcing Functions

Consider an inhomogeneous, second order linear equation with constant coefficients:

$$ay''(t) + by'(t) + cy(t) = g(t).$$

The function $g(t)$ is called the forcing function of the differential equation, because in many physical models $g(t)$ corresponds to the influence of an external force. If $g(t)$ is piecewise continuous, or involves the delta function, then we can solve the equation by the method of Laplace Transforms.

EXAMPLE. Consider the initial value problem:

$$y''(t) + 3y'(t) + y(t) = g(t), \quad y(0) = 1, \quad y'(0) = 1,$$

where

$$g(t) = \begin{cases} 0, & t < 0, \\ 1, & 0 \leq t < 1, \\ -1, & 1 \leq t < 2, \\ 0, & t \geq 2. \end{cases}$$

We can solve this equation in *Maple* with the following sequence of commands.

```
g := t -> Heaviside(t) - 2*Heaviside(t - 1) + Heaviside(t - 2);
eqn3 := diff(y(t), t$2) + 3*diff(y(t), t) + y(t) = g(t);
sol3 := dsolve({eqn3, y(0) = 1, D(y)(0) = 1}, y(t), method = laplace);
```

The solution is too complicated to reproduce here (but you should compute it using *Maple*). Here is a graph of the solution together with the forcing function, produced with the *Maple* command **plot({rhs(sol3), g(t)}, t = 0..5);**

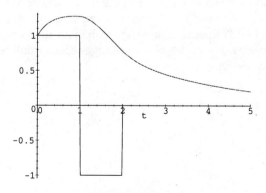

Figure 2

EXAMPLE. We can also use *Maple* to solve nonhomogeneous equations involving the delta function. Consider the initial value problem

$$y''(t) + y'(t) + y(t) = \delta_1(t), \quad y(0) = 0, y'(0) = 0.$$

We can solve this equation with the following sequence of commands.

eqn4 := diff(y(t), t\$2) + diff(y(t), t) + y(t) = Dirac(t − 1);
sol4 := dsolve({eqn4, y(0) = 0, D(y)(0) = 0}, y(t), method = laplace);

The solution is

$$y(t) = \frac{2\sqrt{3}\,\mathrm{Heaviside}(t-1)e^{-(t-1)/2}\sin(\sqrt{3}(t-1)/2)}{3}.$$

Here is a graph of the solution.

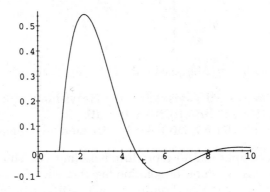

Figure 3

In this graph, you can clearly see the effect of the unit impulse at time $t = 1$. Until $t = 1$, the solution is 0. At time $t = 1$, the unit impulse puts the solution into a nonzero state. After $t = 1$, the impulse function has no further effect. Since the roots of the characteristic polynomial of the homogeneous equation have negative real part, the solution decays exponentially to 0.

Problem Set E

Series Solutions
and Laplace Transforms

1. Consider Airy's equation $y'' - xy = 0$.

   (a) Compute the terms of degree 10 or less in the Taylor series expansion of the solution $y(x)$ to Airy's equation $y'' - xy = 0$ that satisfies $y(0) = 1$, $y'(0) = 0$.

   (b) On the interval $(0, 6)$, graph the Taylor polynomial you obtained, together with the exact solution of the initial value problem.

   (c) Airy's equation can be written as $y'' = xy$. If $x > 1$, then $y'' = xy > y$, so the solutions of Airy's equation grow at least as quickly as the solutions of $y'' = y$. Analyze the latter equation, and predict how well Taylor polynomials will approximate exact solutions of Airy's equation. Relate your analysis to the graph in part (b).

2. Compute the terms of degree 10 or less in the Taylor series expansion of the solution to Problem 23 in Section 5.2 of Boyce & DiPrima:

$$y'' - xy' - y = 0, \quad y(0) = 1, \quad y'(0) = 0.$$

   (a) Graph the Taylor polynomial of degree 10.

   (b) What is the long-term behavior of the Taylor polynomial (as $x \to \pm\infty$)?

   (c) Is the Taylor polynomial an even function? odd? neither?

   (d) Explain purely from the IVP itself why each of your conclusions holds for the actual solution. (*Hints:* In (b), you will have to do a little qualitative analysis—approximate x by a constant; in (c), consider $y_1(x) = y(-x)$.)

3. Compute the terms of degree 10 or less in the Taylor series expansion of the solution to Problem 18 in Section 5.2 of Boyce & DiPrima:

$$(1 - x)y'' + xy' - y = 0, \quad y(0) = -3, \quad y'(0) = 2.$$

The theory suggests the true solution may have a singularity at $x = 1$. Graph the Taylor polynomial you obtained. Do you see any signs of the singularity? Compute the exact solution using **dsolve**. Does the solution have a singularity?

151

4. Use **dsolve** to solve the following Euler equations in Section 5.5 of Boyce & DiPrima (Probs. 3, 6, 8, 13):

   (a) $x^2 y'' - 3xy' + 4y = 0$

   (b) $(x-1)^2 y'' + 8(x-1)y' + 12y = 0$

   (c) $2x^2 y'' - 4xy' + 6y = 0$

   (d) $2x^2 y'' + xy' - 3y = 0, \quad y(1) = 1, \quad y'(1) = 4.$

5. Compute the terms of degree 10 or less in the Frobenius series expansion of the solution to the following problems in Section 5.6 of Boyce & DiPrima (Probs. 2, 5, 8):

   (a) $x^2 y'' + xy' + (x^2 - \frac{1}{9})y = 0$

   (b) $3x^2 y'' + 2xy' + x^2 y = 0$

   (c) $2x^2 y'' + 3xy' + (2x^2 - 1)y = 0.$

6. This problem concerns Bessel's equation, which arises in many physical problems with circular symmetry, such as the study of water waves in a circular pond, vibrations of a circular drum, or the diffraction of light by the circular aperture of a telescope. The Bessel function $J_n(x)$ (where the parameter n is an arbitrary integer) is defined to be the coefficient of t^n in the power series expansion of the function

   $$\exp\left(\frac{1}{2}x\left(t - \frac{1}{t}\right)\right).$$

   (By thinking about what happens to the power series when t and $1/t$ are switched, you can see that $J_{-n}(x) = J_n(x)$ for n even and $J_{-n}(x) = -J_n(x)$ for n odd.) $J_n(x)$ is also a solution to *Bessel's equation of order n*,

   $$x^2 y'' + xy' + (x^2 - n^2)y = 0.$$

   The Taylor series expansion for J_0 is derived in Section 5.9 of Boyce & DiPrima:

   $$J_0(x) = \sum_{j=0}^{\infty}(-1)^j \frac{1}{2^{2j}} \frac{x^{2j}}{(j!)^2}.$$

   (a) *Maple* has a built-in function for $J_n(x)$, called **BesselJ(n, x)**. Use it to plot $J_0(x)$ for $0 \le x \le 10$. (You don't need to graph the function for negative x since J_0 is an even function.) On the same axes, draw the graphs of the 4th order, 10th order, and 20th order Taylor polynomials of J_0. (Use the **series** command in *Maple* (type **?series** for a description) to compute the Taylor expansion of a function to a prescibed order.) How well do the Taylor polynomials approximate the function?

(b) An interesting equality satisfied by the Bessel functions is

$$J_n'(x) = \frac{1}{2}\left(J_{n-1}(x) - J_{n+1}(x)\right).$$

In particular,

$$J_0'(x) = \frac{1}{2}\left(J_{-1}(x) - J_1(x)\right) = \frac{1}{2}\left(-J_1(x) - J_1(x)\right) = -J_1(x).$$

Thus, the maxima and minima of J_0 occur at the zeros of J_1. Using **fsolve**, solve the equations $J_0(x) = 0$ and $J_1(x) = 0$ numerically to find the first five zeros and the first five relative extreme points of J_0, starting at $x = 0$ (you will need lots of different starting values—use your graph for guidance). Compute the differences between successive zeros. Can you make a guess about the periods of the oscillations as $x \to \infty$? (If you did Problem 15 in Problem Set D, you know exactly how the period behaves as $x \to \infty$.)

(c) From the general theory, one knows that Bessel's equation of order n has another linearly independent solution $Y_n(x)$, with a logarithmic singularity as $x \to 0^+$. *Maple* also has a built-in function, **BesselY(n, x)**, for computing $Y_n(x)$. Graph the function $Y_0(x)$ on the interval $0 < x \le 10$. Then compute $\lim_{x \to 0+} Y_0(x)/\ln x$. Graph the function

$$Y_0(x) - c \ln x$$

(on the same interval), where c is the value of the limit you obtained, and observe that it is continuous in a neighborhood of $x = 0$. Thus, the "singular part" of $Y_0(x)$ behaves like $c \ln x$.

7. The first order homogeneous linear differential equation

$$x^2 y' + y = 0$$

has an irregular singular point at $x = 0$ (why?); however, it happens to be an equation that is easy to solve exactly. Find the general solution of the equation for $x > 0$ and for $x < 0$. How do the solutions behave as $x \to 0^+$? as $x \to 0^-$? Use *Maple* to graph a solution for $0 < x < 2$ and a solution for $-2 < x < 0$.

Now find (for $x > 0$ and for $x < 0$) the general solution of the Euler equation

$$xy' + ry = 0,$$

which has a regular singular point at $x = 0$ if $r \ne 0$. How do the solutions behave as $x \to 0^+$? as $x \to 0^-$? Use *Maple* to graph solutions to the right and left of 0 for each of the cases $r = 0.5, r = 1, r = -0.5, r = -1$. What difference do you notice between the behavior of solutions near a regular singular point and the behavior near an irregular singular point?

8. Consider the Legendre equation

$$(1 - x^2)y'' - 2xy' + \alpha(\alpha + 1)y = 0.$$

We assume that $|x| < 1$, because $x = \pm 1$ are regular singular points. We also assume that $\alpha > -1$.

(a) Find series approximations of the two solutions of the Legendre equation with initial conditions $y(0) = 1$, $y'(0) = 0$, and $y(0) = 0$, $y'(0) = 1$. Is this a fundamental set of solutions?

(b) If $\alpha = n$ is a nonnegative integer, the Legendre equation has a polynomial solution of order n. The *Legendre polynomial* $P_n(x)$ is defined to be the unique polynomial solution of the Legendre equation (with $\alpha = n$) such that $P_n(1) = 1$. Use *Maple* to compute the first six Legendre polynomials $P_0(x), \ldots, P_5(x)$. You can do this by using **dsolve** (without the series option and without initial conditions) to solve the Legendre equation for $n = 0, \ldots, 5$; then by inspecting each solution, choose values for the undetermined constants to get polynomial solutions with $P_n(1) = 1$.

(c) Graph $P_0(x), \ldots, P_5(x)$ on the interval $[-1, 1]$. Use different line styles so that you can distinguish the different curves.

(d) In the graph in part (c), you can see that as n increases, the Legendre polynomials are more and more oscillatory on the interval $[-1, 1]$. For x close to zero, the Legendre equation is approximately $y'' + n(n+1)y = 0$. By solving this equation, explain why solutions of the Legendre equation display increasing oscillation (on the interval $[-1, 1]$) as $n \to \infty$.

9. Nonlinear differential equations can sometimes be solved by series methods. Consider, for example, the equation

$$y' = y^2 + x, \qquad\qquad (i)$$

mentioned in Chapter 7 as an example of an equation that cannot be solved in terms of elementary functions. Consider this equation with the initial condition $y(0) = 0$, and let's look for a solution of the form

$$y(x) = \sum_{i=1}^{\infty} a_i x^i. \qquad\qquad (ii)$$

(We know there is no constant term in the Taylor series expansion of y at $x = 0$ because of the initial condition.) Substituting (ii) into (i) and expanding the right-hand side gives a sequence of simultaneous quadratic equations for the coefficients a_i that become increasingly complicated as $i \to \infty$. However, we can solve inductively for the coefficients, by first equating the terms in x, then the terms in x^2, *etc.* *Maple* can carry out this task.

(a) Explain why a_1 must be 0.

(b) Now use **dsolve** to compute a Taylor series expansion of the solution to (i). Make sure you go far enough to get the 11th degree monomial. What pattern do you see?

(c) Plot the 11th degree Taylor polynomial for y, together with a numerical solution of (i) obtained using **dsolve(..., numeric)**, on the interval $-1 < x < 1$. How close are the graphs? Now note that $y(x) > x^2/2$ for $0 < x < 1$, as you can see, for example, from the series. Thus, $y(1) > 0.5$. But for $x > 1$, the right-hand side of (i) is greater than $y(x)^2 + 1$, so the solution grows faster than the solution to the IVP $y' = y^2 + 1$, $y(1) = 0.5$, which is of the form $y(x) = \tan(x - C)$, where $C \approx 0.54$. Since the tangent function blows up when its argument reaches $\pi/2$, this analysis shows that the solution of (i) must become infinite somewhere between $x = 1$ and $x = 2.2$. Is there any way of seeing this from the series solution? Use **odeplot** to locate the point P where the solution blows up. Graph the two approximate solutions (that is, the series solution out to degree 11 and the numerical solution on the interval $[1, 2]$). What do you observe?

10. Suppose $f(t)$ and $g(t)$ are functions with Laplace Transforms $\mathcal{L}(f) = F$ and $\mathcal{L}(g) = G$. Find out which of the following identities *Maple* knows about. (For some of these, you may have to enter the command **assume(c > 0)** to tell *Maple* that the constant is positive. Once you have entered this command, *Maple* will print out the constant c with a tilde after it, as $c\tilde{\ }$, to indicate that c is a *restricted* variable. To clear c, just type **c := 'c'.**)

(a) $\mathcal{L}(af + bg) = a\mathcal{L}(f) + b\mathcal{L}(g)$, where a and b are real numbers.

(b) $\mathcal{L}(u_c(t)f(t - c)) = e^{-cs}F(s)$

(c) $\mathcal{L}(e^{ct}f(t)) = F(s - c)$

(d) $\mathcal{L}(f') = sF(s) - f(0)$

(e) $\mathcal{L}(\int_0^t f(t - u)g(u)\,du) = F(s)G(s)$.

The function $t \to \int_0^t f(t - u)g(u)\,du$ is called the *convolution* of f and g, and is written $f * g$. Thus, the Laplace Transform changes convolution into ordinary multiplication.

11. For each of the following functions, compute the Laplace Transform. Then plot the function and its Laplace Transform over the interval $[0, 10]$. You may want to restrict the vertical range for some of the graphs, and to use different plot styles for the function and its Laplace Transform.

(a) $\sin t$

(b) $\exp t$

(c) $\dfrac{1}{t + 1}$

(d) $\cos t$

(e) $t \cos t$

(f) $u_1(t) \sin t$

On the basis of these graphs, what general conclusions can you draw about the Laplace Transform of a function? In particular, what can you say about the growth or decay of the Laplace Transform of a function? Can you justify your conclusion by looking at the integral formula for the Laplace Transform? (*Hint:* Look at the derivation of $\mathcal{L}(e^{at})$ on the second page of Chapter 11.)

12. This problem illustrates how the choice of method can dramatically affect the time it takes the computer to solve a differential equation. Consider the IVP

$$y'' + y' + y = t^2 e^{-t} \cos t, \qquad y(0) = 1, \qquad y'(0) = 0.$$

This problem could be solved by the method of undetermined coefficients, variation of parameters, or Laplace Transforms.

(a) Try to solve the IVP using **dsolve**. Execute the command **time()** before and after you execute **dsolve** to measure the amount of time *Maple* requires to solve the problem. (*Maple* uses the method of variation of parameters.)

(b) Now use **dsolve** with the option **method = laplace**. Once again, execute **time()** before and after you execute **dsolve**. How does the elapsed time compare to (a)?

(c) Define a new function $g(t)$ to be the output from part (b). Verify that g is a solution to the differential equation. (Don't forget **simplify**.)

(d) Now repeat part (b) with the symbolic initial conditions $y(0) = y0, y'(0) = y1$ (you need not keep track of time). Can *Maple* compute Laplace Transform solutions with symbolic initial conditions?

13. This problem illustrates the dangers of using the ordinary **dsolve** command on differential equations with discontinuous terms. (This problem was written for *Maple* V.3; later versions may give different results.) Consider the following IVP:

$$y'' + y' + \frac{5}{4}y = g(t), \quad y(0) = 0, \quad y'(0) = 0, \quad g(t) = \begin{cases} \sin t, & \text{if } 0 \leq t < \pi \\ 0, & \text{if } t \geq \pi. \end{cases}$$

(a) Solve this equation using **dsolve** (without **method = laplace**). Plot the solution on the interval $[0, 15]$.

(b) Check to see whether the function produced by **dsolve** is actually a solution by substituting it back into the differential equation. The expression you will get is quite complicated. Evaluate it numerically at $t = 0, 0.5$, and 1, to see if both sides of the equation are the same.

(c) Now solve the equation using **dsolve** with **method = laplace**. Plot the solution on $[0, 15]$. Check to see whether this solution is correct by substituting into the original equation.

(d) Find the general solution of the associated homogeneous equation. What is the asymptotic behavior of those solutions as $t \to \infty$? Knowing that the forcing term of the inhomogeneous equation is zero after $t = \pi$, what can you say about the long-term behavior of the solution of the inhomogeneous equation?

In *Maple* V.3, the **dsolve** command gives the wrong answer in part (a) because it uses the method of variation of parameters. The integrands involve discontinuous functions, and *Maple* computes the integrals incorrectly.

14. Use the Laplace Transform method to solve the following IVPs from Sections 6.4 and 6.5 of Boyce & DiPrima. Then graph the solution together with the function on the right hand side of the differential equation (the forcing function) on the interval $[0, 15]$.

(a) $y'' + 2y' + 2y = h(t)$, $\quad y(0) = 0$, $\quad y'(0) = 1$, $\quad h(t) = \begin{cases} 1, & \text{if } \pi \le t < 2\pi \\ 0, & \text{otherwise} \end{cases}$

(b) $y'' + 3y' + 2y = u_2(t)$, $\quad y(0) = 0$, $\quad y'(0) = 1$

(c) $y'' + y = \delta(t - \pi) \cos t$, $\quad y(0) = 0$, $\quad y'(0) = 1$

(d) $y'' + 2y' + 2y = \cos t + \delta(t - \pi/2)$, $\quad y(0) = 0$, $\quad y'(0) = 0$.

15. Use the Laplace Transform method to solve the following IVPs. Then graph the solution on an appropriate interval $(t > 0)$.

(a) $y'''(t) - y''(t) - y'(t) + y(t) = \delta(t - 1)$, $\quad y(0) = y''(0) = 0$, $\quad y'(0) = 1$

(b) $y^{(4)}(t) + 2y''(t) + y(t) = \sin t$, $\quad y(0) = 1$, $\quad y'(0) = y''(0) = y'''(0) = 0$

(c) $y^{(4)}(t) + 5y''(t) + 4y(t) = u_1(t) \sin(3t)$, $\quad y(0) = y'(0) = y''(0) = y'''(0) = 0$

(d) $y'''(t) + y''(t) + y'(t) = \delta(t - 1)$, $\quad y(0) = y''(0) = 0$, $\quad y'(0) = 1$.

Which of these equations has resonance-type behavior?

16. In this problem we investigate the effect of a periodic discontinuous forcing function (a square wave) on a second order linear equation with constant coefficients. Consider the initial value problem

$$y'' + y = h(t), \quad y(0) = 0, \, y'(0) = 1. \tag{i}$$

The associated homogeneous equation has natural period 2π; the general solution of the homogeneous equation is

$$y(t) = A \cos t + B \sin t.$$

Recall that the phenomenon of resonance occurs when the forcing function $h(t)$ is a linear combination of $\sin t$ and $\cos t$. Does resonance occur when the forcing function is periodic of period 2π but discontinuous?

(a) Using step functions, define a *Maple* function $h(t)$ on the interval $[0, 10\pi]$ whose value is $+1$ on $[0, \pi)$, -1 on $[\pi, 2\pi)$, $+1$ on $[2\pi, 3\pi)$, and so on. Plot the function on the interval $[0, 30]$. It should have the appearance of a square wave.

(b) Use **dsolve** with **method = laplace** to solve equation (i) with the function $h(t)$ defined in part (a). Plot the solution together with $h(t)$ on the interval $[0, 30]$. Do you see resonance? Compute and plot a numerical solution to confirm your answer.

(c) In part (a), we constructed a forcing function $h(t)$ with period 2π. The function $h(t/2)$ has period 4π. Repeat part (b) using the forcing function $h(t/2)$. Do you see resonance?

(d) Repeat part (b) using the forcing function $h(2t)$ (this time just plot from 0 to 15). Do you see resonance? What is the period of $h(2t)$?

(e) What can you conclude about the resonance effect for discontinuous forcing functions? Would you expect resonance to occur in equation (i) for *any* forcing function of period 2π? (*Hint*: The function $h(2t)$ has period π as well as period 2π.) Can you venture a guess about when resonance occurs for discontinuous periodic forcing functions? You might try some other periodic forcing functions to check your guess.

17. Do Problem 16 with a sawtooth wave instead of a square wave. More specifically, replace part (a) of Problem 16 with the following, and then do parts (b)–(e) of Problem 16.

(a) Using step functions, define a *Maple* function $h(t)$ on the interval $[0, 10\pi]$, with $h(t) = t$ on $[0, \pi)$, $h(t) = t - \pi$ on $[\pi, 2\pi)$, $h(t) = t - 2\pi$ on $[2\pi, 3\pi)$, and so on. Plot the function on the interval $[0, 30]$. It should have the appearance of a sawtooth wave.

18. This problem is based on Problem 35 in Section 6.2 of Boyce & DiPrima. Consider Bessel's equation
$$ty'' + y' + ty = 0.$$

We will use the Laplace Transform to find some leading terms of the power series expansion of the Bessel function of order zero that is continuous at the origin. Let $y(t)$ be such a solution of the equation, and suppose $Y(s)$ is its transform.

(a) By taking the Laplace Transform of the differential equation, show that $Y(s)$ satisfies the equation
$$(1 + s^2)Y'(s) + sY(s) = 0.$$

(b) Solve the equation in part (a) using **dsolve**. (Use $Y(0) = 1$.)

(c) Use the **series** command to expand the solution in part (b) in powers of $1/s$ out to terms of degree 12. (*Hint*: Expand around $s = \infty$.)

(d) Apply the inverse Laplace Transform to part (c) to obtain the power series expansion of y up to degree 10.

Chapter 12

Higher Order Equations and Systems of First Order Equations

First and second order differential equations arise naturally in many applications. For example, first order differential equations occur in models of population growth and radioactive decay, and second order equations in the study of the motion of a falling body or the motion of a pendulum. There are several techniques for solving special classes of first and second order equations. These techniques produce symbolic solutions, expressed by a formula. For equations that cannot be solved by any of these techniques, we use numerical, geometric, or qualitative methods to investigate solutions.

Equations of higher order, and systems of first order equations, also arise naturally. For example, third order equations come up in fluid dynamics; fourth order equations, in elasticity; and systems of first order equations, in the study of spring–mass systems with several springs and masses. For general higher order equations and systems, there are hardly any techniques for obtaining explicit formula solutions, and numerical, geometric, or qualitative techniques must be used. Nevertheless, for the special class of constant coefficient linear equations and first order linear systems, there are techniques for producing explicit solutions.

In this chapter, we consider higher order equations and first order systems. We outline the basic theory in the linear case. We show how to solve linear first order systems, first by using *Maple* to compute eigenpairs of the coefficient matrix, and then by using **dsolve**. In addition, we discuss the the plotting of phase portraits using *Maple*.

Higher Order Linear Equations

Consider the linear equation

$$y^{(n)} + p_1(x)y^{(n-1)} + \cdots + p_n(x)y = g(x), \qquad (1)$$

and assume the coefficient functions are continuous on the interval $a < x < b$. Then the following are true:

- If $y_1(x), y_2(x), \ldots, y_n(x)$ are n linearly independent solutions of the corresponding homogeneous equation,

$$y^{(n)} + p_1(x)y^{(n-1)} + \cdots + p_n(x)y = 0, \tag{2}$$

and if y_p is any particular solution of the inhomogeneous equation (1), then the general solutions of the equations (1), (2) are, respectively,

$$y = \sum_{i=1}^{n} C_i y_i(x) + y_p(x)$$

and

$$y = \sum_{i=1}^{n} C_i y_i(x).$$

- Given a point $x_0 \in (a, b)$ and initial values $y(x_0) = y_0$, $y'(x_0) = y_0'$, $\ldots$, $y^{(n-1)}(x_0) = y_0^{(n-1)}$, there is a unique solution to equation (1) that satisfies the initial data; the solution has n continuous derivatives and exists on the entire interval (a, b).

- A set of n solutions $y_1(x), y_2(x), \ldots, y_n(x)$ of (2) is linearly independent if and only if the Wronskian

$$W(y_1, y_2, \ldots, y_n) = \det \begin{pmatrix} y_1 & y_2 & \cdots & y_n \\ y_1' & y_2' & \cdots & y_n' \\ \vdots & \vdots & \ddots & \vdots \\ y_1^{(n-1)} & y_2^{(n-1)} & \cdots & y_n^{(n-1)} \end{pmatrix}$$

is nonzero at some point in (a, b); the collection $y_1, \ldots, y_n$ is called a *fundamental set* of solutions of (2).

We see that the general theory of higher order linear equations parallels that of first and second order equations. We note, however, that solutions may be difficult to construct. In practice, we can construct fundamental sets of solutions only for constant coefficient and Euler equations. In these cases, solutions can be constructed by considering trial solutions e^{rx} and x^r, as in the second order case. There is a difficulty even for these equations if n is large, since it is difficult to compute the roots of the characteristic polynomial. We can, however, use *Maple* to find good approximations to the roots.

The **dsolve** command can solve many homogeneous constant coefficient and Euler equations. You can confirm this by solving several linear equations of higher order from your text.

Systems of First Order Equations

Consider the general system of first order equations,

$$\begin{aligned}
x_1' &= F_1(t, x_1, x_2, \ldots, x_n) \\
x_2' &= F_2(t, x_1, x_2, \ldots, x_n) \\
&\vdots \\
x_n' &= F_n(t, x_1, x_2, \ldots, x_n).
\end{aligned} \tag{3}$$

Such systems arise in the study of spring–mass systems with many springs and masses, and in many other applications. Systems of first order equations also arise in the study of higher order equations. A single higher order differential equation

$$y^{(n)} = F(t, y, y', \ldots, y^{(n-1)}),$$

can be converted into a system of first order equations, simply by setting

$$x_1 = y, x_2 = y', \ldots, x_n = y^{(n-1)}.$$

The resulting system is

$$\begin{aligned}
x_1' &= x_2 \\
x_2' &= x_3 \\
&\vdots \\
x_{n-1}' &= x_n \\
x_n' &= F(t, x_1, x_2, \ldots, x_n).
\end{aligned}$$

It is not surprising that the problem of analyzing the general system (3) is quite formidable. Generally, the techniques we can bring to bear will be numerical, geometric, or qualitative. We shall discuss the application of these techniques to nonlinear equations in Chapter 13. For now, we merely observe that we can expect to make some progress toward a formula solution for *linear systems*. So, consider a linear system

$$\begin{aligned}
x_1' &= a_{11}(t)x_1 + \ldots + a_{1n}(t)x_n + b_1(t) \\
x_2' &= a_{21}(t)x_1 + \ldots + a_{2n}(t)x_n + b_2(t) \\
&\vdots \qquad \vdots \\
x_n' &= a_{n1}(t)x_1 + \ldots + a_{nn}(t)x_n + b_n(t).
\end{aligned}$$

We can write this system in matrix notation:

$$\mathbf{X}' = \mathbf{A}(t)\mathbf{X} + \mathbf{B}(t),$$

where

$$\mathbf{X} = \begin{pmatrix} x_1(t) \\ x_2(t) \\ \vdots \\ x_n(t) \end{pmatrix}, \qquad \mathbf{B} = \begin{pmatrix} b_1(t) \\ b_2(t) \\ \vdots \\ b_n(t) \end{pmatrix},$$

and

$$\mathbf{A} = \begin{pmatrix} a_{11}(t) & a_{12}(t) & \cdots & a_{1n}(t) \\ \vdots & \vdots & \ddots & \vdots \\ a_{n1}(t) & a_{n2}(t) & \cdots & a_{nn}(t) \end{pmatrix}.$$

There is a general theory for linear systems, which is completely parallel to the theory for linear differential equations. If $\mathbf{X}^{(1)}, \mathbf{X}^{(2)}, \ldots, \mathbf{X}^{(n)}$ is a family of linearly independent solutions, *i.e.*, a *fundamental set* of solutions, of the homogeneous equation (with $\mathbf{B} = 0$), and if $\mathbf{X}_p$ is a particular solution of the inhomogeneous equation, then the general solutions of these equations are, respectively,

$$\mathbf{X} = \sum_{i=1}^{n} C_i \mathbf{X}^{(i)}$$

and

$$\mathbf{X} = \sum_{i=1}^{n} C_i \mathbf{X}^{(i)} + \mathbf{X}_p.$$

The test for linear independence of n solutions is

$$\det(\mathbf{X}^{(1)} \ldots \mathbf{X}^{(n)}) \neq 0.$$

For linear systems, the constant coefficient case is the easiest to handle, just as it was for single linear equations. Consider the homogeneous linear system

$$\mathbf{X}' = \mathbf{A}\mathbf{X}, \tag{4}$$

where

$$\mathbf{A} = \begin{pmatrix} a_{11} & a_{12} & \cdots & a_{1n} \\ \vdots & \vdots & \ddots & \vdots \\ a_{n1} & a_{n2} & \cdots & a_{nn} \end{pmatrix}$$

is an $n \times n$ matrix of constants. We seek solutions of the form $\mathbf{X}(t) = \boldsymbol{\xi} e^{rt}$; note the similarity to the case of a single linear equation. We find that $\mathbf{X}(t)$ is a nonzero solution of (4) if and only if

$$\mathbf{A}\boldsymbol{\xi} = r\boldsymbol{\xi},$$

i.e., if and only if r is an eigenvalue of $\mathbf{A}$ and $\boldsymbol{\xi}$ is a corresponding eigenvector. We call the pair $r, \boldsymbol{\xi}$ an eigenpair. In order to explain how to construct a fundamental set of solutions, we have to consider three separate cases.

Case I. A has distinct real eigenvalues.

Let $r_1, r_2, \ldots, r_n$ be the distinct eigenvalues of $\mathbf{A}$, and let $\boldsymbol{\xi}^{(1)}, \boldsymbol{\xi}^{(2)}, \ldots, \boldsymbol{\xi}^{(n)}$ be corresponding eigenvectors. Then

$$\mathbf{X}^{(1)}(t) = \boldsymbol{\xi}^{(1)} e^{r_1 t}, \ldots, \mathbf{X}^{(n)}(t) = \boldsymbol{\xi}^{(n)} e^{r_n t}$$

is a fundamental set of solutions for (4), and

$$\mathbf{X}(t) = c_1 \boldsymbol{\xi}^{(1)} e^{r_1 t} + \cdots + c_n \boldsymbol{\xi}^{(n)} e^{r_n t}$$

is the general solution.

Case II. A has distinct eigenvalues, some of which are complex.

Since $\mathbf{A}$ is real, if $r, \boldsymbol{\xi}$ is a complex eigenpair, then the complex conjugate $\bar{r}, \bar{\boldsymbol{\xi}}$ is also an eigenpair. Thus, the corresponding solutions

$$\mathbf{X}^{(1)}(t) = \boldsymbol{\xi} e^{rt}, \ \mathbf{X}^{(2)}(t) = \bar{\boldsymbol{\xi}} e^{\bar{r}t}$$

are conjugate. Therefore, we can find two real solutions of (4) corresponding to the pair $r, \bar{r}$ by taking the real and imaginary parts of $\mathbf{X}^{(1)}(t)$ or $\mathbf{X}^{(2)}(t)$. Writing $\boldsymbol{\xi} = \mathbf{a} + i\mathbf{b}$, where a and b are real, and $r = \lambda + i\mu$, where λ and μ are real, we have

$$\begin{aligned} \mathbf{X}^{(1)}(t) &= (\mathbf{a} + i\mathbf{b})e^{(\lambda + i\mu)t} \\ &= (\mathbf{a} + i\mathbf{b})e^{\lambda t}(\cos \mu t + i \sin \mu t) \\ &= e^{\lambda t}(\mathbf{a} \cos \mu t - \mathbf{b} \sin \mu t) + i e^{\lambda t}(\mathbf{a} \sin \mu t + \mathbf{b} \cos \mu t). \end{aligned}$$

Thus, the vector functions

$$\mathbf{u}(t) = e^{\lambda t}(\mathbf{a} \cos \mu t - \mathbf{b} \sin \mu t)$$
$$\mathbf{v}(t) = e^{\lambda t}(\mathbf{a} \sin \mu t + \mathbf{b} \cos \mu t)$$

are real solutions to (4).

To keep the discussion simple, assume that $r_1 = \lambda + i\mu, r_2 = \lambda - i\mu$ are complex, and that $r_3, \ldots, r_n$ are real and distinct. Let the corresponding eigenvectors be $\boldsymbol{\xi}^{(1)} = \mathbf{a} + i\mathbf{b}, \boldsymbol{\xi}^{(2)} = \mathbf{a} - i\mathbf{b}, \boldsymbol{\xi}^{(3)}, \ldots, \boldsymbol{\xi}^{(n)}$. Then

$$\mathbf{u}(t), \mathbf{v}(t), \boldsymbol{\xi}^{(3)} e^{r_3 t}, \ldots, \boldsymbol{\xi}^{(n)} e^{r_n t}$$

is a fundamental set of solutions for (4). The general situation should now be clear.

Case III. A has repeated eigenvalues.

We restrict our discussion to the case $n = 2$. Suppose $r = \rho$ is an eigenvalue of $\mathbf{A}$ of multiplicity 2, meaning that ρ is a double root of the characteristic polynomial $\det(\mathbf{A} - r\mathbf{I})$. There are still two possibilities. If we can find two linearly independent eigenvectors $\boldsymbol{\xi}^{(1)}$ and $\boldsymbol{\xi}^{(2)}$ corresponding to ρ, then the solutions $\mathbf{X}^{(1)}(t) = \boldsymbol{\xi}^{(1)} e^{\rho t}$ and $\mathbf{X}^{(2)}(t) = \boldsymbol{\xi}^{(2)} e^{\rho t}$ form a fundamental set. The other possibility is that there is only one (linearly independent) eigenvector $\boldsymbol{\xi}$ with eigenvalue ρ. Then one solution of (4) is given by

$$\mathbf{X}^{(1)}(t) = \boldsymbol{\xi} e^{\rho t},$$

and a second by

$$\mathbf{X}^{(2)}(t) = \boldsymbol{\xi}te^{\rho t} + \boldsymbol{\eta}e^{\rho t},$$

where η satisfies

$$(\mathbf{A} - r\mathbf{I})\boldsymbol{\eta} = \boldsymbol{\xi}.$$

The vector η is called a generalized eigenvector of $\mathbf{A}$ for the eigenvalue ρ.

Using *Maple* to Find Eigenpairs

We now show how to use *Maple* to find the eigenpairs of a matrix, and thus to find fundamental sets of solutions and the general solution of a system of linear differential equations with constant coefficients. In order to manipulate matrices with *Maple*, you must first load the **linalg** package.

EXAMPLE 1. Consider the system

$$\mathbf{x}' = \begin{pmatrix} 3 & -2 & 0 \\ 2 & -2 & 0 \\ 0 & 1 & 1 \end{pmatrix} \mathbf{x}.$$

We enter the coefficient matrix in *Maple* as a list of lists:

with(linalg):
A := [[3, −2, 0], [2, −2, 0], [0, 1, 1]];

We can display $\mathbf{A}$ in standard matrix form using the command **matrix(A)**, which produces

$$\begin{array}{ccc} 3 & -2 & 0 \\ 2 & -2 & 0 \\ 0 & 1 & 1. \end{array}$$

We find the eigenpairs of $\mathbf{A}$ with the command **eigenvects(A)**, which produces

$$[-1, 1, \{[-1, -2, 1]\}], [1, 1, \{[0, 0, 1]\}], [2, 1, \{[2, 1, 1]\}].$$

The output of this command is a sequence; each entry of the sequence is a triple $[\rho, m, [eigenvectors]]$ consisting of an eigenvalue ρ, the number m of times it occurs, and a set of independent eigenvectors associated to it. In this example, the eigenpairs are

$$r_1 = -1, \; \boldsymbol{\xi}^{(1)} = \begin{pmatrix} -1 \\ -2 \\ 1 \end{pmatrix}$$

$$r_2 = 1, \; \boldsymbol{\xi}^{(2)} = \begin{pmatrix} 0 \\ 0 \\ 1 \end{pmatrix}$$

$$r_3 = 2, \; \boldsymbol{\xi}^{(3)} = \begin{pmatrix} 2 \\ 1 \\ 1 \end{pmatrix}.$$

Thus, a fundamental set of solutions is

$$\mathbf{X}^{(1)}(t) = \begin{pmatrix} -1 \\ -2 \\ 1 \end{pmatrix} e^{-t}, \quad \mathbf{X}^{(2)}(t) = \begin{pmatrix} 0 \\ 0 \\ 1 \end{pmatrix} e^{t}, \quad \mathbf{X}^{(3)}(t) = \begin{pmatrix} 2 \\ 1 \\ 1 \end{pmatrix} e^{2t},$$

and the general solution is

$$\mathbf{x}(t) = c_1 \begin{pmatrix} -1 \\ -2 \\ 1 \end{pmatrix} e^{-t} + c_2 \begin{pmatrix} 0 \\ 0 \\ 1 \end{pmatrix} e^{t} + c_3 \begin{pmatrix} 2 \\ 1 \\ 1 \end{pmatrix} e^{2t}.$$

Suppose we are seeking the specific solution with initial value

$$\mathbf{x}(0) = \begin{pmatrix} 3 \\ 5 \\ 0 \end{pmatrix}.$$

The constants c_1, c_2, and c_3 must satisfy

$$c_1 \begin{pmatrix} -1 \\ -2 \\ 1 \end{pmatrix} + c_2 \begin{pmatrix} 0 \\ 0 \\ 1 \end{pmatrix} + c_3 \begin{pmatrix} 2 \\ 1 \\ 1 \end{pmatrix} = \begin{pmatrix} -1 & 0 & 2 \\ -2 & 0 & 1 \\ 1 & 1 & 1 \end{pmatrix} \begin{pmatrix} c_1 \\ c_2 \\ c_3 \end{pmatrix} = \begin{pmatrix} 3 \\ 5 \\ 0 \end{pmatrix}.$$

To solve this linear system, we use the command **linsolve**. Let **m** be the coefficient matrix and let **b** be the right-hand side:

  m := [[–1, 0, 2], [–2, 0, 1], [1, 1, 1]];   b := [3, 5, 0];

(Note that the columns of the matrix **m** are the eigenvectors of **A**.) Then to solve the system we type **linsolve(m, b)**, which produces $[-\frac{7}{3}, 2, \frac{1}{3}]$. Thus the solution of the linear system is $c_1 = -7/3$, $c_2 = 2$, $c_3 = 1/3$, and the solution to our initial value problem is

$$\mathbf{x}(t) = -\frac{7}{3} \begin{pmatrix} -1 \\ -2 \\ 1 \end{pmatrix} e^{-t} + 2 \begin{pmatrix} 0 \\ 0 \\ 1 \end{pmatrix} e^{t} + \frac{1}{3} \begin{pmatrix} 2 \\ 1 \\ 1 \end{pmatrix} e^{2t}.$$

EXAMPLE 2. Consider the system

$$\mathbf{x}' = \begin{pmatrix} 3 & -2 \\ 4 & -1 \end{pmatrix} \mathbf{x} \qquad \text{(Boyce \& DiPrima, Sect. 7.6, Prob. 1).}$$

We set **B := [[3, –2], [4, –1]]**, and find the eigenpairs with **eigenvects(B)**, which produces

$$[RootOf(\_Z^2 - 2\_Z + 5), 1, [[1, -\frac{1}{2} RootOf(\_Z^2 - 2\_Z + 5) + \frac{3}{2}]]].$$

As you can see, the **eigenvects** command sometimes prefers not to solve the quadratic equation when it is performing exact arithmetic. You can tell it to solve completely with the option **'radical'** (see the online help for **eigenvects**). You can also circumvent this behavior by forcing *Maple* to work numerically. A single decimal point suffices:

B := [[3.0, −2] [4, −1]]:   eigenvects(B);

$$[1.0 - 2.0I, 1, \{[-0.5 - 0.5I, -I]\}], \quad [1.0 + 2.0I, 1, \{[-0.5 + 0.5I, I]\}]$$

It is sometimes convenient to replace an eigenvector by a constant multiple of itself. In this case, we will multiply the first eigenvector by I and the second by $-I$ to make their second entries equal to 1. After this transformation, we get the eigenpairs

$$1 - 2i, \ \begin{pmatrix} \frac{1}{2} - \frac{1}{2}i \\ 1 \end{pmatrix}$$

and

$$1 + 2i, \ \begin{pmatrix} \frac{1}{2} + \frac{1}{2}i \\ 1 \end{pmatrix}.$$

Note that the second pair is the complex conjugate of the first. Thus a complex fundamental set is

$$\mathbf{X}^{(1)}(t) = \begin{pmatrix} \frac{1}{2} - \frac{1}{2}i \\ 1 \end{pmatrix} e^{(1-2i)t}, \quad \mathbf{X}^{(2)}(t) = \begin{pmatrix} \frac{1}{2} + \frac{1}{2}i \\ 1 \end{pmatrix} e^{(1+2i)t}.$$

The real and imaginary parts of the solution can be extracted by hand, or by using the *Maple* commands **evalc**, **Re**, and **Im**, as in

map(x −> evalc(Re(x*exp((1 − 2*I)*t))), [1/2 − 1/2*I, 1]):
map(x −> evalc(Im(x*exp((1 − 2*I)*t))), [1/2 − 1/2*I, 1]):

Either way, we see that a fundamental set of real solutions is

$$\mathbf{u}(t) = e^t \left[\begin{pmatrix} \frac{1}{2} \\ 1 \end{pmatrix} \cos 2t + \begin{pmatrix} -\frac{1}{2} \\ 0 \end{pmatrix} \sin 2t \right]$$

$$\mathbf{v}(t) = e^t \left[- \begin{pmatrix} \frac{1}{2} \\ 1 \end{pmatrix} \sin 2t + \begin{pmatrix} -\frac{1}{2} \\ 0 \end{pmatrix} \cos 2t \right].$$

EXAMPLE 3. Consider the system

$$\mathbf{x}' = \begin{pmatrix} 3 & -4 \\ 1 & -1 \end{pmatrix} \mathbf{x} \qquad \text{(Boyce \& DiPrima, Sect. 7.7, Prob. 1).}$$

We set **A := [[3, −4], [1, −1]]**. The command **eigenvects(A)** produces

$$[1, 2, \{[2, 1]\}].$$

Even though *Maple* reports that 1 is an eigenvalue with multiplicity 2, it could only find one corresponding eigenvector. Thus $\rho = 1$ and $\boldsymbol{\xi} = \begin{pmatrix} 2 \\ 1 \end{pmatrix}$, and

$$\mathbf{X}^{(1)}(t) = \begin{pmatrix} 2 \\ 1 \end{pmatrix} e^t$$

is one solution. To find a second solution we solve

$$(\mathbf{A} - \rho\mathbf{I})\eta = \begin{pmatrix} 2 & -4 \\ 1 & -2 \end{pmatrix} \eta = \xi = \begin{pmatrix} 2 \\ 1 \end{pmatrix}.$$

Let **m** := [[2, –4], [1, –2]] be the coefficient matrix, and let **b** := [2, 1] be the right-hand side. Then **linsolve(m, b)** produces

$$[2\_t_1 + 1 \quad \_t_1].$$

We can choose one of the infinitely many solutions by taking $\_t_1 = 0$, so

$$\eta = \begin{pmatrix} 1 \\ 0 \end{pmatrix}.$$

Thus, a second solution is

$$\mathbf{X}^{(2)}(t) = \xi t e^{\rho t} + \eta e^{\rho t} = \begin{pmatrix} 2 \\ 1 \end{pmatrix} t e^t + \begin{pmatrix} 1 \\ 0 \end{pmatrix} e^t.$$

The general solution is

$$\mathbf{X}(t) = c_1 \begin{pmatrix} 2 \\ 1 \end{pmatrix} e^t + c_2 \left[\begin{pmatrix} 2 \\ 1 \end{pmatrix} t e^t + \begin{pmatrix} 1 \\ 0 \end{pmatrix} e^t \right].$$

We have shown how to use *Maple*'s linear algebra commands to find eigenpairs, and thus solutions, for linear systems of differential equations with constant co-efficients. The solutions to systems of linear equations can also be found with a direct application of **dsolve**.

EXAMPLE. Consider the system $x' = y$, $y' = -x$. To find its general solution, you would type

   dsolve({diff(x(t), t) = y(t), diff(y(t), t) = −x(t)}, {x(t), y(t)});

The result is

$$x(t) = e^{-it}[c_1 + c_1 e^{2it} + c_2 i - c_2 i e^{2it}]/2$$
$$y(t) = e^{-it}[-c_1 i + c_1 i e^{2it} + c_2 + c_2 e^{2it}]/2.$$

To solve the same system with initial conditions $x(0) = 1$, $y(0) = 0$, you would type

   dsolve({diff(x(t), t) = y(t), diff(y(t), t) = −x(t), x(0) = 1, y(0) = 0}, {x(t), y(t)});

Both methods for solving linear systems are useful. Solving in terms of the eigenpairs of the coefficient matrix is somewhat involved, but yields a simple and useful formula for the solution. The eigenpairs contain valuable information about the solution, which we will exploit further in Problem Set F. On the other hand, it is simpler to use **dsolve**, and for many purposes the solutions generated by **dsolve** are completely satisfactory. We note, however, that **dsolve** sometimes presents the solution in a rather complicated form, as in the example above.

Here are some examples on which you can practice:

(a) $x' = -3x + 2y$, $y' = -x$

(b) $x' = x - 2y$, $y' = -x$

(c) $x' = x + 2y$, $y' = -x$.

Phase Portraits

A solution of a 2×2 linear system is a pair of funtions $x(t)$, $y(t)$. The plot of a solution as a function of t would be a curve in (t, x, y)-space. Generally, such 3-dimensional plots are too complicated to be illuminating. Therefore, we project the curve from 3-dimensional space into the (x, y)-plane. This plane is called the *phase plane*, and the resulting curve in the phase plane is called a *trajectory*. A trajectory is drawn by plotting $(x(t), y(t))$ as the parameter t varies. A plot of a family of trajectories is called a *phase portrait* of the system.

A trajectory is an example of a *parametrized curve*. The *Maple* **plot** command will automatically display **[x(t), y(t), t = a..b]** as a parametric curve. In this section, we describe how to use *Maple*: (1) to solve an initial value problem consisting of a linear system and an initial condition, and plot the corresponding trajectory; (2) to solve a linear system using **dsolve** and draw a phase portrait; (3) to solve a system numerically and draw a phase portrait.

Plotting a Single Trajectory.   Consider the linear system in Example (a) above, with initial condition $x(0) = 1$, $y(0) = 0$. We want to plot the trajectory with this initial condition. First we enter the initial value problem.

   ivp := {diff(x(t), t) = −3*x(t) + 2*y(t), diff(y(t), t) = −x(t), x(0) = 1, y(0) = 0};

Then we type the following:

   solivp := dsolve(ivp, {x(t), y(t)});
   parasol := unapply(subs(solivp, [x(t), y(t), t = trange]), trange);
   traj := trange −> plot(parasol(trange));

This program does two things. First, it produces the solution, **solivp**, of the initial value problem. This solution is a set of equations describing the dependent variables x and y as functions of t. The parametric solution, **parasol**, converts the form of the solution into parametric equations that can be fed into the **plot** command. Next, it defines a function **traj** that plots the trajectory corresponding to **solivp**. The function **traj** takes one argument, a range specifying the endpoints of the time interval for the trajectory. Figure 1 contains the picture generated by the command **traj(−0.3..5)**. To use this program to plot the solution of a different initial value problem, all you have to do is modify the definition of **ivp** appropriately.

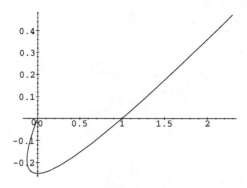

Figure 1

Plotting Several Trajectories. Consider the linear system in Example (b) above. We want to plot trajectories of this system with various initial conditions $x(0) = a$, $y(0) = b$. We can do this by modifying the program above to solve this system with initial conditions $x(0) = a, y(0) = b$.

> **ivp := {diff(x(t), t) = x(t) − 2*y(t), diff(y(t), t) = −x(t), x(0) = a, y(0) = b};**
> **solivp := dsolve(ivp, {x(t), y(t)});**
> **parasol := unapply(subs(solivp, [x(t), y(t), t = trange]), a, b, trange);**

The function **parasol** depends on the initial values a and b and the range of the independent variable. For example, **parasol(1, 2, −3..3)** is a parametric curve, defined for $-3 \le t \le 3$ and determined by the initial values $x(0) = 1$, $y(0) = 2$. Next we define a function **phase** that plots a phase portrait of the linear system. We do this by creating a set of parametric solutions with different initial conditions and passing them to the **plot** command.

> **phase := trange −> plot({seq(seq(parasol(a, b, trange), a = −2..2), b = −2..2)});**

Note that we have chosen a rectangular grid of 25 initial conditions, with a ranging from -2 to 2 and b ranging from -2 to 2 (in integer increments).

To use the function **phase**, simply enter **phase(t0..t1)**, where $t0$ and $t1$ are the endpoints of the time interval $[t0, t1]$ for which you wish to plot the trajectories. This will plot 25 trajectories corresponding to the 25 different initial conditions. The time interval $[t0, t1]$ must be chosen somewhat carefully; a small time interval could result in solution curves that are too short to get an idea of where they're headed, while a large time interval could cause the scale of the graph to get very large, resulting in solution curves that are squeezed together. Moreover, the larger the time interval, the longer it will take for *Maple* to produce the plot. You should start with a small time interval like $[-1, 1]$, and then adjust the interval to get a satisfactory picture. The command **phase(−2..1)** generated the phase portrait shown in Figure 2.

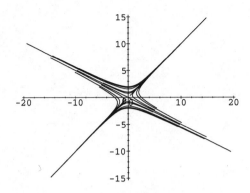

Figure 2

You should be able to plot the phase portraits for any 2×2 linear system with constant coefficients using the procedure above, replacing the differential equations in the definition of **ivp**, and choosing, by trial and error, an appropriate time interval to use with the function **phase**. By combining the phase portrait with a plot of the vector field (see Chapter 13), you should be able to determine the direction of increasing t on the curves. Also, in each case you should be able to decide whether the origin is a *sink* (all solutions approach the origin as t increases), *source* (all solutions move away from the origin), *saddle point* (solutions approach the origin along one direction, then move away from the origin in another direction), or *center* (solutions follow closed curves around the origin).

The procedure for plotting a phase portrait must be modified slightly if you wish to vary only one parameter in the initial data. For example, the program

```
ivp := {diff(x(t), t) = x(t) + 2*y(t), diff(y(t), t) = -x(t), x(0) = a, y(0) = 0};
solivp := dsolve(ivp, {x(t), y(t)});
parasol := unapply(subs(solivp, [x(t), y(t), t = trange]), a, trange);
phase := trange -> plot({seq(parasol(a, trange), a = -4..4)});
```

will yield (upon entering **phase(−4..3)**) the nine curves shown in Figure 3 as a phase portrait for Example (c). (Count the curves! One of the solutions is the equilibrium solution $x(t) = 0, y(t) = 0$.)

Plotting Trajectories of Numerical Solutions. The symbolic solver **dsolve** should be able to solve any homogeneous 2×2 linear system with constant coefficients. For inhomogeneous linear systems, linear systems with variable coefficients, and nonlinear systems, **dsolve** will generally not do the job. In these situations, we turn to the numerical solver **dsolve(..., numeric)**.

A naive approach to using **dsolve(..., numeric)** would be to simply replace **dsolve** with **dsolve(..., numeric)** in the programs above. This will not work,

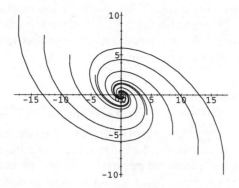

Figure 3

because **dsolve(. . ., numeric)** must have numerical values for the initial conditions before it is evaluated. To circumvent this problem you must prevent *Maple* from evaluating the numerical solution until the initial conditions are available. Here is an example that uses **dsolve(. . ., numeric)** on the linear system in Example (b) above.

> **des := diff(x(t), t) = x(t) − 2*y(t), diff(y(t), t) = −x(t);**
> **numsol := (a, b) −> dsolve({des, x(0) = a, y(0) = b}, {x(t), y(t)},**
> **numeric, maxfun = 1000);**

You cannot apply the plot function **phase** defined above for **dsolve** to produce a phase portrait—the output of **dsolve(. . ., numeric)** is not a set of equations for $x(t)$ and $y(t)$. Instead, it is a procedure that, when evaluated at any number t, returns a set of equations for the corresponding x and y values. We have to modify our program to replace the command to **plot** a set of parametric curves with a command to **display** a set of graphs produced by **odeplot**. We can define

> **curve := (a, b, range) −> odeplot(numsol(a, b), [x(t), y(t)], range);**
> **nphase := range −> display({seq(seq(curve(a, b, range),**
> **a = −2..2), b = −2..2)}, view = [−20..20, −15..15]);**

and run the command **nphase(−3..3)** to produce a phase portrait similar to Figure 2. Note that the x and y ranges must be explicitly given with the option **view** of the **display** command; otherwise, due to a peculiarity of **odeplot**, the x range of the graph will be the same as the t range specified by **range**.

With the above scheme, you can evaluate the numerical solution for particular initial conditions a, b at a particular value $t = t_1$ by using the command

> **numsol(a, b)(t1);**

If you do not need to see the values of the functions, *Maple* has a simpler method for producing phase portraits. The **DEplot** command (which is in the **DEtools** package) was introduced in Chapter 7 for plotting numerical solutions to a single differential equation. (See also Chapter 8 for some additional hints about using **DEplot**.) With a slightly different syntax, **DEplot** can also be used for systems of differential equations. For example, you can type

> **with(DEtools):**
> **iniset := {seq(seq([0, a, b], a = −2..2), b = −2..2)};**
> **pphase := trange −> DEplot([des], [x, y], trange, iniset, stepsize = 0.1);**

It is important to type only [**x, y**], not [**x(t), y(t)**]. The 0 in the initial conditions **iniset** represents the initial value of the independent variable t. Once **pphase** has been defined as above, the command **pphase(−1..1)** will produce a phase portrait. (Recall that it is wise to use the **DEplot** option **stepsize** in order to ensure that the step size used to compute the numerical solution remains small even when the range given for t is large.)

To limit the x and y ranges of the graph, say to [−5, 5] in each direction, you can use the **DEplot** options **x = −5..5** and **y = −5..5**. When you do so, another useful option is **limitrange = true**. This tells **DEplot** to stop computing the numerical trajectories once they leave the specified rectangle, which can make the command run much faster and, in the case of nonlinear equations, can eliminate error messages due to trajectories that blow up in finite time. For example, the command

> **DEplot([des], [x, y], −10..10, iniset, stepsize = 0.1,**
> **x = −5..5, y = −5..5, limitrange = true);**

should produce a good phase portrait in a reasonable amount of time even though the t range specified, [−10, 10], is much larger than it needs to be for the given x and y ranges. Note that the option **limitrange = true** may not be advisable in all cases, especially when the trajectories do a lot of spiraling, because the resulting plot will be incomplete for trajectories that leave and then return to the specified rectangle.

Finally, we note that **DEplot** also works for systems of more than two equations (though this is not documented in the online help), and for time-dependent (nonautonomous) systems. In the latter case, the independent variable t must be given as the first variable in the second argument to **DEplot** (for example, [**t, x, y**] rather than [**x, y**]). When more than two variables are specified in this argument, the option **scene** can be used to specify a pair of variables to plot. For example, you can get a plot of x versus t for a trajectory of the above system by typing

> **DEplot([des], [t, x, y], −3..3, {[0, 1, 1]}, stepsize = 0.1, scene = [t, x], x = −5..5);**

Note that even though the system **des** is not time-dependent, the variable t must be given in the second argument to **DEplot** in order for *Maple* to know that the t in the option **scene** means the independent variable for this system.

REMARK. *Maple* has a command **phaseportrait** (in the **DEtools** package) for plotting phase portraits; however, it is basically a restricted version of **DEplot** with less functionality. We recommend using **DEplot** rather than **phaseportrait**.

Chapter 13

Qualitative Theory for Systems of Differential Equations

In this chapter, we extend the qualitative theory of autonomous differential equations from single equations to systems of two equations. Thus, consider a system of the form

$$\begin{cases} x' = F(x, y) \\ y' = G(x, y). \end{cases} \tag{1}$$

We assume the functions F and G have continuous partial derivatives everywhere in the plane, and the critical points—the common zeros of F and G—are isolated.

We know from the fundamental existence and uniqueness theorems that, corresponding to any choice of initial data (x_0, y_0), there is a unique pair of functions $x(t)$, $y(t)$ that satisfy the system (1) of differential equations and the initial conditions $x(0) = x_0$, $y(0) = y_0$. Taken together, this pair of functions parametrizes a curve, or trajectory, in the *phase plane* that passes through the point (x_0, y_0). Since we are dealing with autonomous systems (*i.e.*, the variable t does not appear on the right side of (1)), the solution curves are *independent of the starting time*. That is, if we consider initial conditions $x(t_0) = x_0$, $y(t_0) = y_0$, then we get the same solution curve with a time delay of t_0 units. Moreover, we also know that two distinct trajectories cannot intersect. Thus, the plane is covered by the family of trajectories; the plot of these curves is the *phase portrait* of (1).

As we know, we can find explicit formula solutions $x(t)$, $y(t)$ only for simple systems. Thus, we are forced to turn to qualitative and numerical methods. It is our purpose here to discuss qualitative techniques for studying the solutions of (1).

In most cases of physical interest, every solution curve behaves in one of the following ways:

 (i) The curve consists of a single critical point;
 (ii) The curve tends to a critical point as $t \to \infty$;
 (iii) The curve is unbounded: the distance from $(x(t), y(t))$ to the origin becomes arbitrarily large as $t \to \infty$, or as $t \to t^*$, for some finite t^*;
 (iv) The curve is periodic: the parametric functions satisfy $x(t + t_p) = x(t)$, $y(t + t_p) = y(t)$ for some fixed t_p;
 (v) The curve approaches a periodic solution, *e.g.*, spiraling in on a circle.

Qualitative techniques may be able to identify the kinds of solutions that appear. In order to keep matters simple, we try to answer the following specific questions:

(1) What can we say about the critical points? Can we make a qualitative guess about their nature and stability? Can we deduce anything about the solution curves that start out close to the critical points?

(2) Can we predict anything about the long-term behavior of the solution curves? This includes those near critical points as well as the solution curves in general.

The list of possible limiting behaviors of solution curves is based on the Poincaré-Bendixson Theorem (*cf.* Theorem 9.7.3 in Boyce & DiPrima), which is valid for autonomous systems of two equations. Systems of three or more equations can have much more complicated limiting behavior. For example, solution curves can remain bounded and yet fail to approach any equilibrium or periodic state as $t \to \infty$. This phenomenon, called "chaos" by mathematicians, was anticipated by Poincaré (and perhaps even earlier by the physicist Maxwell), but most scientists did not appreciate how widespread chaos is until the arrival of computers. See Problem 13 in Problem Set F for an example.

There are two qualitative methods for analyzing systems of equations: one based on the idea of a *vector field*; and the other based on the principle of *linearized stability*. The latter method is treated in detail in Sections 9.3–9.5 of Boyce & DiPrima; it provides information about the stability of critical points of a nonlinear system by studying associated linear systems. In this chapter, we focus on the former method: the use of vector fields in qualitative analysis. Some of the problems in Problem Set F involve linearized stability analysis.

Here is the basic idea. For any solution curve $(x(t), y(t))$, and any point t, we have the differential equations

$$\begin{cases} x'(t) = F(x(t), y(t)) \\ y'(t) = G(x(t), y(t)). \end{cases}$$

If we employ vector notation

$$\mathbf{x}(t) = \begin{pmatrix} x(t) \\ y(t) \end{pmatrix}, \quad \mathbf{f}(\mathbf{x}) = \begin{pmatrix} F(\mathbf{x}) \\ G(\mathbf{x}) \end{pmatrix},$$

then the system is written

$$\mathbf{x}' = \mathbf{f}(\mathbf{x}).$$

Moreover, the vector $\mathbf{x}'(t) = \mathbf{f}(\mathbf{x}(t))$ is just the tangent vector to the curve $\mathbf{x}(t)$. Since knowledge of the collection of tangent vectors to the solution curves would give a good idea of the curves themselves, it would be useful to have a plot of these vectors. Thus, corresponding to any vector $\mathbf{x}$, we draw the vector $\mathbf{f}(\mathbf{x})$, translated so that its foot is at the point $\mathbf{x}$. This plot is called the vector field of the system (1). Since we cannot do this at every point of the phase plane, we only draw the vectors at a set of regularly chosen points. Then we step back and look at the resulting vector field. We do not have the solution curves sketched, but we do have a representative collection of their tangent vectors. From the tangent vectors, we can get a good idea of the curves themselves. Indeed, we can often answer the questions above by a careful examination of the vector field.

Vector fields can be drawn by hand for simple systems, but the command **fieldplot** can draw vector fields of any first order system of two equations. We illustrate the use of this command by examining two specific systems, namely

$$\begin{cases} x' = x(1 - x - y) \\ y' = y(0.75 - 0.5x - y); \end{cases} \tag{2}$$

and

$$\begin{cases} x' = x(5 - x - y) \\ y' = y(-2 + x). \end{cases} \tag{3}$$

System (2) is a competing species model that is discussed in Boyce & DiPrima in Section 9.4, Example 1. System (3) is a predator-prey model from Section 7.4 of Edwards & Penney, **Elementary Differential Equations with Applications**, 3rd edition, Prentice-Hall, Inc., 1994.

The **fieldplot** command is contained in the **plots** package. The syntax of the command is

fieldplot([F(x, y), G(x, y)], x = x0..x1, y = y0..y1, (options));

We first consider system (2). To draw the vector field we enter

fieldplot([x*(1 − x − y), y*(0.75 − 0.5*x − y)], x = 0..1.1, y = 0..0.8, arrows = SLIM, axes = BOXED);

The result is shown in Figure 1.

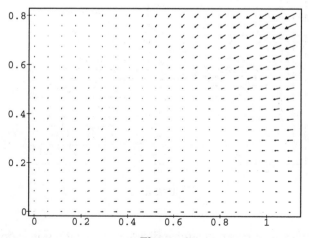

Figure 1

In a vector field, the vector at the point $\mathbf{x} = (x, y)$ is $\mathbf{f}(\mathbf{x})$, indicating both the direction and length of $\mathbf{f}(\mathbf{x})$. The vector at $\mathbf{x}$ drawn by **fieldplot** faithfully represents the direction of $\mathbf{f}(\mathbf{x})$ but, for the sake of visual effectiveness, its length is only proportional to the length of $\mathbf{f}(\mathbf{x})$. The critical, or equilibrium, points are those points at which the vector field vanishes, *i.e.*, those points where $F(x, y) = G(x, y) = 0$. Thus, the vectors are very short near the critical points. In the plot above we can approximately identify the critical points, but it is difficult to see the directions of the very short vectors near the critical points.

A simple way to see the directions of vectors near the critical points is to replace the **fieldplot** command with the **dfieldplot** command. This command is contained in the **DEtools** package; we used it previously to plot the direction field of a single first order differential equation. It produces plots in which every vector has the same length. The drawback, of course, is that it may be harder to locate the critical points (since there are no short arrows); the compensating benefit is that you can see the directions more clearly.

Here is the command we use to plot the "equal length" vector field.

> **dfieldplot([x*(1 − x − y), y*(0.75 − 0.5*x − y)], [x, y], 0..1, x = 0..1.5, y = 0..1, arrows = SLIM, axes = BOXED);**

(The third argument **0..1** specifies a range for t; this is irrelevant to the vector field plotted in this example but the syntax of **dfieldplot** requires that some range be specified.) The result is shown in Figure 2.

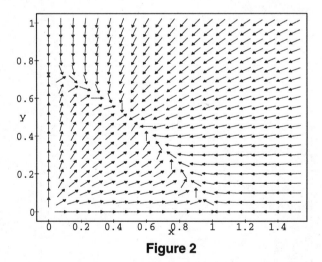

Figure 2

This picture gives us a much clearer indication of what's going on, but it still doesn't allow us to identify the critical points precisely. To do this we actually have to solve the equations $x' = 0$ and $y' = 0$ simultaneously. We can do this with the **solve** command,

> **solve({x*(1 − x − y) = 0, y*(0.75 − 0.5*x − y) = 0}, {x, y});**

which produces the answer

$$\{x = 0.500, y = 0.500\}, \{x = 0, y = 0.750\}, \{y = 0, x = 1.\}, \{x = 0, y = 0\}$$

Thus, the critical points are $(0,0)$, $(0, 0.75)$, $(1, 0)$, and $(0.5, 0.5)$. Knowing the critical points, we can deduce from the vector field that $(0, 0)$ is an unstable node, $(0, 0.75)$ and $(1, 0)$ are unstable saddle points, and $(0.5, 0.5)$ is an asymptotically stable node. Solutions starting near the saddle points (but not on the axes) tend away from them, and those starting near the point $(0.5, 0.5)$ tend toward it. In fact, the vector field strongly suggests that every solution curve starting in the first quadrant (but not on the axes) tends toward $(0.5, 0.5)$. Hence $(0.5, 0.5)$, which corresponds to equal populations, is apparently the limiting state that all positive solutions approach as t increases. We have thus answered both questions (1) and (2) on the basis of the vector field. Figure 3 provides a closer look at the vector field near the point $(0.5, 0.5)$.

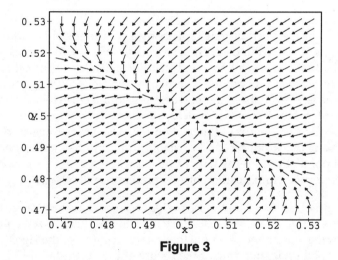

Figure 3

Now consider the predator-prey system (3). Here $x(t)$ represents the population of prey and $y(t)$ the population of predators. The critical points of this system are $(0, 0), (5, 0), (2, 3)$. As in system (2), our goal is to use the vector field to answer questions (1) and (2). Here is the appropriate *Maple* command :

> **dfieldplot([x*(5 − x − y), y*(−2 + x)], [x, y], 0..1, x = 0..6, y = 0..4,**

axes = BOXED, arrows = SLIM);

The output is shown in Figure 4.

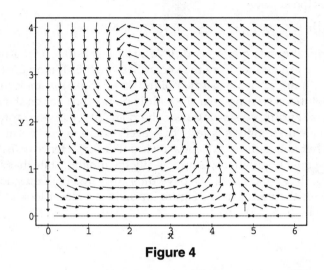

Figure 4

It is evident from the portrait that $(0,0)$ and $(5,0)$ are unstable saddle points and that solutions spiral around $(2,3)$. The vectors near $(2,3)$ suggest that the solutions spiral into $(2,3)$, and a linearized stability analysis confirms that $(2,3)$ is an asymptotically stable spiral point. In particular, solutions starting near the first two critical points tend away from them, whereas solution curves starting near the latter tend toward it. In fact, the vector field suggests strongly that every solution curve starting in the first quadrant (but not on the axes) tends toward the critical point $(2,3)$. This is the strongest kind of stable equilibrium—namely, no matter what the initial populations are, as long as they are both positive, the population tends toward the equilibrium position of 40% predators and 60% prey.

Remarks.   We indicated above that vector fields could be drawn by hand. It would be difficult, however, to draw as satisfactory a vector field as we have produced with *Maple*. On the other hand, we note that a careful study of the signs of F and G can lead to a good understanding of the nature of the vector field. This is done for Example (2) in Section 9.4 in Boyce & DiPrima. See in particular Figures 9.4.1 and 9.4.2 there.

The essential idea in Chapter 6 for a single autonomous first order equation

$$x' = f(x)$$

is to determine the qualitative nature of the solutions purely on the basis of the sign of $f(x)$ for various x's. Actually, we have done the same thing here: namely, determine the qualitative nature of the solutions (trajectories) of a system from information on the signs of F and G.

As mentioned above, according to the principle of linearized stability, the nature of critical points for nonlinear systems can be deduced from the associated linear systems. If the point is asymptotically stable for the associated linear system (the case if the eigenvalues are negative, or have negative real parts), then the point is asymptotically stable for the original nonlinear system. If it is unstable for the linear system, it is unstable for the nonlinear system. Centers are ambiguous. This analysis is valid in exactly the same way for a single equation. Suppose $\bar{x}$ is a critical point for $x' = f(x)$. Then letting $u(t) = x(t) - \bar{x}$, we see that

$$u' = f(u + \bar{x}) \approx f(\bar{x}) + f'(\bar{x})u = f'(\bar{x})u,$$

so the associated linear equation is $u' = f'(\bar{x})u$. The solutions are $u(t) = ce^{\lambda t}$, where $\lambda = f'(\bar{x})$. Therefore, $x(t) = \bar{x} + ce^{\lambda t}$. It is clear that $\bar{x}$ is asymptotically stable if $\lambda < 0$ and unstable if $\lambda > 0$. The same is true of the nonlinear system (with the situation for $\lambda = 0$ being ambiguous). Thus, we see that this assessment of stability parallels the situation for systems.

Conclusion.   Solutions of systems can be calculated with **dsolve(..., numeric)** and their trajectories plotted. Suggestions on convenient ways to do this are made in Chapter 12. Taken together, the information provided by a vector field, by a plot of the trajectories, and by linearized stability analyses, gives a complete understanding of the behavior of the solutions of a system of two first order equations. The information provided by these three approaches is similar, but each approach yields information the other approaches don't provide. For example, a vector field provides a good global indication of what the phase portrait will look like, as well as indicating the approximate location of the critical points and their type; a plot of the trajectories gives a precise indication of the solution curves; and a linearized stability analysis determines the type of the critical points.

In using these approaches to study a system, it is almost always best to start with a vector field plot or with linearized stability analyses. Typically, it takes a long time to plot trajectories of nonlinear systems. But by using the information from a vector field plot or from linearized stability analyses you can choose appropriate initial data points to use with **dsolve(..., numeric)**. A vector field plot will also help you choose an appropriate time interval (*e.g.*, positive or negative time).

Problem Set F

Systems of Equations

A number of suggestions for using *Maple* to solve these problems may be found in Chapter 12. The parameters in those suggestions may need to be modified according to the problem at hand. In particular, you may have to change the time interval or the set of initial conditions.

1. In this problem, we study three systems of equations taken from Boyce & DiPrima:

$$\mathbf{x}' = \begin{pmatrix} 2 & -1 \\ 3 & -2 \end{pmatrix} \mathbf{x} \qquad \text{(Prob. 3, Sect. 7.5)} \qquad (i)$$

$$\mathbf{x}' = \begin{pmatrix} 1 & -1 \\ 5 & -3 \end{pmatrix} \mathbf{x} \qquad \text{(Prob. 5, Sect. 7.6)} \qquad (ii)$$

$$\mathbf{x}' = \begin{pmatrix} -3 & 5/2 \\ -5/2 & 2 \end{pmatrix} \mathbf{x} \qquad \text{(Prob. 4, Sect. 7.7).} \qquad (iii)$$

(a) Use *Maple* to find the eigenvalues and eigenvectors of each linear system. Use the eigenvectors and eigenvalues to write down the general solution of the system.

(b) Use **dsolve** to compute the solution of system (i). Compare the general solution you obtained in part (a) with the solution generated by **dsolve**. Are they the same? If not, explain how they are related (that is, match up the constants).

(c) Using the solution formulas obtained above, plot several trajectories of each system. On your graphs, identify the eigenvectors (if relevant), the direction of increasing time on the trajectories, and the type and stability of the origin as a critical point. You may find that the quality of your portraits can be enhanced by modifying the t-interval or the range of values assumed by the initial data. (A word of caution: If you request too many curves, *Maple* will take a long time to generate the plot.)

2. Do Problem 1 but replace the three systems listed there by the following three from Boyce & DiPrima:

$$\mathbf{x}' = \begin{pmatrix} 5/4 & 3/4 \\ 3/4 & 5/4 \end{pmatrix} \mathbf{x} \qquad \text{(Prob. 6, Sect. 7.5)} \qquad (i)$$

$$\mathbf{x}' = \begin{pmatrix} 2 & -5/2 \\ 9/5 & -1 \end{pmatrix} \mathbf{x} \qquad \text{(Prob. 4, Sect. 7.6)} \qquad (ii)$$

$$\mathbf{x}' = \begin{pmatrix} -3/2 & 1 \\ -1/4 & -1/2 \end{pmatrix} \mathbf{x} \qquad \text{(Prob. 3, Sect. 7.7).} \qquad (iii)$$

3. Use the command **eigenvects** to find the eigenvalues and eigenvectors of the following systems. Use the eigenvalues and eigenvectors to write down the general solutions.

(a)

$$\mathbf{x}' = \begin{pmatrix} 2 & -1 \\ 1 & -2 \end{pmatrix} \mathbf{x}.$$

Let $\mathbf{x}(t) = (x(t), y(t))$. Determine the possible limiting behavior of $x(t)$, of $y(t)$, and of $x(t)/y(t)$ as t approaches $+\infty$.

(b)

$$\mathbf{x}' = \begin{pmatrix} 4 & 3 \\ -3 & -2 \end{pmatrix} \mathbf{x}.$$

(c)

$$\mathbf{x}' = \begin{pmatrix} 0 & 0 & -1 \\ 2 & 0 & 0 \\ -1 & 2 & 4 \end{pmatrix} \mathbf{x} \qquad \text{(Prob. 19, Sect. 7.5, Boyce \& DiPrima).}$$

Find the solution with initial condition

$$\mathbf{x}(0) = \begin{pmatrix} 7 \\ 5 \\ 5 \end{pmatrix}.$$

(d) Now solve the initial value problem in (c) with **dsolve** and compare the answer with the solution you obtained in (c).

4. *Maple* can solve some inhomogeneous linear systems. Here are three such systems (taken from Boyce & DiPrima, Sect. 7.9, Problems 1, 3, & 10).

$$\mathbf{x}' = \begin{pmatrix} 2 & -1 \\ 3 & -2 \end{pmatrix} \mathbf{x} + \begin{pmatrix} e^t \\ t \end{pmatrix} \qquad (i)$$

$$\mathbf{x}' = \begin{pmatrix} 2 & -5 \\ 1 & -2 \end{pmatrix} \mathbf{x} + \begin{pmatrix} -\cos t \\ \sin t \end{pmatrix} \qquad (ii)$$

$$\mathbf{x'} = \begin{pmatrix} -3 & \sqrt{2} \\ \sqrt{2} & -2 \end{pmatrix} \mathbf{x} + \begin{pmatrix} e^{-t} \\ -e^{-t} \end{pmatrix}. \tag{iii}$$

(a) Solve the three systems using **dsolve**.

(b) Now impose the initial data

$$\mathbf{x}(0) = \begin{pmatrix} 1 \\ 1 \end{pmatrix}$$

on each system. For each of (*i*)–(*iii*), draw the solution curve using a time interval $-1 \leq t \leq 1$. Based on the differential equation, indicate the direction of motion through the initial value. Then expand the time interval and, purely on the graphical evidence, venture a guess as to the behavior of the solution curve as $t \to -\infty$ and as $t \to \infty$.

5. Here we reconsider the pendulum models examined in Problems 3–6 of Problem Set D. (See also the discussion in Section 9.3 of Boyce & DiPrima.)

(a) Consider first the undamped pendulum

$$\theta'' + \sin\theta = 0, \quad \theta(0) = 0, \quad \theta'(0) = b.$$

Let $x = \theta$ and $y = \theta'$; then x and y satisfy the system

$$\begin{cases} x' = y \\ y' = -\sin x \end{cases} \qquad \begin{cases} x(0) = 0 \\ y(0) = b. \end{cases}$$

Solve this system numerically and plot, on a single graph, the resulting trajectories for the initial conditions $x(0) = 0$, and $y(0) = 0.5, 1, 1.5, 2, 2.5$. Use a positive time range (*e.g.*, **t = 0..20**) and the option **scaling = CONSTRAINED** to improve your pictures.

(b) Based on your pictures in part (a), describe physically what the pendulum seems to be doing in the three cases $\theta'(0) = 1.5, 2$, and 2.5.

(c) The energy of the pendulum is defined as the sum of kinetic energy $(\theta')^2/2$ and potential energy $1 - \cos\theta$, so

$$E = \frac{1}{2}(\theta')^2 + 1 - \cos\theta = \frac{1}{2}y^2 + 1 - \cos x.$$

Show, by taking the derivative dE/dt, that E is constant when $\theta(t)$ is a solution to the pendulum equation. What basic physical principle does this represent?

(d) Use **contourplot** (with the option **grid = [100, 100]**) to plot the contour lines for the energy. Explain how your picture is related to the trajectory plot from part (a).

(e) If the pendulum reaches the upright position (*i.e.*, $\theta = \pi$), what must be true of the energy? Now explain why there is a critical value E_0 of the energy, below which the pendulum swings back and forth without reaching the upright position, and above which it swings overhead and continues to revolve in the same direction. What is E_0? What must the pendulum do when $E = E_0$? Explain. Next, consider the solution curve corresponding to initial data $\theta(0) = 0, \theta'(0) = b$. What is the value of the energy on that curve? Do your conclusions from part (b) agree with your analysis in this part?

(f) Now consider the damped pendulum

$$\theta'' + 0.5\theta' + \sin\theta = 0, \quad \theta(0) = 0, \quad \theta'(0) = b.$$

Numerically solve the corresponding first order system (which you must determine) and plot the resulting trajectories for the initial velocities $b = 0, 0.5, 1, \ldots, 6$. You will notice that all the trajectories in your graph tend toward the critical points $(0,0)$ or $(2\pi, 0)$. Explain what this means physically. There is a value b_0 for which the trajectory tends toward the critical point $(\pi, 0)$. Estimate, up to two-decimal accuracy, the value of b_0. What would this correspond to physically?

(g) Recall the energy defined in part (c). Compute E' and determine which of the following are possible: (1) E is increasing, (2) E is decreasing, (3) E stays the same. Explain how the possibilities are reflected in the solutions from part (f).

6. Consider the *competing species* model (from Boyce & DiPrima)

$$\begin{cases} \dfrac{dx}{dt} = x(1.5 - x - 0.5y) \\ \dfrac{dy}{dt} = y(2 - 1.5x - 0.5y) \end{cases} \qquad \text{(Prob. 2, Sect. 9.4).}$$

(a) Find all critical points of the system. At each critical point, calculate the corresponding linear system and find the eigenvalues of the coefficient matrix; then identify the type and stability of the critical point.

(b) Plot the vector field.

(c) Use several initial data points (x_0, y_0) in the first quadrant to draw a phase portrait for the system. Identify the direction of increasing t on the trajectories you obtain. Use your vector field plot from part (b) to choose a representative sample of initial conditions. Then combine the vector field and phase portrait on a single graph.

(d) Suppose the initial state of the population is given by

$$x(0) = 2.5, \, y(0) = 2.$$

Find the state of the population at $t = 1, 2, 3, 4, 5, \ldots, 20$.

(e) Explain why practically speaking there is no "peaceful coexistence"; *i.e.*, with the exception of an atypical set of starting populations (the *separatrix* curve), one or the other population must die out. For which nonzero initial populations is there no change? Sketch (by hand) on your plot the separatrices; *i.e.*, the solution curves that approach the unstable equilibrium point where both populations are positive and form the boundary between the solution curves that approach each of the two stable points where only one population survives. (In Problem 11, we investigate how to approximate the separatrix using *Maple*.)

(f) The vertical line $x = 1.5$ cuts the separatrix. By experimenting with the long-term behavior of solutions emanating from several points on this line, find an approximation to two-decimal point accuracy of the value $\bar{y}$ such that $(1.5, \bar{y})$ is on the separatrix. Could you verify numerically whether the point is in fact on the separatrix? Why or why not?

7. Consider the *competing species* model (from Boyce & DiPrima)

$$\begin{cases} \dfrac{dx}{dt} = x(1.5 - 0.5x - y) \\ \dfrac{dy}{dt} = y(0.75 - 0.125x - y) \end{cases} \qquad \text{(Prob. 4, Sect. 9.4)}.$$

(a) Find all critical points of the system. At each critical point, calculate the corresponding linear system and find the eigenvalues of the coefficient matrix; then identify the type and stability of the critical point.

(b) Plot the vector field.

(c) Use several initial data points (x_0, y_0) in the first quadrant to draw a phase portrait for the system. Identify the direction of increasing t on the trajectories you obtain. Use your vector field plot from part (b) to choose a representative sample of initial conditions. Then combine the vector field and phase portrait on a single graph.

(d) Suppose the initial state of the population is given by

$$x(0) = 0.1, \ y(0) = 0.1.$$

Find the state of the population at $t = 1, 2, 3, 4, 5, \ldots, 20$.

(e) Explain why, practically speaking, "peaceful coexistence" is the only outcome; *i.e.*, with the exception of the situation in which one or both species starts out without any population, the population distributions always tend toward a certain equilibrium point. Sketch (by hand) on your plot the separatrices that connect the stable equilibrium point to the two unstable points at which one population is zero; these separatrices divide the solution curves that tend toward the origin as $t \to -\infty$ from those that are unbounded as $t \to -\infty$. (In Problem 11, we investigate how to approximate the separatrix using *Maple*.)

(f) The vertical line $x = 2.5$ cuts a separatrix. By experimenting with the behavior of solutions for *negative* time emanating from several points on this line, find an approximation to two-decimal point accuracy of the value $\bar{y}$ such that $(2.5, \bar{y})$ is on the separatrix. (*Hint:* $-3 \le t \le 0$ should suffice.) Could you verify numerically whether the point is in fact on the separatrix? Why or why not?

8. Consider the *predator-prey* model

$$\begin{cases} \dfrac{dx}{dt} = x(2-y) \\ \dfrac{dy}{dt} = y(x-1) \end{cases}$$

in which x represents the population of the prey and y represents the population of the predators.

(a) Find all critical points of the system. At each critical point, calculate the corresponding linear system and find the eigenvalues of the coefficient matrix; then identify the type and stability of the critical point.

(b) Plot the vector field.

(c) Use several initial data points (x_0, y_0) in the first quadrant to draw a phase portrait for the system. Identify the direction of increasing t on the trajectories you obtain. Use your vector field plot from part (b) to choose a representative sample of initial conditions. Then combine the vector field and phase portrait on a single graph.

(d) Explain from your phase portrait how the populations vary for initial data close to the equilibrium point $(\bar{x}_0, \bar{y}_0)$ (the unique critical point inside the first quadrant). What about initial data far from the critical point?

(e) Suppose the initial state of the population is given by

$$x(0) = 1, \; y(0) = 1.$$

Find the state of the population at $t = 1, 2, 3, 4, 5$.

(f) Estimate the period of the solution curve with initial data $(1, 1)$.

9. Consider a *predator-prey* model where the behavior of the prey is governed by a logistic equation (in the absence of the predator). Such a model is typified by the following system from Boyce & DiPrima:

$$\begin{cases} \dfrac{dx}{dt} = x(1 - 0.5x - 0.5y) \\ \dfrac{dy}{dt} = y(0.5x - 0.25) \end{cases} \qquad \text{(Prob. 3, Sect. 9.5),}$$

where x represents the population of the prey, and y represents the population of the predators.

(a) Find all critical points of the system. At each critical point, calculate the corresponding linear system and find the eigenvalues of the coefficient matrix; then identify the type and stability of the critical point.

(b) Plot the vector field.

(c) Use several initial data points (x_0, y_0) in the first quadrant to draw a phase portrait for the system. Identify the direction of increasing t on the trajectories you obtain. Use your vector field plot from part (b) to choose a representative sample of initial conditions. Then combine the vector field and phase portrait on a single graph.

(d) Explain from your phase portrait how the populations vary over time for initial data near the equilibrium point $(\bar{x}_0, \bar{y}_0)$ (the unique critical point inside the first quadrant, not on the axes). What happens when the initial condition is far from the equilibrium point?

(e) Suppose the initial state of the population is given by

$$x(0) = 1, \ y(0) = 1.$$

Find the state of the population at $t = 1, 2, 3, 4, 5$.

(f) Estimate how long it takes for both populations to arrive simultaneously within 0.01 of their equilibrium values if we start with initial data $(1, 1)$.

10. Consider a modified predator-prey system where the behavior of the prey is governed by a logistic/threshold equation (in the absence of the predator). Such a model is typified by the following system from Boyce & DiPrima:

$$\begin{cases} \dfrac{dx}{dt} = x(-1 + 2.5x - 0.3y - x^2) \\ \dfrac{dy}{dt} = y(-1.5 + x) \end{cases} \quad \text{(Prob. 5, Sect. 9.5),}$$

where x represents the population of the prey, and y represents the population of the predators.

(a) Find all critical points of the system. At each critical point, calculate the corresponding linear system and find the eigenvalues and eigenvectors of the coefficient matrix; then identify the critical points as to type and stability.

(b) Plot the vector field.

(c) Use several initial data points (x_0, y_0) in the first quadrant to draw a phase portrait for the system. Use your vector field plot from part (b) to choose a representative sample of initial conditions. Then combine the vector field and phase portrait on a single graph.

(d) In parts (a), (b), and (c), you obtained information about the solutions of the system using three different approaches. Combine all of this information by combining the plots from parts (b) and (c) with the **display** command, and then drawing in by hand the critical points, the eigenvectors from part (a), and any separatrices. What information does the graph in part (a) provide that is not provided by the other approaches? Answer the same question for parts (b) and (c).

(e) Interpret your conclusions in terms of the populations of the two species.

11. Some of the nonlinear systems of differential equations we have studied have more than one asymptotically stable equilibrium point. In such cases, it can be difficult to predict which (if any) equilibrium point the solution with a given initial condition will approach as time increases. Generally, the solution curves that approach one stable equilibrium will be separated from the solutions that approach another stable equilibrium by a separatrix curve. The separatrix is itself a solution curve that does not approach either stable equilibrium—often it approaches a saddle point instead. (See, for example, Figure 9.4.8 in Section 9.4 of Boyce & DiPrima.)

Having located a relevant saddle point, one can approximate the separatrix by choosing an initial condition very close to the saddle point and solving the differential equation *backwards* in time. The reason for going "back in time" is to find (approximately) a solution curve that approaches very close to the saddle point as time increases. For two population dynamics models, we will use this idea to get a fairly precise map of which initial conditions go to which equilibria.

(a) Consider the system

$$\begin{cases} \dfrac{dx}{dt} = x(1.5 - x - 0.5y) \\ \dfrac{dy}{dt} = y(2 - 1.5x - 0.5y) \end{cases}$$

studied in Problem 6 above. There are two asymptotically stable equilibria, $(1.5, 0)$ and $(0, 4)$, a saddle point at $(1, 1)$, and an unstable node at $(0, 0)$. Plot a family of solution curves in the first quadrant (positive x and y) on the same graph; use a time interval from $t = 0$ to a positive time large enough that you can clearly see where the solutions curves are headed, but not so large that your plot takes forever to compute. (We suggest a set of initial values between 0.5 and 4.5. It also may be useful to adjust the range of the plot until you get a reasonably square graph.) Observe where the solution curves seem to be heading and where the separatrix seems to be.

(b) Draw an approximate separatrix by plotting a solution curve with initial values for x and y very close to the saddle point (1,1), using a *negative* range of values for t. This should give you a good picture of the separatrix on one side of the saddle point; to approximate the rest of the separatrix you will need to choose a set of initial conditions on the other side of (but still very close to) the saddle point. In each case, you may need to fine-tune the time interval, since a time interval that is too small will only show you a small part of the separatrix, while too large an interval may cause the solution to blow up. Finally, show all of your plots on one graph, and make sure the separatrix really does separate the different asymptotic properties of the solution curves found in part (a). (To help in distinguishing the separatrix, you can use the option **linestyle = 4** in making your separatrix plots.) Discuss how the possible limiting values of the species depend on the initial values of the species.

(c) Repeat part (a) using the system

$$\begin{cases} \dfrac{dx}{dt} = x(-1 + 2.5x - 0.3y - x^2) \\[2mm] \dfrac{dy}{dt} = y(-1.5 + x) \end{cases}$$

from Problem 10 above. This time there are asymptotically stable equilibria at the origin and $(3/2, 5/3)$, and saddle points at $(0.5, 0)$ and $(2, 0)$.

(d) Repeat part (b) for the system in part (c). It is up to you to decide whether one or both of the saddle points are relevant to drawing the separatrix or separatrices that divide those solution curves that approach one equilibrium from those that approach the other as time increases; your picture from part (c) may be helpful. Also, keep in mind that since the saddle points are on the x-axis in this case, you need only consider nearby initial conditions above the x-axis because we are only interested in solutions in the first quadrant.

12. This problem is based on Problems 7.3.34–35 of Edwards and Penney, **Elementary Differential Equations with Applications**, 3rd edition, Prentice-Hall, Inc., 1994. (See also Boyce & DiPrima, Problem 17, Section 9.3.)

(a) Consider the linear system

$$\begin{cases} \dfrac{dx}{dt} = -x + hy \\[2mm] \dfrac{dy}{dt} = x - y. \end{cases}$$

Draw phase portraits for the system for the values $h = 0$, 0.5, and -0.5. What can you deduce about the change in the type and/or stability of the equilibrium point $(0,0)$ corresponding to relatively small perturbations of the system?

(b) Now consider the system

$$\begin{cases} \dfrac{dx}{dt} = y + hx(x^2 + y^2) \\[2mm] \dfrac{dy}{dt} = -x + hy(x^2 + y^2). \end{cases}$$

Draw phase portraits (using numerical solutions this time) for $h = 0$, 1, and -1. (*Note:* For $h = 1$, you may have to keep the initial data close to the origin and keep the time interval very short. Even with $t = 1$, *Maple* complains; but be patient, you will get a nice picture eventually.) Illustrate how the linear approximation method (*cf.* Chapter 9 of Boyce & DiPrima) is inconclusive in the case of a *center* by citing the evidence in your portraits. (To decide which way the solution curves are going, you can examine the signs of dx/dt and dy/dt at a particular point, say $x = 1$, $y = 0$, or use *Maple* to plot the vector field in each case.)

13. In Chapter 5 we investigated the sensitivity to initial values of solutions of a single differential equation. In this problem, we investigate the same issue for two systems of equations. The systems we study are said to be *chaotic* because the solutions are sensitive to initial values, but in contrast to the examples in Chapter 5 and Problems 14 and 15 of Problem Set C, the solutions remain bounded.

   Since we do not know the exact solutions for the systems we will study, in order to judge the time it takes for a small perturbation of the system to become large, we will compare pairs of numerical solutions whose initial conditions are close, but still relatively far apart compared with the local error (*cf.* Chapter 7) of our numerical method. To be safe we only consider perturbations as small as 10^{-4}.

   (a) Consider the Lorenz system

$$x' = 10(y - x)$$
$$y' = 28x - y - xz$$
$$z' = -(8/3)z + xy$$

   studied in Section 9.8 of Boyce & DiPrima. We investigate the idea illustrated in Figure 9.8.3, that small changes in the initial conditions can lead to large changes in the solution after a relatively short period of time. For $a = 0.1$, plot on the same graph the first coordinate $x(t)$ of the solutions corresponding to the initial conditions $(5, 5, 5)$ and $(5 + a, 5, 5)$ from $t = 0$ to $t = 20$. (We recommend that you use the **DEplot** command with **scene = [t, x]** and **stepsize = 0.01**; the latter option is necessary to ensure that the local truncation error is small, but it will also cause the numerical solver to take longer than usual to compute the approximate solutions. Since you will be using the initial condition $(5, 5, 5)$ again below, it may save time to use a separate **DEplot** command for each initial condition and combine the plots later with the **display** command. This approach also allows you to use an option like **linestyle = 4** in one of the **DEplot** commands in order to better distinguish between the two curves.) Observe the time at which the solutions start to differ noticeably. Repeat for $a = 0.01, 0.001, 0.0001$. (The criterion for a "noticeable" difference between the two solutions is up to you; just try to be consistent from one observation to the next.)

   (b) Make a table or graph of the number of decimal places in which the initial condition was perturbed (that is, 1, 2, 3, and 4 for the four given values of a) versus the amount of time the solutions stayed close to each other. This graph shows roughly how long we should trust a numerical solution to be close to the actual solution for a given number of digits of accuracy in each step of our numerical method. Describe how the amount of time we can trust a numerical solution seems to depend on the number of digits of accuracy per time step, judging from your data. If a numerical method has 16 digits of accuracy, about how long do you think the numerical solution can be trusted? What if the accuracy were 100 digits?

(c) Repeat part (a) for the Rössler system

$$x' = -y - z$$
$$y' = x + 0.36y$$
$$z' = 0.4x - 4.5z + xz.$$

This time plot from $t = 0$ to $t = 100$, and use $(2, 2, 2)$ as the initial condition. (With the longer time interval, the option **stepsize = 0.01** may make **DEplot** take intolerably long—it should be alright to increase the step size to 0.05.)

(d) Repeat part (b) for the Rössler system. Judging from the results of parts (b) and (d), is there a common principle you can draw for systems of differential equations of this type?

Complex Systems. In the following three problems, we consider a special class of 2×2 systems, namely, those that may be represented as a differential equation involving a single complex variable z. Consider, for example, the equation

$$z' = z(e^{i\phi} + z\bar{z}). \tag{1}$$

Here $z(t) = x(t) + iy(t)$ is a complex-valued function of the independent variable t, ϕ is a real parameter, and $\bar{z}$ is the complex conjugate of z. If we compute the real and imaginary parts of (1), we obtain the equivalent nonlinear 2×2 system

$$\begin{cases} x' = x \cos \phi - y \sin \phi + x^3 - xy^2 \\ y' = x \sin \phi + y \cos \phi + x^2y - y^3. \end{cases} \tag{2}$$

In spite of the fact that these are equivalent, the expression (1) offers several advantages over (2). First, (1) is "one-dimensional" in the sense that there is only one dependent variable z. Second, there are certain properties of the equation (1) that are apparent in the complex form, but obscure in the 2×2 form. For example, (1) is invariant by rotations through any angle (see the following problem), and therefore its set of solutions is rotationally symmetric. Symmetry plays a large role in the theory of differential equations, and complex-valued equations like (1) are the simplest kind of differential equations displaying rotational symmetry. Third, equations like (1) exhibit a phenomenon called *bifurcation* when the parameter ϕ varies. A parametrized family of differential equations is said to *bifurcate* at a parameter value ϕ_0 if the qualitative behavior of the differential equation changes as the parameter passes through ϕ_0. Examples of bifurcations are: loss of stability of a critical point; and creation or annihilation of limit cycles, or periodic solutions.

You may have noticed that for certain real-valued differential equations **dsolve** returns complex-valued solutions. In fact, many *Maple* commands do not distinguish between real and complex numbers. This is true of the commands **dsolve** and **dsolve(..., numeric)**. In particular, we can use these commands on equations like (1) without worrying about the fact that these equations are complex-valued. *Maple* will report its solutions in exactly the same form as for real-valued differential equations, except that now the solutions will almost always be complex-valued (whereas in the case of real-valued equations, complex-valued solutions were rarely reported).

Unfortunately, the *Maple* command **DEplot** *does* distinguish between complex- and real-valued functions, so if we want to use **DEplot** to draw the phase portraits of the solutions in the complex plane, we first have to extract the real and imaginary parts of the complex equations, and then use **DEplot** on the real and imaginary parts. In order to save you a considerable amount of trouble figuring out exactly how to do this, we give you the following program:

```
with(DEtools):
complexsystem := proc(phi, trange) local x, y, z, zrhs, eqns, j, r, inits;
  zrhs := subs(z = x + I*y, z*(exp(I*phi) + z*conjugate(z)));
  eqns := [evalc(Re(zrhs)), evalc(Im(zrhs))];
  inits := seq(seq([0, r*cos(2*Pi*j/6), r*sin(2*Pi*j/6)], r = [0.25, 0.75]), j = 0..5);
  DEplot(eqns, [x, y], trange, inits, x = -2..2, y = -2..2, limitrange = true,
    stepsize = 0.1);
end;
```

This program is designed to solve equation (1) numerically and plot solutions for a given value of the parameter ϕ. The other argument of the function specifies the time interval on which to solve the differential equation. For example, typing **complexsystem(Pi, -5..5)** will plot a phase portrait for $\phi = \pi$ using values of t from -5 to 5.

In order to use and modify this program, you should note the following features:

- The right-hand side of the complex differential equation (1) appears in the second line of the program, defining **zrhs**. Note that **I** is *Maple*'s notation for $\sqrt{-1}$.
- We have included initial values corresponding to the complex initial condition $z(0) = re^{i\theta}$, given in polar coordinates. Note that multiplication by $e^{i\theta}$ corresponds in the complex plane to counterclockwise rotation by the angle θ. The idea is to use a set of initial points which, like the differential equation, are rotationally symmetric around the origin (see parts (a) of the problems below). In this particular example, the initial conditions consist of points on the circles of radius 0.25 and 0.75, spaced evenly at angles $2\pi j/6$, for $j = 0, \ldots, 5$.
- The syntax we have used in **DEplot** may be different from what you are used to. In the first argument **eqns**, we give only the right-hand sides of

the equations for the real and imaginary parts **x** and **y** of **z**. This syntax is generally optional, but is important in this program.

To summarize, the only things you'll have to modify to use this program in the following problems are:

- the actual differential equation used to define **zrhs**,
- the list of initial conditions **inits**, and
- possibly the x and y ranges in the **DEplot** command.

14. This exercise concerns the equation mentioned above,

$$z' = z(e^{i\phi} + z\bar{z}). \tag{i}$$

(a) Show that equation (i) is rotationally invariant in the following sense: If we let $w = e^{i\theta}z$, for any angle θ, then w satisfies the same differential equation as z; that is, $w' = w(e^{i\phi} + w\bar{w})$. You may show this by hand or by using *Maple* (but it's easier to do it by hand).

(b) Plot the trajectories of the differential equation for parameter values $\phi = 0, \pi/4, \pi/3, 2\pi/3$. Determine the direction of the trajectories by evaluating the right-hand side at various values of z. (We suggest plotting the trajectories on the time interval $[-3, 2]$.) What kind of symmetries can you see in the plots?

(c) Examine the results of (b). Can you detect whether the parameter has passed through a bifurcation value? What exactly is the qualitative change in the behavior of the solutions?

(d) Plot the trajectories of the system for the two parameter values $\phi = \pi/2 \pm 0.2$. (You should also change the time interval to $[-5, 3]$.) Estimate the bifurcation value of the parameter.

(e) Let $\rho = z\bar{z}$. Note that ρ is the square of the distance from the origin to z. In particular, ρ is a real-valued positive function of t. Moreover, one can show that ρ satisfies the differential equation $\rho' = 2\rho(\mathrm{Re}(e^{i\phi}) + \rho)$. Note that a critical point of this differential equation corresponds to a solution of (i) that stays a fixed distance from the origin. By finding the critical points of the differential equation for ρ, explain the results of (c) and (d).

15. Consider the complex-valued differential equation

$$z' = e^{i\phi}z + \bar{z}^2. \tag{i}$$

Refer to the text preceding Problem 14 for general remarks concerning complex-valued differential equations.

(a) Show that equation (i) is rotationally invariant through an angle of $2\pi/3$ in the following sense: If we let $w = e^{2\pi i/3}z$, then w also satisfies the differential equation (i), *i.e.*, $w' = e^{i\phi}w + \bar{w}^2$. You may show this by hand or by using *Maple*.

(b) Plot the trajectories of the differential equation for parameter values $\phi = 0, \pi/4, \pi/2$. You should use a set of initial conditions consisting of 12 evenly spaced points on each of the circles of radius 0.5 and 1.5. Determine the direction of the trajectories by evaluating the right-hand side at various values of z. (We suggest plotting the trajectories on the time interval $[-3, 2]$.) What symmetries can you detect in the plot? (*Note*: These plots may take five minutes or longer to draw.)

(c) Look at the results of (b). On which interval does the parameter pass through a bifurcation value? What exactly is the qualitative change in the behavior of the solutions?

(d) Set $z = x + iy$ in equation (i), expand the equation in terms of x and y, and take the real and imaginary parts to obtain an equivalent real-valued 2×2 system.

(e) Using the result of (d), for each of the parameter values $0, \pi/4, \pi/2$, find the critical points of the system (there are 4 in each case). Indicate these critical points on your plots in (b).

16. Consider the complex-valued differential equation

$$z' = 0.3e^{i\phi}z - (1+i)z^3\bar{z}^2 + \bar{z}^4.$$ (i)

Refer to the text preceding Problem 14 for general remarks concerning complex-valued differential equations.

(a) Show that equation (i) is rotationally invariant through an angle of $2\pi/5$ in the following sense: If we let $w = e^{2\pi i/5}z$, then w also satisfies the differential equation (i).

(b) Plot the trajectories of the differential equation for parameter values $\phi = 0, \pi/4, \pi/2$. You should use a set of initial conditions consisting of 20 evenly spaced points on each of the circles of radius 0.25 and 0.75. Determine the direction of the trajectories by plotting the vector field associated with this equation. (We suggest plotting the trajectories on the time interval $[-8, 10]$, with the range restricted to $[-1, 1]$.) What symmetries can you detect in the plots?

(c) Examine the results of (b). On which interval or intervals does the parameter pass through a bifurcation value? What exactly is the qualitative change in the behavior of the solutions? Using the **display** command, plot the vector fields and integral curves on the same graph for each parameter value. By examining these plots, try to figure out how many critical points there are inside the unit square. (*Note*: The stable critical points are easy to find. The unstable ones are not so obvious.)

Glossary

We list here the *Maple* objects that arise in the various input statements encountered in this book. We list them according to five types: commands, options, built-in functions, constants, and programming statements. The distinction between the first and third is somewhat artificial, as *Maple* makes no distinction between them. However, for the purposes of this course, it is convenient to think of a *Maple* built-in function as we normally think of functions, in particular as something that can be evaluated or plotted; while a command is something that manipulates data or expressions, or initiates a process.

Each command and option is followed by a brief description of its effect, and then one or more examples. To find a full description of a command you can type **?command** in a Worksheet.

Maple Commands

@ (at sign)   Composition operator.
   (cos@arcos)(x);

@@ (double at sign)   Repeated composition operator.
   (cos@@2)(0);
   (D@@3)(sin);

conjugate   Gives the complex conjugate of a complex number.
   conjugate(2 + 3*I);

contourplot (in the **plots** package)   Plots the level curves of a function of two variables.
   with(plots):
   contourplot(x^2 + y^2, x = −2..2, y = −2..2);

convert   Converts an expression to a specified form.
   convert(0.425, rational);
   convert(series(sin(x), x), polynom);

D   Differentiation operator for functions; used to describe initial conditions on derivatives.

    D(sin);
    dsolve({diff(y(x), x$2) = y(x), y(0) = 1, D(y)(0) = 1}, y(x));

DEplot (in the **DEtools** package)   Plots one or more numerical solutions of a differential equation or system of differential equations.

    with(DEtools):
    DEplot(diff(y(x), x$2) = x^3*y(x) + 1, [x, y], x = −3..2, {[0, 0.5, 2]});
    DEplot([2*x − y, x + 2*y], [x, y], −1..1, {[0, 2, 0], [0, 1, 0], [0, 0, 1], [0, 1, 1],
        [0, 0, 2]}, x = −10..10, y = −10..10, limitrange = true);

dfieldplot (in the **DEtools** package)   Plots the direction field of a differential equation or system of equations.

    with(DEtools):
    dfieldplot(exp(−t) − 2*x, x(t), t = −2..3, x = −1..2);
    dfieldplot(x − 3*y, [x, y], x = −2..2 y = −2..2, axes = BOXED, arrows = LINE);
    dfieldplot([x*(2 − y), y*sin(x)], [x, y], 0..1, x = −3..3, y = −3..3, axes = BOXED,
        arrows = THICK);

diff   Differentiation operator.

    diff(f(x), x);
    diff(x^3 − 3*x, x);
    diff(cos(x), x$2);

display   Combines and displays several previously generated graphics.

    display({graph1, graph2});

$ (dollar sign)   Sequence operator.

    [j^2 $ j = 0..5];
    diff(sinh(x), x$2);

dsolve   Symbolic ODE solver.

    dsolve(diff(y(x), x$2) − x*y(x) = 0, y(x));
    dsolve({diff(y(x), x) + y(x)^2 = 0, y(0) = 1}, y(x));
    dsolve({diff(x(t), t) = 2*x(t) + y(t), diff(y(t), t) = −x(t)}, {x(t), y(t)});

dsolve(. . ., method = laplace)   Computes symbolic solutions of differential equations using the Laplace Transform. Useful for differential equations involving discontinuous functions.

    dsolve({diff(y(x), x) + y(x) = Dirac(x − 1), y(0) = 1}, y(x), method = laplace);

dsolve(. . ., numeric)   Numerical ODE solver.

    dsolve({diff(y(x), x) = x + y(x)^2, y(0) = 1}, y(x), numeric, maxfun = 1000);
    dsolve({diff(y(x), x$2) − x*y(x) = 0, y(0) = 1, D(y)(0) = 0}, y(x), numeric,
        maxfun = 1000);

dsolve(. . ., series)   Computes series solutions of differential equations.

    dsolve({diff(y(x), x$2) = x*y(x)^2, y(0) = 1, D(y)(0) = 0}, y(x), type = series);

eigenvects (in the **linalg** package)   Computes eigenvalues and eigenvectors of a matrix.
> **with(linalg):**
> **eigenvects([[a, b], [c, d]]);**
> **eigenvects([[1, 0, 0], [1, 1, 1], [1, 2, 4]], radical);**

evalc   Evaluates an expression containing complex numbers, assuming that unknown variables represent real numbers.
> **evalc(Re(x + I*y));**
> **evalc(abs(x + I*y));**

evalf   Evaluates numerically; gives a decimal approximation of a number.
> **evalf(Pi, 15);**
> **evalf(solve(x^2 − 4*x + 9 = 0, x));**

evalf(Int())   Numerical integration.
> **evalf(Int(f(x), x = 0..5));**
> **evalf(Int(sin(x)/x, x = 0..infinity));**

evalm   Evaluates a matrix expression. Often used with the matrix multiplication operator **& ***.
> **evalm([[a, b], [c, d]] &* [u, v]);**

expand   Expands products and powers in an algebraic expression.
> **expand((x + y)^3);**

factor   Factors a polynomial.
> **factor(x^4 − y^4);**

fieldplot (in the **plots** package)   Draws a vector field plot given a pair of functions of two variables; lengths of vectors are proportional to their magnitudes.
> **with(plots):**
> **fieldplot([y, −x], x = −1..1, y = −1..1);**
> **fieldplot([f(x, y), g(x, y)], x = 0..2, y = 0..5, arrows = SLIM, axes = BOXED);**

Float   Creates a floating point constant using exponential notation. For example, the following yields 3×10^{-8}.
> **abserr = Float(3, −8);**

fsolve   Finds a single numerical solution to an equation or system of equations. If an interval is specified, looks for a solution in that interval.
> **fsolve(cos(x) = x, x, 0..1);**
> **fsolve({x*y = 2, y = x}, {x, y});**

implicitplot (in the **plots** package)   Plots a curve defined implicitly.
> **with(plots):**
> **implicitplot(y^2 + y = x^3 − x, x = −2..3, y = −3..3);**

int   Integration operator for both definite and indefinite integrals.
> **int(1/(1 + x^2), x);**
> **int(exp(−x), x = 0..infinity);**

invlaplace   Computes the inverse Laplace Transform.
  invlaplace(exp(−s)/s, s, t);

laplace   Computes the Laplace Transform.
  laplace(sin(t), t, s);

limit   Finds a limit.
  limit(sin(x)/x, x = 0);
  limit(1/x, x = 0, left);

linsolve (in the **linalg** package)   Solves a matrix equation.
  with(linalg):
  linsolve([[1, 2], [3, 4]], [6, 7]);

map   Applies a function to each element of a list or set.
  map(sqrt, {1, 2, 3});
  map(x −> x^2, [1, 2, 3]);

matrix (in the **linalg** package)   Converts a list into a matrix, and displays it accordingly.
  with(linalg):
  matrix([[1, 2, 3], [4, 5, 6]]);

odeplot (in the **plots** package)   Plots a numerical solution produced by **dsolve(..., numeric)**.
  with(plots):
  sol := dsolve(diff(y(x), x) = x^2 − y(x), y(0) = 1, y(x), numeric, maxfun = 1000);
  odeplot(sol, [x, y(x)], 0..2);

op   Extracts elements of a list, set, sequence or expression. Can be used to remove extra levels of brackets or braces.
  op([[1, 2], 3, [4, 5, 6, [7]]]);
  map(op, [[1, 2], 3, [4, 5, 6, [7]]]);

plot   Basic plot command. Plots functions of one variable, expressions, lists of points, parametric curves, or sets containing any of the previous objects.
  plot(sin, 0..Pi);
  plot(f(x), x = 0..1);
  plot({x^2, x^3}, x = −2..2);
  plot([[1, 1], [2, 4], [3, 10]]);
  plot([cos(t), sin(t), t = 0..2*Pi]);
  plot({f(t, j) $ j = 1..10}, t = 0..5);

print   Shows the value of an expression; useful for displaying lists as tables.
  map(print, [1, 2, 3, 4]):

rhs   Gives the right-hand side of an equation.
  rhs(y = 2*x);
  rhs(dsolve(diff(y(x), x) = x*y(x), y(x)));

seq   Builds a sequence; useful for constructing lists of initial conditions.
    seq(x^2 + c, c = −3..3);
    seq(i*(i + 1), i = [1, 2, 3, 5, 7]);
    seq(seq([i, j], i = 1..5), j = 1..5);

series   Generates terms of a power series expansion about a point.
    series(exp(−x), x = 0, 10);

simplify   Simplifies an expression.
    simplify(1/(1 + x)^2 − 1/(1 − x)^2);

solve   Algebraically solves an equation or set of equations; works best on polynomials.
    solve(2*x^2 − 3*x + 6 = 0, x);
    solve({x + 3*y = 4, −x − 5*y = 3}, {x, y});

subs   Substitutes for parts of an expression.
    subs(x = 2, x^3 − 4*x + 1);
    subs(sin(x) = z, sin(x)^2 + cos(x));
    subs({x(t) = t^2, y(t) = cos(t)}, {x(t), y(t)});

sum   Sums a sequence.
    sum((i − 1)/(i + 1), i = 1..10);
    sum(g(0.1*j), j = 20..30);

textplot (in the **plots** package)   Plots text strings (for labeling).
    with(plots):
    textplot([1, 1, `The point (1, 1)`]);

unapply   Converts an expression into a function.
    f := unapply(x^2 + 3, x);
    f := unapply(x^2 + k, x, k);

with   Loads a *Maple* package.
    with(plots):
    with(DEtools):
    with(linalg):

Global Variables and Options to Maple Commands

abserr   Controls the local absolute error in **dsolve(. . ., numeric)**.
    dsolve({diff(x(t), t) = t*x(t), x(0) = 1}, x(t), numeric, abserr = Float(1, −10));

arrows   Controls the shape of the arrows in a vector field or direction field.
    dfieldplot(exp(−t) − 2*x, x(t), t = −2..3, x = −1..2, arrows = LINE);
    fieldplot([f(x, y), g(x, y)], x = 0..2, y = 0..5, arrows = SLIM);

axes   Controls how the axes of a plot are displayed.
    plot(sin(x), x = 0..2*Pi, axes = FRAMED);
    dfieldplot(exp(−t) − 2*x, x(t), t = −2..3, x = −1..2, axes = BOXED);

contours   Specifies how many contours to use in a contour plot.
    contourplot(f(x, y), x = 0..1, y = 0..2, contours = 12);

Digits   This global variable controls the number of digits used in numerical computations; default is 10.
    Digits := 20;

grid   Controls the number of points plotted by **contourplot, implicitplot,** and **dfieldplot**; default is 25×25 for **implicitplot** and **contourplot**, and 20×20 for **dfieldplot**.
    contourplot(x^2 − y^3, x = −2..2, y = −2..2, grid = [50, 50]);

limitrange   Controls whether **DEplot** stops calculating when the curve leaves the displayed part of the graph; default is false.
    DEplot(diff(y(x), x\$2) = x^3*y(x) + 1, [x, y], x = −3..2, {[0, 0.5, 2]},
        limitrange = true);

maxfun   Limits the number of steps used by **dsolve(..., numeric)**; default is $30,000$.
    dsolve({diff(y(x), x) = x^2 − y(x)^2, y(0) = 1}, y(x), numeric, maxfun = 1000);

numpoints   The minimum number of points used by a plotting routine; default is 49.
    plot(sin(x*Pi/49), x = 0..1, numpoints = 100);

Order   This global variable controls the order of series calculations; default is 6.
    Order := 11;

relerr   Controls the local relative error in **dsolve(..., numeric)**.
    dsolve({diff(x(t), t) = t*x(t), x(0) = 1}, x(t), numeric, relerr = Float(1, −10));

scaling   Controls whether the axes in a plot have the same scale. Default is **UNCONSTRAINED**, so axes may have different scales.
    plot([cos(t), sin(t), t = 0..2*Pi], scaling = CONSTRAINED);

scene   Controls which variables are plotted. Used in the plotting commands from the **DEtools** package.
    DEplot([diff(x(t), t) = −t*cos(y(t)), diff(y(t), t) = cos(x(t))], [t, x, y], t = 0..10,
        {[0, 1, 1]}, x = 0..3, y = 1..3, scene = [x, y], stepsize = 0.1);

stepsize   Controls the step size in **DEplot**.
    DEplot(diff(y(x), x\$2) = x^3*y(x) + 1, [x, y], x = −3..2, {[0, 0.5, 2]},
        stepsize = 0.1);

title   Specifies a title for a graph.
    plot(sin(x), x = 0..4*Pi, title = 'Another sine wave');

Built-In Functions

abs $|x|$.

Ai The solution $\mathrm{Ai}(x)$ to Airy's equation $y'' - xy = 0$.

Bi The solution $\mathrm{Bi}(x)$ to Airy's equation.

arcsin $\arcsin x$.

BesselJ(0, ·) The solution $J_0(x)$ to Bessel's equation of order zero, $x^2 y'' + xy' + x^2 y = 0$.

BesselY(0, ·) The solution $Y_0(x)$ to Bessel's equation of order zero.

cos $\cos x$.

cosh $\cosh x$.

Dirac The Dirac delta function.

erf The *error function* $\mathrm{erf}(x) = (2/\sqrt{\pi}) \int_0^x e^{-t^2}\, dt$.

exp e^x.

Heaviside The unit step function.

Im $\Im(z)$, the imaginary part of a complex number.

ln The natural logarithm $\ln x = \log_e x$.

Re $\Re(z)$, the real part of a complex number.

Si The *sine integral* $\mathrm{Si}(x) = \int_0^x \sin(t)/t\, dt$.

sin $\sin x$.

sinh $\sinh x$.

sqrt $\sqrt{x}$.

tan $\tan x$.

Built-In Constants

E e, the base of the natural logarithm.

I $i = \sqrt{-1}$.

infinity ∞.

Pi π.

Maple Programming

do ... od   Marks a block of statements for repetition.
   j := 10; while j > 0 do j := j − 1; od;

for   Repeats a command a certain number of times.
   a := [ ]; for j from 0 to 1 by 0.2 do a := [op(a), [j, j^2]]; od;

global   Specifies that certain variables in a program are global, *i.e.*, their values may come from outside the program.

if ... fi   Introduces a conditional.
   checksign := x −> if x < 0 then print(negative); else print(nonnegative); fi;

local   Specifies that certain variables in a program are local, *i.e.*, are only used inside the program.

proc ... end   Defines a *Maple* procedure or program.
   eqn := diff(y(x), x) = x^2 − y(x);

   compareplots := proc(b) local exact, approx; global eqn;
     exact := plot(rhs(dsolve({eqn, y(0) = b}, y(x))), x = 0..5, style = POINT):
     approx := odeplot(dsolve({eqn, y(0) = b}, y(x), numeric,
         maxfun = 1000), [x, y(x)], 0..5):
     display({exact, approx});
   end;

   compareplots(1);

Sample Worksheet Solutions

Problem Set B, Problem 1.

We are interested in the differential equation xy' + 2y = sin(x), with initial
condition y(Pi/2) = c. Here is the general solution:
> restart:
> sol := dsolve({x*diff(y(x), x) + 2*y(x) = sin(x), y(Pi/2) = c}, y(x));

$$sol := y(x) = \frac{\sin(x)}{x^2} - \frac{\cos(x)}{x} - \frac{1}{4}\frac{\left(4\frac{1}{\pi^2} - c\right)\pi^2}{x^2}$$

Here is a function that gives, for fixed c, the solution of the IVP with initial
condition y(Pi/2) = c.
> f := unapply(simplify(rhs(sol)), c);

$$f := c \rightarrow \frac{1}{4}\frac{4\sin(x) - 4\cos(x)\,x - 4 + c\,\pi^2}{x^2}$$

The solution with y(Pi/2) = 1 is given by:
> y1 := unapply(f(1), x);

$$y1 := x \rightarrow \frac{1}{4}\frac{4\sin(x) - 4\cos(x)\,x - 4 + \pi^2}{x^2}$$

(a)
Here is a table of values for the solution of the IVP with c = 1.
> point := x -> [x, evalf(y1(x))]:
> list_of_points := [point(0.5*x) $ x = 1..10]:

> map(print, list_of_points):

$$[.5, 6.032141434]$$

$$[1.0, 1.768569780]$$

$$[1.5, 1.048351238]$$

$$[2.0, .8022480500]$$

$$[2.5, .6509971652]$$

$$[3.0, .5087220664]$$

$$[3.5, .3587115329]$$

$$[4.0, .2078233180]$$

$$[4.5, .07103467064]$$

$$[5.0, -.03639336405]$$

(b)

We graph the solution y1(x) on several intervals.

> plot(y1(x), x = 0..2);

> plot(y1(x), x = 1..10);

> plot(y1(x), x = 10..100);

By inspecting the function y1(x), we see that the solution approaches positive infinity as x goes to 0, and approaches 0 as x goes to infinity. This analysis is borne out by the graphs above.

(c)

Here is a table of the solutions of the IVP with initial conditions y(Pi/2) = 0.2j for j = 1, ..., 5, and a plot of these solutions over two different intervals. Note that the index j = 1 corresponds to the lowest solution, and the index j = 5 corresponds to the highest.

> map(print, [[[j], f(0.2*j)]] $ j = 1..5]):

$$\left[[1], \frac{1}{4} \frac{4 \sin(x) - 4 \cos(x) x - 4 + .2 \pi^2}{x^2} \right]$$

$$\left[[2], \frac{1}{4} \frac{4 \sin(x) - 4 \cos(x) x - 4 + .4 \pi^2}{x^2} \right]$$

$$\left[[3], \frac{1}{4} \frac{4 \sin(x) - 4 \cos(x) x - 4 + .6 \pi^2}{x^2} \right]$$

$$\left[[4], \frac{1}{4} \frac{4 \sin(x) - 4 \cos(x) x - 4 + .8 \pi^2}{x^2} \right]$$

$$\left[[5], \frac{1}{4} \frac{4 \sin(x) - 4 \cos(x) x - 4 + 1.0 \pi^2}{x^2} \right]$$

> plot({f(0.2*j) $ j = 1..5}, x = 0.1..0.2);

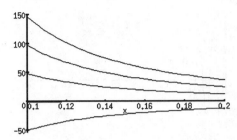

> plot({f(0.2*j) $ j = 1..5}, x = 0.2..10, y = -1..1);

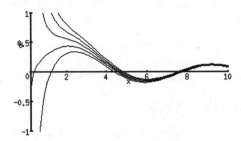

(d)

The solutions in (c) approach plus or minus infinity as x approaches 0 from the right, and approach 0 as x approaches infinity. Can we find a solution that has no singularity at x = 0? The general solution is given at the beginning of this problem. The only way that a solution could possibly be nonsingular at x = 0 is if c = 4/Pi^2. We can check using L'Hopital's rule that in this case the function is continuous at 0. Here is a graph of this solution.

> plot(f(4/Pi^2), x = -5..5);

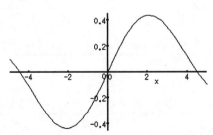

Problem Set B, Problem 4.

We are interested in solutions to y' = (x - e^(-x))/(y + e^y), particularly the solution with y(1.5) = 0.5.

(a)
```
> restart:
> dsolve(diff(y(x), x) = (x - exp(-x))/(y + exp(y)), y(x));
```

$$\frac{1}{2}\,y(x)^2 + e^{y(x)} - \frac{1}{2}\,x^2 - e^{(-x)} = \_C1$$

(b)
The solutions of this equation are implicit; to use them, we define a function f(x, y) equal to the left-hand side of the equation reported by Maple. The solution of the IVP is obtained by setting this function equal to f(1.5, 0.5).
```
> f := (x,y) -> y^2/2 + exp(y) - x^2/2 - exp(-x);
```

$$f := (x, y) \rightarrow \frac{1}{2}\,y^2 + e^y - \frac{1}{2}\,x^2 - e^{(-x)}$$

```
> c := f(1.5, 0.5);
```

$$c := .4255911109$$

We can use contourplot to see some of the solution curves.
```
> with(plots):
> contourplot(f(x, y), x = -1..3, y = -2..2, axes = BOXED, grid = [40, 40]);
```

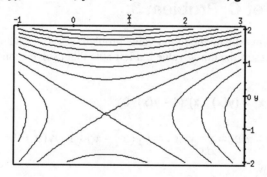

(c), (d)
Here are the values of the solution of the IVP at the points x = 0, 1, 1.8, and 2.1.
```
> fsolve(f(0, y) = c);
```

$$.3183856549$$

```
> fsolve(f(1, y) = c);
```

$$.2356325919$$

```
> fsolve(f(1.8, y) = c);
```

$$.6821874213$$

> **fsolve(f(2.1, y) = c);**

$$.8662118724$$

The following graph shows the solution corresponding to the value f(1.5, 0.5). The top curve corresponds to the solution of the IVP because it passes through the point (1.5, 0.5). We have marked the points with x-coordinates 0, 1, 1.8, 2.1.

> **curve := implicitplot(f(x, y) - c, x = -1..3, y = -2..2):**
> **points := plot([[0, 0.318], [1, 0.236], [1.8, 0.682], [2.1, 0.866]],**
>   **style = POINT, symbol = BOX):**
> **display({curve, points});**

Problem Set C, Problem 3.

We are going to investigate the initial value problem y' = (y - x)(1 - y^3), y(0) = b for various choices of the initial value b. First note that dsolve cannot find an exact solution.

> **restart:**
> **de := diff(y(x), x) = (y(x) - x)*(1 - y(x)^3);**

$$de := \frac{\partial}{\partial x} \, \mathrm{y}(x) = (\mathrm{y}(x) - x)\left(1 - \mathrm{y}(x)^3\right)$$

> **dsolve(de, y(x));**
>   **(a)**
  We will thus use dsolve(..., numeric) and odeplot to graph the solutions of the IVP for the initial conditions y(0) = -0.5, 0, 0.5, 1, 1.5, 2. The next command creates a function of b that represents the solution of our initial value problem with the initial condition y(0) = b.

> **sol := b -> dsolve({de, y(0) = b}, y(x), numeric, maxfun = 1000);**

$$sol := b \rightarrow \mathrm{dsolve}(\{\, de, \mathrm{y}(0) = b \,\}, \mathrm{y}(x), \textit{numeric}, \textit{maxfun} = 1000)$$

We now define a function that creates a plot of the solution with a given initial value.

> **with(plots):**

> **graph1 := b -> odeplot(sol(b), [x, y(x)], 0..4);**

$$graph1 := b \rightarrow \text{odeplot}(\text{sol}(b), [x, y(x)], 0 .. 4)$$

Next we make a list of plots for the values of b mentioned above.

> **list1 := seq(graph1(0.5*i), i = -1..4):**

Finally, we display these plots on the same graph.

> **display({list1});**

(b)

The plots in part (a) indicate that if b = 1, the corresponding solution is y = 1; if
0 < b < 1, the solution first increases and then decreases to -infinity; if b <= 0, the
solution decreases to -infinity; and if b > 1, the solution first decreases and then
increases to infinity. That y = 1 is a solution can be verified by plugging y = 1 into
the differential equation. If b < 1, it appears that there is a number x*(b) such that
the solution approaches -infinity as x -> x*(b). One cannot be certain about this on
the basis of the plots, but it is in fact true. To get a better idea about the long-term
behavior of solutions corresponding to b > 1, we plot some solutions over a longer
interval.

> **graph2 := b -> odeplot(sol(b), [x, y(x)], 0..10);**

$$graph2 := b \rightarrow \text{odeplot}(\text{sol}(b), [x, y(x)], 0 .. 10)$$

> **list2 := seq(graph2(i), i = 1..4):**
> **display({list2});**

(c)

Now we'll combine the preceding graph with a plot of the line y = x.

> **line := plot(x, x = 0..10, style = POINT):**

```
> display({list2, line});
```

It appears that the solutions for b > 1 are asymptotic to the line y = x. Note that the function y = x is not itself a solution of the differential equation. Along the line y = x, the slope y' is zero; above the line, y' is negative; and below the line, y' is positive. Thus, it is plausible that the solutions are pushed toward the line y = x. (A careful analysis of the differential equation confirms this.) Here is a plot of the direction field together with several solutions. We see that the direction field confirms the observations we have made about the solutions.

```
> with(DEtools):
> dfield := dfieldplot((y - x)*(1 - y^3), [x, y], 0..4, y = -1..4,
       arrows = LINE, axes =  BOXED):
> display({dfield, list1});
```

We can also study this problem with the command DEplot.

```
> DEplot(diff(y(x), x) = (y(x) - x)*(1 - y(x)^3), [x, y], 0..4, {[0, 1.5], [0, 2]},
       stepsize = 0.02);
```

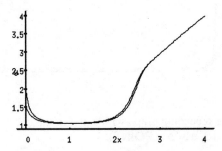

If we try to plot over a longer interval, DEplot exhibits the type of numerical instability discussed in Chapter 7.

> DEplot(diff(y(x), x) = (y(x) - x)*(1 - y(x)^3), [x, y], 0..10, {[0, 2], [0, 5]}, y = 0..10, limitrange = true, stepsize = 0.02);

Problem Set D, Problem 1.

> restart:

We consider the second order differential equation

> airy := diff(y(x), x$2) = x*y(x);

$$airy := \frac{\partial^2}{\partial x^2} y(x) = x\, y(x)$$

(a)

When x is close to 0, we want to compare the solution of Airy's equation with the solution of the IVP y''(x) = 0, y'(0) = 1, y(0) = 0. The solution of this IVP is y = x. Here is a plot of the numerical solution of Airy's equation together with the function y = x.

> with(plots): with(DEtools):
> fac1plot := plot(x, x = -2..2):
> airy1plot := DEplot(airy, [x, y], -2..2, {[0, 0, 1]}):
> display({fac1plot, airy1plot});

The facsimile solution agrees well with the actual solution in a neighborhood of 0.

(b)

For x close to -16 = -(4^2), we want to compare the solution of Airy's equation to the facsimile solution

```
> fac2 := (c1, c2) -> c1*sin(4*x + c2);
```

$$fac2 := (c1, c2) \rightarrow c1 \sin(4\,x + c2)$$

First, we'll plot a numerical solution of Airy's equation.

```
> airy2plot := DEplot(airy, [x, y], -18..-14, {[0, 0, 1]}, stepsize = 0.1):
> airy2plot;
```

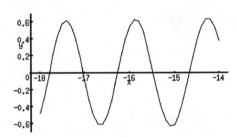

This certainly looks like a sine wave. Let's see how well it matches up with an appropriate sine wave. We have to choose constants c1 and c2 in the facsimile solution to make it match up. Note first that c1 is the amplitude of the facsimile solution, and we can see from the graph that the amplitude of the solution of Airy's equation is about 0.61 on this interval. The constant c2 determines the phase shift, and can be read off from the zeros of the solution. In particular, the solution of Airy's equation has a zero at about -16.3, so we should choose c2 to satisfy 4*(-16.3) + c2 = 0.

```
> fac2plot := plot(fac2(0.61, 4*16.3), x = -18..-14, style = POINT):
> display({fac2plot, airy2plot});
```

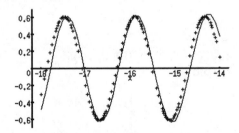

The plots match up well. Why did we have to choose the values of c1 and c2 by hand? Our analysis suggests that the facsimile solution should approximate the actual solution near x = -K^2. But the initial condition that we used for Airy's equation is at the point x = 0, where the facsimile solution is not a good approximation. Thus, the undetermined constants in the facsimile solution are unrelated to the initial conditions in Airy's equation, and we needed to choose them by hand to get a good match. Nevertheless, the frequency of the facsimile solution is determined by K, and is independent of the undetermined constants. Thus, we can at least conclude that the frequency of the solutions of Airy's equation in a neighborhood of x = -K^2 will be roughly proportional to K.

(c)

```
> fac3 := (c1, c2) -> c1*sinh(4*x + c2);
```

$$fac3 := (c1, c2) \rightarrow c1 \sinh(4x + c2)$$

```
> airy3plot := DEplot(airy, [x, y], 14..18, {[0, 0, 1]}):
> airy3plot;
```

We'd like to compare this with the graph of the hyperbolic sine function. Again, we have to choose c1 and c2 by hand. We'll use an arbitrary choice: c1 = 1, c2 = 0.

```
> plot(fac3(1, 0), x = 14..18);
```

The graphs are remarkably similar. Note, however, that the values in the second graph are about 10^9 greater than in the first, which means that we should have chosen c1 to be about 10^(-9).

(d)

Finally, we want to produce a graph of the numerical solution on the interval from -20 to 2.

> DEplot(airy, [x, y], -20..2, {[0,0,1]}, stepsize = 0.1);

This graph indicates that the frequency increases and the amplitude decreases as x goes to -infinity. The increasing frequency is predicted by our facsimile analysis; the decreasing amplitude is harder to explain.

Note: We used DEplot instead of odeplot in this problem because we wanted to plot the solution to the left of the initial condition.

Problem Set E, Problem 1.

(a)
We are interested in the series solution of Airy's equation.
> restart:
> airyeqn:=diff(y(x), x$2) - x*y(x) = 0;

$$airyeqn := \left(\frac{\partial^2}{\partial x^2} y(x) \right) - x\, y(x) = 0$$

> Order := 11:
> seriessol := dsolve({airyeqn, y(0) = 0, D(y)(0) = 1}, y(x), series);

$$seriessol := y(x) = x + \frac{1}{12} x^4 + \frac{1}{504} x^7 + \frac{1}{45360} x^{10} + O(x^{11})$$

> taylorsol := convert(rhs(seriessol), polynom);

$$taylorsol := x + \frac{1}{12} x^4 + \frac{1}{504} x^7 + \frac{1}{45360} x^{10}$$

(b)
Here is the exact solution of Airy's equation.

> **exactsol := dsolve({airyeqn, y(0) = 0, D(y)(0) = 1}, y(x));**

$$exactsol := y(x) = \frac{2}{9} \frac{3^{5/6} \pi \sqrt{x} \; \text{BesselI}\left(\frac{1}{3}, \frac{2}{3} x^{3/2}\right)}{\Gamma\left(\frac{2}{3}\right)}$$

Here is a plot comparing the exact solution to the (truncated) series solution.
> **plot1 := plot(taylorsol, x = 0..6, linestyle = 4):**
> **plot2 := plot(rhs(exactsol), x = 0..6):**
> **with(plots):**
> **display({plot1, plot2});**

(c)
The general solution of the comparison equation y'' = y is c1*exp(x) + c2*exp(-x).
The solution blows up exponentially (when c1 is nonzero). Thus, the exact solution
of Airy's equation will diverge exponentially from any Taylor polynomial
approximation.

Problem Set E, Problem 16.

(a)
> **restart:**
We define a square wave on the interval [0, 10Pi] by using a sum of Heaviside
functions.
> **h := t -> -1 + 2*sum((-1)^i*Heaviside(t - Pi*i), i = 0..10);**

$$h := t \to -1 + 2\left(\sum_{i=0}^{10} (-1)^i \, \text{Heaviside}(t - \pi i)\right)$$

> **h(t);**

$$-1 + 2\,\text{Heaviside}(t) - 2\,\text{Heaviside}(t - \pi) + 2\,\text{Heaviside}(t - 2\pi)$$
$$- 2\,\text{Heaviside}(t - 3\pi) + 2\,\text{Heaviside}(t - 4\pi)$$

$$- 2\,\text{Heaviside}(t-5\,\pi) + 2\,\text{Heaviside}(t-6\,\pi)$$

$$- 2\,\text{Heaviside}(t-7\,\pi) + 2\,\text{Heaviside}(t-8\,\pi)$$

$$- 2\,\text{Heaviside}(t-9\,\pi) + 2\,\text{Heaviside}(t-10\,\pi)$$

> **plot(h(t), t = 0..30);**

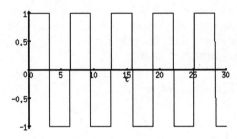

(b)
> **eqnlhs := diff(y(t), t$2) + y(t);**

$$eqnlhs := \left(\frac{\partial^2}{\partial t^2}\, y(t)\right) + y(t)$$

> **ic := y(0) = 0, D(y)(0) = 1;**

$$ic := y(0) = 0,\, D(y)(0) = 1$$

> **solb := dsolve({eqnlhs = h(t), ic}, y(t), method = laplace):**
> **plot({rhs(solb), h(t)}, t = 0..30);**

We do see resonance. The solution appears to grow without bound. Let's check the solution by using dsolve(..., numeric).
> **numsolb := dsolve({eqnlhs = h(t), ic}, y(t), numeric, maxfun = 5000);**

```
numsolb := proc(rkf45_x) ... end
```
> **with(plots):**

> **odeplot(numsolb, [t, y(t)], 0..30, numpoints = 100);**

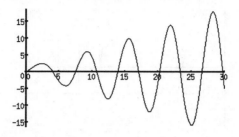

(c)
> **solc := dsolve({eqnlhs = h(t/2), ic}, y(t), method = laplace):**
> **plot({rhs(solc), h(t/2)}, t = 0..30);**

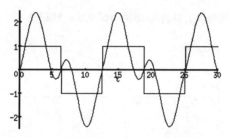

This solution does not exhibit resonance. The solutions remain bounded.
> **numsolc := dsolve({eqnlhs = h(t/2), ic}, y(t), numeric, maxfun = 5000);**

```
numsolc := proc(rkf45_x) ... end
```
> **odeplot(numsolc, [t, y(t)], 0..30, numpoints = 100);**

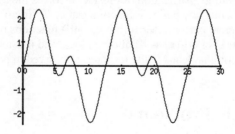

(d)
Now we examine the solution with forcing function h(2t), which has period Pi.
> **sold := dsolve({eqnlhs = h(2*t), ic}, y(t), method = laplace):**

> **plot({rhs(sold), h(2*t)}, t = 0..15);**

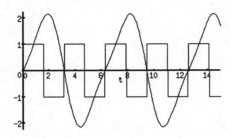

This solution does not exhibit resonance.
> **numsold := dsolve({eqnlhs = h(2*t), ic}, y(t), numeric, maxfun = 5000);**

```
numsold := proc(rkf45_x) ... end
```
> **odeplot(numsold, [t, y(t)], 0..15, numpoints = 100);**

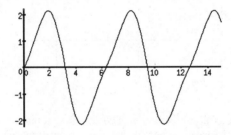

(e)
The results of (b), (c), and (d) indicate that resonance may be a consequence of the period of the forcing function, regardless of the actual shape of the function. This is, in fact, true. A rigorous justification of this fact involves the theory of Fourier analysis, which shows that any periodic function can be "built up" out of cosine and sine functions of different periods. Most (but not all!) functions with minimal period 2Pi contain sin(x) or cos(x) as a building block, and it is the occurrence of the sin(x) or cos(x) term that leads to the resonance observed in part (b).

Problem Set F, Problem 6.

(a)
First, we find the critical points of the system.
> **restart:**
> **sys := x*(1.5 - x - 0.5*y), y*(2 - 1.5*x - 0.5*y);**

$$sys := x\,(1.5 - x - .5\,y),\ y\,(2 - 1.5\,x - .5\,y)$$

> critpoints := solve({sys}, {x, y});

$$critpoints := \{ x = 0, y = 0 \}, \{ x = 0, y = 4. \}, \{ y = 0, x = 1.500000000 \},$$
$$\{ y = 1., x = 1.000000000 \}$$

We want to compute the eigenvalues of the associated linear system at each critical point. First, we define an expression that gives the matrix of first order partial derivatives of the system at a point (x, y).

> with(linalg):
  derivative := [[diff(sys[1], x), diff(sys[1], y)],
            [diff(sys[2], x), diff(sys[2], y)]];

```
Warning: new definition for    norm
Warning: new definition for    trace
```

$$derivative := [[1.5 - 2x - .5y, -.5x], [-1.5y, 2 - 1.5x - 1.0y]]$$

> eigenvals(subs(critpoints[1], derivative));

$$1.5, 2.$$

> eigenvals(subs(critpoints[2], derivative));

$$-2.0, -.5$$

> eigenvals(subs(critpoints[3], derivative));

$$-1.500000000, -.250000000$$

> eigenvals(subs(critpoints[4], derivative));

$$-1.651387819, .1513878188$$

Thus, we find that the types of the four equilibrium points are:
(0, 0) --   unstable node
(0, 4) --   asymptotically stable node
(1.5, 0) --   asymptotically stable node
(1, 1) --   unstable saddle point
(b)
> with(DEtools):
> vfield := dfieldplot([sys], [x, y], -10..10, x = 0..3, y = 0..5):

> **vfield;**

The vector field confirms what we found in part (a).

(c)

We're going to use the DEplot command to plot a phase portrait for this nonlinear system. We start with a rectangular grid of 42 different initial conditions. Note that an initial condition for the system consists of a triple [t0, x0, y0], where t0 is the initial time, and (x0, y0) is the initial position. We take t0 = 0 in each case.

> **initials := seq(seq([0, 0.5*i, j], i = 0..6), j = 0..5);**

$$initials := [0, 0, 0], [0, .5, 0], [0, 1.0, 0], [0, 1.5, 0], [0, 2.0, 0],$$
$$[0, 2.5, 0], [0, 3.0, 0], [0, 0, 1], [0, .5, 1], [0, 1.0, 1],$$
$$[0, 1.5, 1], [0, 2.0, 1], [0, 2.5, 1], [0, 3.0, 1], [0, 0, 2],$$
$$[0, .5, 2], [0, 1.0, 2], [0, 1.5, 2], [0, 2.0, 2], [0, 2.5, 2],$$
$$[0, 3.0, 2], [0, 0, 3], [0, .5, 3], [0, 1.0, 3], [0, 1.5, 3],$$
$$[0, 2.0, 3], [0, 2.5, 3], [0, 3.0, 3], [0, 0, 4], [0, .5, 4],$$
$$[0, 1.0, 4], [0, 1.5, 4], [0, 2.0, 4], [0, 2.5, 4], [0, 3.0, 4],$$
$$[0, 0, 5], [0, .5, 5], [0, 1.0, 5], [0, 1.5, 5], [0, 2.0, 5],$$
$$[0, 2.5, 5], [0, 3.0, 5]$$

> **portrait := DEplot([sys], [x, y], 0..10, {initials}, x = 0..3, y = 0..5,**
> **stepsize = 0.1):**

> **portrait;**

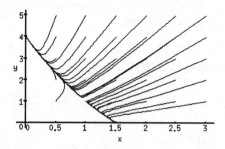

This graph is not ideal. The problem is that a rectangular grid of initial conditions is not the best choice for this system. By looking at the vector field, we see that a better choice of initial conditions would be a collection of evenly spaced points along lines parallel to, and above and below, the line from $(0, 4)$ to $(1.5, 0)$. Since that line has slope about -2.5, we redefine our initial conditions as follows.

> **initials := seq(seq([0, j*(0.1*i), j*(2.5 - 2.5*(0.1*i))], i = 0..10), j = [0.6, 2.6]):**
> **portrait := DEplot([sys], [x, y], 0..10, {initials}, x = 0..3, y = 0..5):**
>   **portrait;**

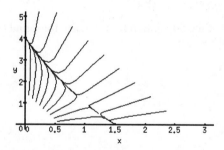

Much better! By superimposing the vector field from part (b), we can get a clear idea of the directions of the trajectories.

> **with(plots):**
> **display({vfield, portrait});**

(d)
To find particular values of the population we have to use dsolve(..., numeric).
> **tsys := subs({x = x(t), y = y(t)}, [sys]);**

$$tsys := [\,x(t)\,(1.5 - x(t) - .5\,y(t)),\, y(t)\,(2 - 1.5\,x(t) - .5\,y(t))\,]$$

> **dsys := diff(x(t), t) = tsys[1], diff(y(t), t) = tsys[2];**

$$dsys := \frac{\partial}{\partial t}\,x(t) = x(t)\,(1.5 - x(t) - .5\,y(t)),$$

$$\frac{\partial}{\partial t}\,y(t) = y(t)\,(2 - 1.5\,x(t) - .5\,y(t))$$

We're interested in the population as a function of t, given initial conditions
x0 = a, y0 = b.
> **popn := (a, b) -> dsolve({dsys, x(0) = a, y(0) = b}, {x(t), y(t)},**
    numeric, maxfun = 1000);

$$popn := (a, b) \to dsolve(\{\,dsys, x(0) = a, y(0) = b\,\}, \{\,y(t), x(t)\,\},$$

$$numeric,\; maxfun = 1000)$$

Here is a list of values of the population for t = 1..20, for initial conditions (2.5, 2).
> **population := popn(2.5, 2):**

> array([seq(evalf(population(u), 4), u = 1..20)]);

$$
\begin{bmatrix}
t = 1. & x(t) = 1.294 & y(t) = .7611 \\
t = 2. & x(t) = 1.203 & y(t) = .6295 \\
t = 3. & x(t) = 1.204 & y(t) = .5699 \\
t = 4. & x(t) = 1.222 & y(t) = .5205 \\
t = 5. & x(t) = 1.245 & y(t) = .4718 \\
t = 6. & x(t) = 1.269 & y(t) = .4230 \\
t = 7. & x(t) = 1.294 & y(t) = .3746 \\
t = 8. & x(t) = 1.318 & y(t) = .3275 \\
t = 9. & x(t) = 1.342 & y(t) = .2826 \\
t = 10. & x(t) = 1.364 & y(t) = .2408 \\
t = 11. & x(t) = 1.384 & y(t) = .2028 \\
t = 12. & x(t) = 1.403 & y(t) = .1688 \\
t = 13. & x(t) = 1.420 & y(t) = .1390 \\
t = 14. & x(t) = 1.434 & y(t) = .1134 \\
t = 15. & x(t) = 1.446 & y(t) = .09178 \\
t = 16. & x(t) = 1.457 & y(t) = .07375 \\
t = 17. & x(t) = 1.465 & y(t) = .05891 \\
t = 18. & x(t) = 1.472 & y(t) = .04682 \\
t = 19. & x(t) = 1.478 & y(t) = .03706 \\
t = 20. & x(t) = 1.483 & y(t) = .02924
\end{bmatrix}
$$

We see that the solution is converging to the equilibrium point at $(1.5, 0)$.

(e)

There is no peaceful coexistence because almost all the trajectories tend toward an equilibrium point representing a positive population of one species and a zero population of the other. For example, in (d) we saw that the population of x tends to 1.5 and the population of y tends to 0. The only nonzero initial population distribution that results in no change is $x = 1$, $y = 1$.

Looking back at the phase portrait in part (c), we see that the separatrices lie in the corridor separating the curves that bend toward the equilibrium $(1.5, 0)$ and those that bend toward (0, 4). This corridor extends from the origin to the saddle point (1, 1) and from there toward the upper right of the plot.

(f)

We want to focus in on the place where the separatrix crosses the line x = 1.5. We can see from the plot above that the y-value of the intersection is between 1 and 2.

```
> initials := seq([0, 1.5, 1 + 0.1*j], j = 0..10):
> DEplot([sys], [x, y], 0..15, {initials}, x = 0.5..1.5, y = 0..2, stepsize = 0.5);
```

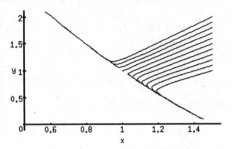

We see that the separatrix lies near the fourth curve from the top, corresponding to y = 1.7. Let's focus in a little more and use a smaller stepsize.

```
> initials := seq([0, 1.5, 1.65 + 0.01*j], j = 0..10):
> DEplot([sys], [x, y], 0..20, {initials}, x = 0.9..1.1, y = 0.9..1.1,
      stepsize = 0.2);
```

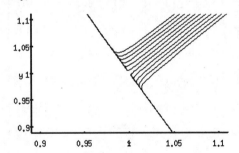

We see that the separatrix is between the fifth and sixth curves, so we conclude that the line x = 1.5 cuts the separatrix between y = 1.69 and y = 1.70. Of course, we cannot numerically determine an exact value on the separatrix because our numerical procedure will always introduce errors.

Index

The index uses the same conventions for fonts that are used throughout the book. *Maple* commands, such as **dsolve**, are printed in boldface. Menu options, such as `File`, are printed in a monospaced typewriter font. Trademarked names, such as *Macintosh*, are printed in a slanted font. Everything else is printed in a standard font.

@ 92.

$ 45, 59, 69, 91, 93, 94, 95, 96.

abs 63.

abserr 78.

accuracy 73, 74, 75, 77, 78, 80, 81, 107, 115, 129, 131, 184, 185, 191.

Ai 120, 125.

air resistance 128, 129, 131.

Airy function 120, 125.

Airy's equation 117, 119, 120, 124, 125, 127, 135, 136, 151.

algebra 67, 137.

algebraic equation 138.

amplification factor 82.

amplitude 125, 126, 129, 133, 134.

analytic 138.

anames 86.

antiderivative 33, 67, 112, 137.

application 11, 14.

approximate solution 68, 73, 75, 77.

approximation, Euler 73, 113, 114, 115.

approximation, tangent line 71, 73.

arbitrary constant 43, 46, 138.

array 96.

arrow 26.

arrow vs. **unapply** 88.

assigned 86.

assignment 24, 90.

associated linear system 179.

assume 155.

asymptote 55, 63, 107.

asymptotically stable 56, 58, 177, 178, 179, 188, 189.

autonomous 172.

autonomous equation 54, 57, 62, 173, 174, 178.

`Axes` 37, 41.

`Balloon Help` 15.

`Below` 36.

Bessel function 120, 126, 128, 136, 152, 153, 158.

Bessel's equation 117, 119, 120, 124, 125, 126, 127, 134, 136, 152, 153, 158.

BesselI 126.

BesselJ 120, 126, 136, 139, 152.

BesselK 126.

BesselY 120, 126, 136, 139, 153.

Bi 120, 125.

bifurcation 66, 191, 193, 194.

`Bold` 41.

boundary conditions 130.

boundary value problem 130.

Boxed 37.

built-in function 106, 111, 112, 115, 120, 152, 153.

catenary 130.

census data 66.

center 170, 179, 190.

chaos 174, 190.

Character 38.

characteristic equation 123, 132, 160, 163.

circular drum 152.

circular membrane 117.

circular symmetry 117.

clearing values 24, 29, 106.

click 11.

coefficients, constant 117, 118, 123, 128, 131, 135, 137, 145, 157, 159, 160, 162, 164, 167, 170.

coefficients, variable 117, 118, 123, 131, 135, 137, 138, 170.

coherent English 6.

collaboration 6.

colon 29, 96, 98, 105.

colon equals 24.

comparison method 5, 117, 118.

competing species 1, 175, 184, 185.

complex eigenpair 163.

complex variables 138.

constant coefficient 117, 118, 123, 128, 131, 135, 137, 145, 157, 159, 160, 162, 164, 167, 170.

constant solution 62.

constant, arbitrary 43, 46, 138.

continuous dependence 2, 47, 49, 61, 132.

contourplot 29, 32, 60, 61, 97, 99, 100, 183.

convergent 138.

convert 139.

convolution 155.

coordinates, finding 37.

coprocessor, numeric 7.

Copy 13, 16, 19, 35, 36.

copying files 15.

cos 25, 33, 122.

critical point 54, 56, 58, 64, 173, 174, 176, 177, 178, 179, 181, 184, 185, 186, 187, 191, 193, 194.

curve, parametric 98, 168, 173.

Cut 36.

D 91, 92.

damping 125, 126, 129, 132, 184.

decay 123, 124, 125.

definite integral 33.

delete 15, 18.

DEplot 29, 68, 75, 76, 77, 81, 82, 84, 97, 100, 101, 102, 103, 104, 105, 109, 113, 127, 171, 172, 190, 191, 192, 193.

Desktop 16.

DEtools 29, 51, 100, 101, 122, 171, 172, 176.

DEtools[options] 77.

dfieldplot 29, 51, 53, 54, 63, 97, 100, 101, 122, 176, 177.

diff 32, 43, 44, 46, 50, 68, 70, 79, 83, 91, 111, 167, 168, 169, 170, 171.

diffraction 117, 152.

Digits 78, 81.

Dirac 148.

Dirac delta function 147, 148.

direction field 5, 51, 52, 53, 54, 55, 56, 62, 63, 64, 66, 110, 121, 122, 124, 125, 135, 136.

directory 18, 19.

Disk 12.

diskette 12, 13, 14, 15, 16, 17.

display 29, 63, 64, 81, 97, 99, 101, 171, 187, 190, 194.

Display Region Boundaries 38.

do 73.

document 21.

documentation, online 23.

dollar sign 45, 59, 69, 91, 93, 95, 96.

dollar sign vs. **seq** 94.

double quotes 27.

double-click 11.

drag 11.

drive 13.

dsolve 43, 44, 45, 46, 50, 61, 62, 63, 65, 66, 68, 77, 79, 81, 91, 101, 106, 111, 112, 128, 132, 137, 138, 139, 141, 145, 146, 151, 152, 154, 156, 157, 158, 159, 160, 167, 168, 169, 170, 171, 181, 182, 183, 192.

dsolve(. . ., numeric) 68, 69, 70, 71, 75, 76, 77, 78, 79, 80, 81, 82, 83, 84, 102, 103, 106, 109, 111, 112, 113, 114, 115, 119, 126, 128, 131, 155, 170, 171, 179, 192.

E 25.

Edit 12, 13, 16, 17, 19, 35, 36, 37.

eigenpair 162, 163, 164, 165, 166, 167.

eigenvalue 162, 163, 164, 166, 179, 181, 182, 184, 185, 186, 187.

eigenvector 162, 163, 164, 165, 166, 181, 182, 187.

eigenvects 164, 165, 166, 182.

Eject Disk 17.

elasticity 130, 159.

elementary function 67, 70, 111.

Empty Trash 15.

end 73.

energy 183.

Enter 21, 22, 40.

Enter Text 36.

equation 90, 100.

equation, Airy's 117, 119, 120, 124, 125, 127, 135, 136, 151.

equation, algebraic 138.

equation, autonomous 54, 57, 62, 173, 174, 178.

equation, Bessel's 117, 119, 120, 124, 125, 126, 127, 134, 136, 152, 153, 158.

equation, characteristic 123, 132, 160, 163.

equation, logistic 186.

equation, logistic/threshold 64, 187.

equation, parabolic cylinder 135.

equilibrium 55, 57, 58, 62, 110, 122, 123, 174, 176, 178, 185, 186, 187, 188, 189.

Erase 16.

erf 111.

error message 104, 106, 107.

error, global 48, 78, 81, 82.

error, local 48, 78, 81, 190.

error, round-off 75, 80, 83, 96.

error, truncation 75, 80, 83, 190.

errors, recovering from 106.

Euler 77.

Euler approximation 73.

Euler equation 140, 141, 152, 153, 160.

Euler Method 71, 72, 73, 74, 82, 113, 114, 115.

evalc 166.

evalf 22, 25, 34, 59, 69, 73, 78, 96.

evaluate worksheet 28.

evaluation, full 85.

evaluation, order of 94, 96.

evaluation, suppressing 86, 94, 96.

exact solution 68, 69, 79.

execute worksheet 28.

existence 2, 43, 45, 46, 55, 62, 63, 173.

Exit 12, 19, 20.

exp 24, 51, 79, 115, 166.

expand 23, 25.

experimental data 2.

explicit formula 68.

exponential decay 123.

exponential growth 123.

exponential order 144.

expression 26.

expressions vs. functions 26, 27, 86, 87, 91, 106.

external force 129.

factor 24, 25.

falling body 159.

family of solutions 44, 101.

fieldplot 100, 175, 176.

File 12, 13, 14, 16, 17, 18, 19, 20, 36, 40, 41.
Filter 19.
Finder 14, 15, 17.
finite time 53, 56, 57, 70, 109, 113, 173.
first order method 72.
Float 78.
floating-point 22.
fluid dynamics 159.
folder 14.
Font 41.
for 73.
forcing function 133, 156, 157, 158.
forcing, periodic 130, 133, 157.
format 12, 15.
Format 35, 36, 37, 38, 40, 41.
Format Disk 12.
fourth order method 75.
Frame 37.
Frobenius series 141, 152.
fsolve 25, 32, 60, 61, 62, 65, 66, 153.
function keys 35.
function, Airy 120, 125.
function, Bessel 120, 126, 128, 152, 153, 158.
function, built-in 106, 111, 112, 115, 120, 152, 153.
functions vs. expressions 26, 27, 86, 87, 91, 106.
fundamental law 1.
fundamental set 103, 120, 126, 160, 162, 163, 164, 165, 166.
general solution 43, 120, 121, 125, 153, 160, 162, 163, 164, 165, 167, 181, 182.
generalized eigenvector 164.
generalized function 148.
geometric method 8, 121.
global behavior 60.
global error 48, 78, 81, 82.
Gompertz model 64.
Gompertz-threshold model 110.
grading 8.
graphics coordinates 37.

graphics region 36.
graphics window 37.
grid 183.
grow 122, 123, 124, 125.
hardware 7.
Heaviside 146, 147, 149.
help 12, 14, 15, 18, 23.
Help 12, 23, 37.
Help for Selection 37.
Help On 37.
Hi-res Print 38.
higher derivative 91.
higher order 102.
homogeneous 119, 121, 123, 127, 132, 137, 138, 153, 160, 162.
I 25, 192.
icon 12, 14, 15, 16, 17.
Im 166.
implicit 60, 61, 63.
implicitplot 29, 32, 60, 61, 63, 97, 100.
improper integral 138, 143, 144.
Improved Euler Method 73, 74, 75, 82, 113, 114.
indefinite integral 33.
indicial equation 140, 141.
infinity 25.
inflection point 53, 56.
inhomogeneous 137, 138, 142, 143, 149, 157, 160, 162, 170, 182.
initial condition 44, 45, 46, 47, 55, 59, 60, 61, 63, 76, 122, 127, 129, 130, 131, 133, 134, 135, 173.
initial value 1, 44, 46, 47, 48, 71, 73, 138.
initial value problem 1, 43, 46, 48, 59, 60, 61, 62, 66, 67, 68, 70, 71, 73, 76, 78, 80, 109, 128, 132, 133, 145, 157.
Initialize 16.
Input 36, 39.
input region 21, 22, 28, 35, 40.
Insert New Region 36.
Insert Page Break 37, 41.
Insert Prompt 36.
Insert Separator Line 37.

Insert Text 36.
insertion point 36.
int 33, 34, 34.
integral 67.
integral curve 51.
integral transform 143.
integral, definite 33.
integral, improper 138, 143, 144.
integral, indefinite 33.
integration, numerical 34.
interface 11.
interlaced zeros 119, 120.
interpolate 73.
interrupt 17.
Interrupt 20, 26.
intersection point 32.
interval of existence 70.
Inverse Laplace Transform 143, 145, 158.
invlaplace 145.
iris 28, 106.
irregular singularity 141, 153.
jump discontinuity 144.
kernel 28, 143.
keyboard equivalent 35.
kinetic energy 183.
label 98.
Label 12.
laplace 145, 156.
Laplace Transform 137, 143, 144, 145, 146, 148, 149, 155, 156, 157, 158.
Legendre equation 153, 154.
Legendre polynomial 154.
level curve 32, 99, 100.
lhs 91.
library 28.
limit 33, 64.
limit cycle 191.
limiting behavior 62, 63, 66, 113, 133, 134, 174, 177, 182, 189.
limitrange 104, 172.
linalg 164.
linear system 161.
linearized stability 174, 178, 179.
linearly dependent 120.

linearly independent 119, 137, 153, 160, 162, 163.
linestyle 189.
linsolve 165, 167.
list 92, 95.
ln 24, 25.
Load 19.
local 73.
local behavior 60.
local error 48, 78, 81, 190.
log 25.
logarithmic singularity 153.
logistic equation 186.
logistic/threshold equation 64, 187.
long-term behavior 64, 114, 115, 123, 133, 151, 174, 185.
Lorenz system 190.
Macintosh 3, 11, 14, 15, 16, 17, 21, 22, 35, 36, 37, 38, 39, 40, 41.
manual pages 18.
map 69, 95, 96, 97, 166.
maple leaf 12, 15.
Math Style 35, 37, 38.
matrix 164.
maxfun 68, 70, 71, 133.
maximum 52, 112, 123, 130, 153.
measurement 48.
memory 12, 15.
menu 14.
method 77.
minimum 56, 65, 123, 153.
mistakes, common 106.
mixing 65.
model 1, 2, 5, 65, 117, 128, 159, 175, 184, 185, 186, 187, 188.
mouse 11.
moving files 15.
multiple solutions 101.
multiplicity 163.
network 11, 12, 13, 16.
New 13, 19.
node 177, 188.
nonautonomous 172.

nonlinear 62, 129, 130, 133, 161, 170, 174, 179, 188, 191.

Normal 37.

numeric coprocessor 7.

numerical integration 34.

numerical method 5, 6, 8, 67, 68, 71, 75, 78, 80, 81, 112, 113, 118, 131, 190, 191.

numerical solution 69, 79, 80, 81, 111, 118, 127, 129, 131, 133, 135, 155, 190, 191.

numpoints 71, 101, 113, 130, 133.

od 73.

odeplot 29, 68, 69, 70, 71, 75, 76, 79, 81, 83, 84, 97, 100, 101, 109, 113, 114, 155, 171.

op 73, 93, 97, 105.

Open 13, 16, 19, 36, 40.

optics 117, 127.

Options 12, 37, 38, 41.

Order 139.

ordinary point 138.

oscillatory 118, 123, 124, 125, 126, 127, 132, 133, 134, 135, 153, 154.

Output 37, 38, 39.

Output Fontsize 37.

Output Mode 38.

output region 21, 22, 23, 28, 35.

packages 29.

parabolic cylinder equation 126, 135.

parameter 65, 94, 95, 96, 131, 152, 168, 170, 181, 191, 192, 193, 194.

parametric curve 98, 168, 169, 171, 173.

partial differential equation 1.

particular solution 160, 162.

Paste 13, 17, 19, 36.

peaceful coexistence 184, 185.

pencil and paper 4.

pendulum 128, 129, 130, 183, 184.

periodic 129, 133, 173, 174, 191.

periodic forcing 133.

perturbation 189, 190.

phase plane 168, 173, 174.

phase portrait 5, 159, 168, 169, 170, 171, 173, 179, 184, 185, 186, 187, 189, 192.

phase shift 129, 133, 134.

phaseportrait 172.

physical model 1, 5, 48, 54, 65, 80, 117, 126, 129, 152, 183, 184.

Pi 25.

piecewise continuous 144, 146.

piecewise linear function 73.

platform 2, 3, 5, 6, 11.

plot 26, 27, 31, 45, 73, 79, 95, 97, 98, 101, 113, 114, 115, 149, 168, 169, 170, 171.

plots 29, 32, 63, 64, 69, 99, 100, 175.

Poincaré-Bendixson Theorem 174.

pointer 11.

polar coordinates 192.

pole 140.

polynom 139.

polynomial 31, 32.

population 1, 65, 66, 177, 178, 184, 185, 186, 187, 188.

population growth 64, 66, 159.

potential energy 183.

power series 138, 152, 158.

predator-prey 175, 177, 186, 187.

predict the future 48.

Pretty Print 38.

print 11, 14, 17, 19.

print 69, 96.

Print 14, 17, 19.

proc 73, 88.

procedure 88.

Program Manager 11, 12.

Prüfer substitution 121.

quantum mechanics 126, 127.

Quit 12, 14, 17.

quotes, double 27.

quotes, left 99.

quotes, right 85, 86, 94, 96.

radical 165.

radioactive decay 159.

radius of convergence 138, 139.

range 135.
Re 166.
readlib 29.
recovering from errors 106.
recursion 71, 73, 74, 138.
recursion relation 138.
recursive definition 25.
reduction of order 137.
region 21, 35.
regular singularity 140, 141, 153.
relerr 78.
reliability 81.
removable singularity 112.
Remove Separator Lines 38.
resonance 130, 133, 157, 158.
restart 29, 38, 86.
Return 16, 21, 22, 23, 41.
Revert 41.
rhs 44, 91, 139, 149.
Riccati equation 121.
RootOf 165.
rotational invariance 193, 194.
rotational symmetry 191.
round-off error 75, 80, 83, 96.
Runge-Kutta Method 74, 75, 82.
Rössler system 191.
saddle point 170, 177, 178, 188, 189.
save 11, 12, 13, 14, 15, 16, 17, 18, 19, 20.
Save 13, 16, 19.
Save a Copy In 16.
Save As 13, 16, 18, 19.
sawtooth 158.
scaling 183.
scene 172, 190.
second order 91, 96, 102, 117, 119, 123.
second order method 74.
select 14.
semicolon 21, 29, 98, 105, 106.
semicolon vs. colon 29.
sensitivity 46, 48, 49, 50, 60, 80, 132, 133, 190.
Separator Lines 38.
separator region 36.
separatrix 184, 185, 186, 187, 188, 189.

seq 93, 94, 95, 96, 97, 169, 170, 172, 192.
sequence 92, 95.
sequence operator 45, 93, 95, 96.
series 139, 141, 152, 158.
series solution 137, 138, 141.
set 92, 95, 97.
Settings 41.
Shift-Return 21.
Show Balloons 15.
Show Page Breaks 41.
Si 112.
simplify 24, 32, 156.
Simpson's rule 67.
sin 25, 33, 122.
singularity 59, 104, 105, 107, 125, 128, 138, 140, 151.
singularity, irregular 141, 153.
singularity, logarithmic 153.
singularity, regular 140, 141, 153.
singularity, removable 112.
sinh 127.
sink 170.
Size 41.
Small 35, 37, 38.
solve 22, 25, 32, 66, 94, 177.
source 170.
Special 15, 17.
special function 139.
spiral 173, 178.
spring–mass system 159, 161.
sqrt 25, 69.
square wave 157.
stability 5, 43, 110, 174, 179, 181, 184, 185, 186, 187, 189, 191.
stable 48, 49, 50, 62, 64, 66, 78, 80, 81, 122, 178, 185, 188, 194.
Status 39.
step size 71, 72, 74, 75.
stepsize 77, 104, 113, 172, 190, 191.
Stop 26.
Sturm Comparison Theorem 118, 119, 120, 133, 134, 135.
Sturm-Liouville 121.

Style 40, 41.

subs 26, 69, 70, 77, 83, 89, 90, 169, 170.

Subscript 40.

substitution, simultaneous 90.

sum 86.

syllabus 8.

Symbol 41.

symbolic computation 8, 137.

symbolic solution 43, 159.

syntax error 22, 23, 97, 106, 107.

tangent line approximation 71, 72, 73.

tangent vector 174, 175.

Taylor polynomial 139, 151, 152, 155.

Taylor series 151, 152, 154.

terminal velocity 131.

Text 36, 39.

text region 35.

Text Region 36.

textplot 97, 99.

thinking 4.

third order 102.

time 48.

time 156.

time delay 173.

Title 41.

titlebar 11, 17.

Tool Bar 39.

trajectory 168, 169, 173, 179, 181, 183, 184, 185, 186, 187, 193, 194.

transform 143.

transformation rule 26.

trapezoidal rule 67.

troubleshooting 106.

truncation error 75, 80, 83, 190.

tutorial 12, 15.

tutorial 23.

type 139.

typing 4.

unapply 44, 87, 88, 169, 170.

undetermined coefficients 137, 146, 156.

union 93.

uniqueness 2, 43, 45, 46, 55, 60, 61, 62, 120, 160, 173.

unit impulse function 147.

unit step function 146, 147.

UNIX 11, 17, 18.

unstable 48, 49, 56, 58, 62, 64, 78, 80, 82, 122, 177, 178, 179, 185, 188.

variable coefficient 117, 118, 131, 135, 137, 138, 170.

variable step sizes 75.

variation of parameters 137, 146, 156, 157.

vector field 170, 174, 175, 176, 177, 178, 179, 184, 185, 186, 187, 194.

vibration 117.

view 171.

View 38, 39.

warning message 106.

waves 117, 127, 152.

Windows 12, 37, 39.

Windows 3, 11, 12, 35, 36, 37, 39.

with 29, 32, 51, 69, 122.

Worksheet 3, 4, 5, 6, 12, 13, 14, 15, 16, 17, 18, 19, 20, 21, 22, 25, 28, 29, 31, 35, 36, 37, 38, 39, 40, 41, 98, 106.

Worksheet 13.

Wronskian 119, 120, 160.

X Window System 3, 11, 17, 35, 36, 37, 38.

zeros, interlaced 119, 120.